FREE SPIRIT

MICHAEL CHAMBERS

Free Spirit

A Brush with a Fox

Methuen London

First published in Great Britain in 1990
by Methuen London
Michelin House, 81 Fulham Road, London SW3 6RB
Copyright © 1990 Michael Chambers

A CIP catalogue record for this book
is available from the British Library
ISBN 0–413–62980–5

Photoset by Rowland Phototypesetting Ltd
Bury St Edmunds, Suffolk
Printed in Great Britain by
St Edmundsbury Press Ltd,
Bury St Edmunds, Suffolk

To the three who made this tale possible,
and to all who fight the frustrating
and uphill battle to gain respect
and better treatment for those
who live on the wild side

Contents

Contents

List of Illustrations

When I took these pictures I had little idea that they would later be reproduced in a book. Taken with unsophisticated equipment, some even lifted from ciné film, they are consequently not always of the highest quality. I hope you will bear with us.

M.C.

Acknowledgements

I would like to acknowledge the generously donated time and typing skills of Barbara Griffiths; the equally generous use of Jon Twiggs's photocopier and his interest and suggestions on matters 'arty'; and similarly Rex Darby's contribution on matters photographic, intended to improve my chances of lifting black-and-white stills from a colour ciné film.

FREE SPIRIT

Prologue

At the events that closely preceded this story I can no more than conjecture. The only facts upon which a reconstruction can be based are that a tiny fox cub was wandering alone in the middle of the night, along a village street, which is when I started my involvement; and that, as I learned later, two or three men with spades and terriers had been seen walking along the river bank during that weekend.

Foxes are, in a country that styles itself 'animal loving', subjected to a variety of very unpleasant practices: they are hunted, shot, trapped (even the evil gin trap is still used), snared, poisoned and baited with terriers, often being held, helpless, while the dogs savage them. I have heard reports of gratuitous cruelties so appalling as to challenge the reasonable imagination. This creature, beautiful, interesting and largely beneficial to man, is perhaps more than any other the plaything of the sadist and the victim of tradition.

Probably trapped underground by the terriers, while the men dug steadily towards them, what became of the other cubs and the vixen? Whatever the answer, that the cub's experience of man and dog had, up to that moment when I caught my first fleeting glimpse of it, been a wholly terrifying one, is almost certain, and makes our subsequent relationship the more remarkable. That something so worthwhile should have had such ill beginnings, does perhaps give cause for hope in even the blackest circumstances.

1

A Fox
Joins the Family

It was a big seven-a-side tournament and by the time we had lost in the final round, we had taken part in six games of rugby, starting what now seemed a long time ago on a bright Sunday morning. The games, as always, had come with increasing frequency as we progressed. As the choice of teams to watch became less, so the crowds became bigger, until a fine congregation, well lubricated and pulsating with 'Oggy, Oggy, Oggy' had manfully, but vainly, tried to lift the underdogs, as for the second year running we surrendered the final to the only first class club in the tournament.

We had some fifty miles to travel and our convoy stopped at several watering holes before, having been evicted from a final pub, we arrived at my cottage for a last bevy. Two guys who had taken knocks about the head were feeling groggy and, deciding that beer and bonhomie would not help their condition, had split off much earlier. This left a shortage of transport to get the remainder back to the city, eight miles away. So I drove in with them.

I had left the lighted streets well behind and was wandering along the lanes towards Thame Lea Village and a fateful meeting. It was 2 am. As the lane swept s-shaped through the village, a furry bundle tumbled out of the long grass of the verge and straight in front of my car, so close that I merely conceived an impression, rather than a clear sighting, before it vanished under the dipping bonnet. The fluffy bundle trundled back into sight, and made off down the headlights' beam. It was not a kitten that I had nearly run down, but a very young fox cub.

I got out and caught it, when it turned into a driveway and couldn't get past the gates. The fact that I could catch it at all indicates how young it was, although still capable of loud protests and sinking needle-like puppy teeth into my hand. I plonked it down on the front passenger seat, which it dived beneath. I thought about the situation; there was almost certainly something untoward for such a tiny cub to be wandering on its own. I did not want to take it away if the vixen was about; this seemed unlikely since under her influence the cub would not have got itself into such a situation.

There lay in the field behind my cottage several large cages, some almost rusted away, a few still in reasonably sound condition. I rapidly drove the remaining two miles to my home and returned with the cub inside a large wire mesh cage. I set this down near the spot where I had found him. I then backed the car off for fifty or sixty yards, parked on the grass verge and extinguished the lights. If the vixen was about, I was fairly sure she would soon find the cub, and at one stage I thought this had happened, but it was only an inquisitive cat. I kept my vigil for an hour, by which time I was decidedly chilly and fairly sure the vixen was not there, so I retrieved the cage and headed home.

My wife got up to share a much looked forward to brew, and the cub was liberated in the kitchen. Our washing machine had about two inches of ground clearance; too small for the cub to get through one thought. He dived for this gap, seemed to flow through it rather like a spilt cup of water, and vanished. Eyes upturned in resignation – it seemed bed was still some time away – we finished out tea. 'Do we leave him to find his own way out and clean up the mess before breakfast, or do we try to extract him now?' Since as we entered the kitchen he would probably merely dive back into his new sanctuary, we might as well do it now.

We gently eased the washing machine away from the wall and slowly tipped it on to its side. The fox did not appear, but this manoeuvre induced the washing machine to pour several pints of water on to the kitchen floor. My wife made a most unladylike suggestion. I doubted the possibility of following such a directive, so I merely paddled through the spreading puddle and peered into the bowels of the machine.

The inside was a concentration of electric motors, vee belts, pulleys, pumps, pipes, cables and control gear. The cub, when I did eventually spot him, was tucked away in a shadowy corner beyond this tangled barrier.

Half an hour later the cub was back in the cage, which stood on a generous thickness of newspaper. My hand was scraped and sore from having been thrust through tiny spaces, between sharp bits of washing machine.

We went to bed.

Thank God for Easter Monday – it seemed a very appropriate sentiment all round but particularly so under these circumstances. A day to recover. I stretched and rolled over, then made a suggestion, to which my wife responded that I had better make up my mind whether I wanted tea or sympathy, because I wasn't having both. Before I could choose, she added, 'First I'm going to see what that monster has done to my kitchen, so you might as well settle for tea while I'm down there.' I could hear her chatting to the cub and Sniff, as I stretched and explored various bumps and bruises, all stiffening nicely.

The cub, now known as Ferdi, was in his cage on the lawn when I emerged. Touching noses with Sniff who lay alongside, he was flanked by the two cats and apparently quite composed, until either of us went into the garden, when he obviously became very scared. The first concern was as to whether or not he was weaned. If he wouldn't take food for himself, then feeding him was going to be a difficult problem and in his present state most traumatic for Ferdi. I ran a large circle of heavy wire netting on the lawn. This was a good move because it gave the cub a fair area for exercise and, better still, let Sniff join him – the latter being a very significant fact in what was to follow. Sniff became a substitute mother and willing playmate.

Apart from a break, when I went for a walk to try to loosen up a few stiff joints, Sniff spent virtually all day in the playpen. Attempts to get Ferdi to eat dog food failed inconclusively, since he was most relaxed, and so likely to eat, while Sniff was with him, but was inhibited by whoever placed the food for him. Sniff slurped up these tiny offerings before he recovered his composure. In fact, she was having a great day, having found a new playmate and also getting regular snacks served to her. We decided that if

Ferdi hadn't eaten by the next day, we would have to try to feed him milk and egg, slightly warmed, through a syringe.

My animals get one large meal a day. I don't believe in doggie breakfasts, dinners and teas, and a choccy drop to go to bed with. So as evening approached, we decided to feed the dog, cats and fox simultaneously on the lawn, dog and cats outside the wire and fox inside.

The bowls were set down, Ferdi's containing dog food yet again, puddled into a very moist paste with milk and egg. We set it down and stood well back. The dog and cats fell to immediately; the cub seemed to give long consideration to the situation, before approaching the bowl for an enquiring sniff, then a lap at the liquid that had been forced to the top, before finally bolting down the whole lot. Arms around each other, we laughed our relief at this let-off.

That night he slept in deep straw in a box I had made for him, placed inside a large external cupboard that had once been used for riding tack.

He seemed likely to survive.

2

'If You Love it, Set it Free . . .'

I hate to see animals caged; I believe they are all as entitled to be as free as man himself, probably more so since man's problems are of his own creation; entitled to a large enough piece of this world left undisturbed, to provide for the environmental needs of all species, before, one by one, we push them over the brink to join so many others that have recently tumbled into the abyss of extinction.

I believe man should – must – adjust his numbers to redress the massive imbalance between the human population on one hand, the other animal populations and available resources on the other.

The task gets more awesome by the minute; it will have to be tackled eventually, so why not now while there is still a little left that is worth preserving? I am appalled to reflect upon the changes that have occurred during the time I have taken to consider and commit to paper these dozen lines – how many square miles of rain forest have gone forever? How many more millions of mouths to feed?

I used to watch the tragedy of a brown bear. Once a week I would take some ski coaching on a nylon slope in the grounds of a zoo. The sloping carpet of bristles was just above the bears' enclosure. Whether this was intended to provide the pupils with incentive not to fall, I'm unsure.

One of the bears, always the same one, was kept in a tiny concrete cell beneath the open enclosure. Why, I do not know, but I never saw that creature granted even the appallingly inadequate freedom of the enclosure itself. It took him four shuffling paces to cross that dreadful cell; immediately he made the fourth step he turned with a great ponderous swing and paced four times to swing again. He never glanced at the iron grill through which I looked at him. On my side of the door were millions of square miles, yet man had condemned him, not for any crime, to shuffle his life away, four and four and four and four, nothing to look at but concrete, nothing to do but eat and endure. There was an injustice and a tragedy of immense sadness in that concrete cave.

What an amazing paradox, and sadly so oft repeated, that Teddy, Rupert, Poo and that other famed for his addiction to marmalade sandwiches, find near universal affection, while a real-life prototype should be treated so differently.

Throughout the session, every session, when voices were still for the moment, the scuff, scuff, scuff of great rough feet drifted up to where I was free to indulge in idle pleasure; free to practise something as frivolous, as contrived, as sliding over nylon bristles on planks of wood.

I took to arriving early and going to see him, exactly as I had last seen him; to pushing buns or fruit through the grill, but he never interrupted his pacing. He was right: how could tit-bits compensate him?

I would think what I had done during the week since last I'd looked into his cell. It would probably be singularly unexciting. Then I would consider what he had done.

Yes! I hate the caging of animals.

From the first moment there was a commitment to conditioning Ferdi for as full and normal a foxy life as possible. There was also a lurking awareness that if things went badly, I might produce an animal, not tame enough for one world and not competent enough for the other. This would inevitably condemn him to a life of confinement of some sort. That sad brown bear shuffled across my mind. What I wanted was a fox capable of living free in either world, the final choice to be his own.

'If you love a thing set it free. If it comes back to you it's yours; if it does not, it never was.'

A couple of days later Sniff and Ferdi had become great friends, enthusiastic greetings were exchanged each time they met: strange soprano noises from the cub and standard doggy responses from Sniff. They played for hours. The roll-about rough-house was a bit one sided – Sniff, who obviously had a fair amount of Corgi in the cocktail of her lineage, but was longer in the leg and tail, weighed in at a stocky twenty-eight pounds. At about two pounds, Ferdi was a game competitor who never gave in, and occasionally showed a flash of squeaky-voiced temper. Sometimes the cats would join, briefly, in the game, but it was really too undignified for them. When they hopped into the playpen it was usually for some decorous touching of noses or some licking. Between the cats and Sniff, the cub used to get so much washing, it's a wonder there was anything left to wash. When he objected to this excess of hygiene, he would often be held down by a heavy paw until the bath had been concluded to Sniff's satisfaction, while Ferdi would flop out in tolerant resignation.

From the start, Sniff seemed to know just what the cub needed, making him work hard but always allowing him enough success to keep him encouraged. She would succumb to his roly-poly, fumble-footed attacks, flopping over on to her side, when the cub would scramble over her, worrying at her ears with white needle teeth, while she tried to paddle him off with her front paws. Those slender teeth were very sharp. A couple of days after finding Ferdi, although it was not my birthday, I took a bath. I had developed a sore finger, and with the skin softened by the soaking, I was exploring the offending spot. I was pressing firmly around it when out popped a slim white cone. One of Ferdi's teeth left there by the bite he had taken when I first grabbed him – I believe the only time he ever bit me.

By now, familiarity had made Ferdi much more relaxed towards Carol and me. Our approach was always very gentle and quiet. We talked to him in smooth even tones, avoiding sudden changes of voice or movement, always prefixing by his name anything offered to him. Our approaches were usually beneficial to the cub – feeding times – or tempting him to take a tit-bit from our fingers. For a long while this was a test of courage – a slow nervous approach, then straining forward at full stretch to snatch the morsel and scamper away. I think that most influential of all was Sniff's complete trust in us, being transmitted to the cub.

Although things were going quite well, each night Ferdi had to be caught. There was no submitting to being collected and shut up for the night. Each advance set us back initially.

It was with grave doubts that I decided to put a collar on him. If he escaped and survived, the implications were horrible to contemplate. He would be a full grown fox by the end of the year. A collar tight enough to prevent him slipping it now, would slowly strangle the growing fox long before then. However, since walking on a line would be prelude to going free, there didn't seem much alternative to a collar.

Ferdi did not like the collar.

I got it on him without much trouble, but when I put him down and this thing retained its loose hold on his neck, he went berserk; hissing, spitting, growling his juvenile growl, he tumbled around the playpen, shaking himself, scrabbling with front claws at this thing beneath his chin, rolling on his back in a wild mixture of fright and anger. So extreme was his reaction that I thought of removing the collar, but he had to get used to it sometime. Then, by an unfortunate fluke, he pushed one of his front paws through the collar so that it became stuck beneath his chin. If he had been scared before, he now seemed terrified. I grabbed him, released the trapped foot, sat down on the grass, plopped him into the hollow of my lap and contained him with both hands. He quickly calmed, and I started scratching his ears. When I released him again there was little reaction; occasional grumblings and shaking of the head. After this, he quickly adapted to the collar and soon appeared unaware of it.

The next move in the progression was to tie him on a line. I wanted something light, and used a length of sea fishing line, not nylon. I tied it to his collar, and letting the line run through my fingers, I moved off a few yards. Ferdi ambled off quite unconcerned until he felt the check on his neck, he whirled round and appeared not to realise what was causing the restraint; whether his very young eyes were not focusing critically, I do not know, but he reacted as though under attack from an invisible enemy. Rearing on to his hind legs, sparring at the air with his front paws, growling and spitting furiously, he bounced and jerked backwards as he fought the restraining cord. For several minutes he raged at the end of the line, obviously bewildered and frightened by this strange force he could not understand or identify. When there was no sign of his terror abating, I took the line off his collar. We went though the same procedure several times in the next few days before he could accept it calmly.

Once this had been achieved I started walking him on a line, initially around the garden and then into the field. He didn't walk at all well on a lead, and by dog standards, never was to. It was a patience-testing exercise, and had to be conducted at his design. Only rarely were we keeping station with slack line between us. He would be either diving into the hedge bottom and setting me the problem of untangling the line from deep within the hedge, where he'd weaved it like a cat's cradle; or straining away in front so that I'd run with him, usually in pursuit of Sniff, who, as soon as she came within the radius of the line, would be attacked and in the ensuing tumble often became entangled. When she made off again the cub, legs braced stiffly in front of him, would be dragged along like a child's toy that had lost its wheels.

At this period I spent a lot of time untangling. This indiscipline on the line was of no importance, I was not trying to train a fox to the lead, merely to get him used to being about the countryside in the company of Sniff and me. It was at this stage, when he was at ease in our company, quite willing to play a rather painful game of counting fingers, and easily handled, that we discovered our 'Boy named Sue', or in this case a girl named 'Ferdi'.

Ferdi was a vixen!

Things were progressing very well and there was little that she was afraid of; when she touched noses with inquisitive cows it was not Ferdi but Sniff who became anxious for her safety and would drive the cows off a few paces. The exception to this rule was people; strangers were treated with great suspicion. She would retreat to the limit of her line; if they then advanced she would become frightened, and eventually if they closed with her, her fear would drive her to aggression. It was a trait that disappointed many people, but one that I found desirable, against the day when she might once again be a wild fox. I did nothing to alter it.

As the spring and summer progressed, Ferdi grew rapidly and became increasingly more fun to observe. The fishing line had been replaced by a length of sash cord to which was attached a good springy piece of wood cut from the hedge, about eighteen inches long. It was the last step before real freedom. Tied to her collar, the cord was twelve to fifteen feet long and the wood formed a yoke at the other end which jammed if Ferdi tried to go through the dense hedges around my field.

11

Now began the really exuberant period of Ferdi's life. Already getting the leggy, supple-spined attributes of the quadruped athlete, she was very quick and agile. She would race around the field with the stick cartwheeling after her, and Sniff, without any such handicap, in keen pursuit but already in danger of being outpaced. Sniff, a great retriever of sticks, especially from water, would try to grab the bouncing yoke, and when she succeeded would then career around in tandem with the fox, or would attempt to bring the stick back for me to throw, giving the appearance of taking a very reluctant fox for a walk. In a straight pull Sniff would eventually bring both stick and fox back to me; but there rarely was a straight pull. When she felt the check, Ferdi would turn to see what the dog was up to, and launch a playful attack on her. Their tussles were, by now, very much more evenly balanced affairs; still outweighed and outpowered, Ferdi's speed gave her a distinct edge unless she deliberately opted for a close-quarter rough and tumble, when they would roll all over each other, the one underneath forever trying to paddle the other off with her feet.

Sniff would endeavour to ignore the attack and keep a grip on the precious stick, but the fox would persist until, in order to defend herself, Sniff would have to drop it. The fox would immediately break off the engagement and rush away, with Sniff once again chasing the elusive stick.

For the first time I observed what I considered to have been an action based on reason rather than innate instinct. Since I left them on their own in the field, I cannot be certain how long the thought process took or indeed if initially she was merely mimicking Sniff's habit, but when after an hour Sniff came back into the garden, Ferdi followed her carrying the yoke. With her mouth partly open, she always appeared to be grinning, and now, bright eyed and vital with energy and enthusiasm, she gave the impression of being highly amused. Having so quickly solved this silly little problem I'd set for her, the joke, it seemed, was on me.

Several times after that I saw her pick up the stick, then easily outrun the pursuing dog. It was an interesting but disturbing development, because she was much more likely to wriggle through the hedge with the stick held in her mouth, than to pull it through on the end of the line where she had no control over it. If in my absence she once got out of the field with the yoke attached to

her, it would become a serious hazard. If she wandered any
distance and it became tangled she would be at the mercy of
anyone who happened upon her. I decided only to run her like that
when I could be with her.

3

First Visitors

We had moved into the cottage in the short dark days before Christmas four years earlier. Our very first visitor had called to pay his respects that same evening. Carol had opened the kitchen door and standing just on the fringe of the wedge of yellow light that drove into the darkness was a vague huge shape, 'like the hound of the Baskervilles', was her description. I reopened the door, which had been closed so abruptly, and there was Blackie, slightly hurt by such an ill-mannered display towards a neighbour who had come to introduce himself, and check that we were safely installed. He came in to see how we were managing and graciously accepted a few biscuits, as would any visitors, while making it quite clear that it mattered not to him that the place was like a tip; and we were really not to worry about it.

Big, rangy, raw boned with a rough coat; almost entirely black but greying a bit around the muzzle with maturity. He gave the impression of a tough, rugged forty year old with a touch of hoar frost about the temples. This turned out to be exactly what he was. This was his patch, he was top of the pecking order and woe betide any dog that forgot it. Shaped like a miniature Irish Wolfhound, but no hound of the Baskervilles, Blackie was all heart and good-will. He became a very regular visitor and escort.

A couple of years later little Sniff, an abandoned Christmas present, had slotted into Blackie's kingdom; it seemed that the great despot could always find a place for a new young bitch. We didn't seek his opinion or permission before having her spayed. But he didn't seem to bear a grudge. I suspect he was getting a wee bit past his peak and probably had more than he could cope with already. Nevertheless, they became firm friends on a purely platonic basis, and so she slipped under the mantle of his patronage and protection; this I guess in turn brought him under mine, an office I discharged some time later when he stood falsely accused of stock worrying. I had, fortunately, witnessed the entire incident: the miscreant, who had really done very little harm had been a large, very yellow labrador. Subsequently I'd managed to out bluff a gun-toting farmer in an exchange of unpleasantries reminiscent of the junior school playground. After he'd told me what he was about to do to me with his gun, and with similar eloquence I'd told him where I would place the gun so that he might carry it home leaving both hands free, we each put out our tongues and declared that my brother is bigger than your brother and there the matter ended.

I had long ago introduced Blackie to Ferdi quite without qualms, since he would never harm so small and openly friendly a creature. Now that Ferdi was regularly racing about the field, Blackie got into the habit of joining in the chase.

In my field, which now did no more than provide grazing for someone else's horses, there stood a stock compound, its posts and rails were still sound. Part of this skirted with chainlink fencing, and with wire netting laid in the ground and over the top would provide a most suitable place for the vixen. We provided a straw filled wooden sleeping box with hinged roof, and clad in thin zinc sheet to minimise wear and provide weather-proofing. Working days she spent in the enclosure, and after her evening's liberty was shut up again each night.

The first priority on arriving home from work was to set her free; even at this tender age she was very noisy in her greeting.

The famous 'scream' of the vixen (I'm not sure that is the word I'd choose to describe Ferdi's vocalising, but it seems to be well established in the glossary of foxy matter), experienced for the first time, unexpectedly, at close quarters, can certainly make the senses prickle and add an extra chill to night time in the January woodlands. It is not solely a mating call. I know a couple of clandestine prowlers of the darkened countryside who claim that it is not even peculiar to the vixen. One, whom I shall call Cyril because that's not his name, told me a tale to support his opinion.

Cyril is not averse to wandering through the woods at night, about his own business. This particular night business had been poor and, not wanting to go home empty handed, he decided to skirt a certain farmyard where he had discovered that several marans had forsaken their nestboxes and begun laying 'loose' in the hedge bottom. Half a dozen beautiful dark brown, rich-tasting maran eggs would adequately reward him for the several fruitless cross country miles he had put in that evening.

There was a steady breeze blowing and Cyril took a wide circuit to bring it into his face as he approached the farm. Several times as he worked quietly along the hedge bottom, he heard the rattle as a farm dog dragged its chain on the cobbled farmyard.

Cyril had collected his breakfast, when nearby and without warning the 'scream' of a vixen sent ice water down his back. Cyril dropped to a low crouch to search the skyline. A large dog fox was sitting on top of a wheel-about hen coop. As Cyril watched, he called again and jumped lightly down, immediately vanishing against the dark back drop.

Cyril explained, 'The bugger really blew the whistle on me. The farm dog started a hell of a racket just t'other side o' t'edge. A bloody great shaft o' light floods out from the kitchen door and cuts right across the track just behind me. Trapped in a dead end between two hedges, I 'ad t'goo through a real wild patch o'bramble, and bloody quick, afore they lets the dog loose. I come out t'other side wi' more prickles than a bloody hotchie; lovely maran eggs dribblin' out o' me shirt front, past me belt and down inside me breeches.

'Oh yes! I can tell ye a dog fox can make the same scream as a vixen; or summat damn like it.'

Ferdi's 'scream' was really quite a short call, but she repeated it with such rapidity that it sounded almost continuous, rising to a crescendo. It was undoubtedly stimulated by excitement, which is presumably why this part of the fox's vocabulary is generally associated with the mating period. It was one very excited vixen that heard our nightly approach to release her. She would start screaming her welcome long before I got to the enclosure. Usually one or more dogs would be dashing round and round the wire, keen to start the game. To my ear there was nothing particularly distinctive about the engine note of my car; but both the fox and the dogs unerringly recognised it.

Blackie had taken to bringing a mate along, and the passage of my car along the lane was a signal for the dogs to pop out of a gateway or from under a hedge and dash along in my wake, while Sniff would scamper to her station at the end of my drive, and the fox would probably be already serenading. One felt really welcomed home.

With her yoke attached and freed from the compound, Ferdi would observe a short ritual – there would be enthusiastic greetings for all of us in turn; she dashed from one to another, tail held low and furiously brushing the ground.

'Butch' was smooth-coated and black; labrador was one of the ingredients. He was not much more than a pup and about two-thirds of Blackie's size. If either dog got impatient and pawed at Ferdi before the welcoming ceremony was concluded, she would turn on the offender with jaws open and yak, yak, yak at him from the back of her throat. Sniff never offended in this way; unable to compete once the tail chase started, she would quickly go through a rather more intimate form of greeting, usually involving some mutual sniffing and licking. She had probably already spent a lot of time at the compound during the day, doing a bit of nose touching through the wire. Now, craftily, she spent the rest of the brief ceremony trying to get a grip on the stick at the end of Ferdi's line.

Whether Ferdi had first to get rid of Sniff or not, eventually, either carrying or dragging the yoke, she led them off in a furious energy extravaganza, up, down and around the field until they all piled into a worrying, kicking, rolling heap and finally into open-mouthed, heaving-flanked, dripping-tongued rest, stretched out forelegs straight in front, hind legs straight behind, bellies to the ground, they resembled collapsed rocking horses. They panted like steam locos. Then they would troop across to the old, spring-fed stone trough, and with a slap slap slapping of pink tongues they would, again like steam loco's, take on prodigious quantities of cold, clear water.

As it became the normal rather than the exception for Ferdi to carry her stick, I decided it was time for her to go free.

We had a nice, safe routine that provided the fox with a lot of exercise, fun and company; and me with much interest and pleasure. But I wanted more for her, and to this end I was about to put it all at hazard.

All she had to do was keep running and she could not be recaught.

For a little vixen with too much trust and too little experience, even with the resource of her kind, it would be an unnecessarily dangerous countryside she would wander. Who would notice the collar before he squeezed the trigger? Who, with a gun in his hands, would care?

I was holding Ferdi, the dogs bounding excitedly about me, looking up at her, tails fit to fall off. I agonised a few more seconds. I was about to relinquish the control, to hand her all the options; there would be only whatever bond had been established between us to hold her. Anyone who has trained a hawk knows well the feeling before he casts it off for the first time. I had made my decision, and she was beginning to struggle in my arms. I threw her lightly down. But she knew this was different; the greetings were very brief and away she went.

Released from her handicap, her performance was dramatic; she put on a scintillating display of speed and agility. Then, on the third circuit of the field, she passed through the hedge as though it did not exist, and led the dogs, streaming in her wake, across two fields and out of my sight. I thought: that's it, you did it too soon. I whistled piercingly through my fingers. I had been using the whistle as well as her name for some time. I ran across to the hedge but could see neither dogs nor fox. I suspected that they had swung left along the line of a hedge three fields away, because I could see a group of cattle on the far side of that field, all heads turned in typically inquisitive fashion.

I was about to follow, when the fox shot into view, having now come through the next hedge along and turned back towards my field, but far out to my left. I whistled again and she came on a straight run for my top hedge. The first dog to appear was Blackie, followed by Butch with little Sniff going gamely, but well behind. Ferdi was out of sight again for several seconds, then emerged from a patch of thistles at the top end of my field and came at a good fast lope, straight to me, where, evidently very well pleased with herself, panting so that she appeared to be grinning broadly, she dusted vigorously with her brush, while making soft yuck yucking noises deep in her throat.

The last to arrive was Sniff, and not bothering to join the group, she headed straight for the trough, where the others all joined her. Blackie was the only one who could get a drink without standing on his hindlegs, so the other three stood in line and slurped away.

Ferdi remained free until dusk, when she quite happily trotted behind me across the field to her compound.

As if to celebrate the event, Blackie next turned up with two more mates; a border collie from a local farm, and a real thoroughbred 'Allsorts', a large shaggy chap, white with two almost perfect black circles in his rough coat. I christened him Bull's Eye. I never knew his real name or from where he came. Whether the boss had held auditions, I can't tell, but they were well chosen and slotted happily into the ritual without any problems.

Now, like a mechanised, latterday Pied Piper, as I drove the last quarter mile home, the enchanting note of my exhaust pipe had dogs appearing like magic and bounding gleefully after me. The collie's owner asked one evening, 'What do you keep in your boot, a hundredweight of sausage?'

4

In Quest of Fun and Food

On reflection, I can well believe that Ferdi's training in the skills of the wild fox was going on continually as an adjunct to the overt, frivolous life of fun she enjoyed with the dogs and ourselves. Certainly the wild race with the dogs, and the daily rough-housing with heavier opponents was honing reflexes and strengthening muscle.

Now she was running free for several hours each day. I've little doubt that judged purely by athletic performance, she was as fit as any wild cub at the same stage of development. But there is much more to being equipped to survive in the wild than merely being fit. If she was ever to succeed as a wild fox she had to achieve the two fundamental elements which made up the other side of the survival equation: she must be able to acquire a regular food supply; she must not expose herself to unnecessary danger in doing so. In man's plastic-wrapped, clock-ticking, micro chip existence, orderly routine is the efficient way, the way to success. In the natural world it's an invitation to disaster.

With several of our original objectives achieved and the wind set fair for future progress, my concern centred increasingly upon one particular aspect of a wild cub's education, which I could see no way of simulating. When parent foxes lead half grown cubs on hunting forays, they are not only demonstrating hunting and foraging skills but, probably more importantly, by their own caution and transmitted anxieties in certain circumstances, they are conditioning the cubs to react in the same way as themselves, relieving the need for the cubs to go through the hazardous and often fatal exercise of acquiring conditioned reflexes through first-hand experience. The fox is a versatile opportunist and only really vulnerable if an earth is discovered in which there are very young cubs; for the vixen will take great personal risks to try to move them. It is easy to imagine that a cub, having missed this natural conditioning and as yet not skilled enough to obtain his supper from the wild larder, would find easy pickings at the farmyard take-away, and would, having once discovered the secret of soft living, break the basic rule and become predictable. It would then be a matter of time, and little of that, before he found the trap or snare, the poisoned bait, or hail of lead shot; man's endearing devices.

Ferdi was going to learn little of value in the arts of actually bringing a quarry to her paws either from me or from the dogs. The dogs' hunting instincts had been dulled. For generations dogs have depended on man to provide. There was, of course, great en-thusiasm and excitement when they found a rabbit sitting out. It was flushed and chased with a great sense of fun. When it had dived for cover into its air-raid shelter under the hedge, they would mill around the entrance with thrashing tails discussing what might have been, if only they'd not tripped over that bit of bramble. Never mind, in the pantry was always this week's special offer, and the old boy was a dab hand with the tin opener.

I'm sure that the cub does learn hunting skills from its parents and under their influence masters its craft more quickly than the self-taught cub. But after observing Ferdi's development, I'm certain that the foundations of these skills are innate – instinctive and, given the time to learn by trial and error, the DIY cub will acquire a comprehensive competence in the vital art.

In this respect, at least, I could act the surrogate parent fox, being the provider while she practised providing for herself. In this, also, she had a minor advantage over her wild equivalents – it certainly could not offset their advantages over her – but it was something. The wild cub is on a tight schedule, like all things in the precisely integrated world of nature, and he had better be master of his craft by October/November time, for his parents will not tolerate him around after that. In the modern vernacular he will be given the 'Big E'. Ferdi was on no such timetable. I would provide, for as long as she required the service. So, if the self-teaching process were to take longer it did not matter.

The fare of a wild fox is very varied, ranging from earthworms – he will sit on a lawn in a rain storm, gobbling them down as they surface – through a great range of insects and small game, comprising mostly rats, mice, rabbits and, according to legend, dead cats. I've heard it opined that 'There's nowt to touch a dead cat if ye batin' for a fox.' Except in extremes, I doubt that the dead cat would have much attraction.

There is so much cliché and myth bound up with tales of poaching, 'keeping and the amazing cunning of various individual animals, that at times the whole thing assumes fairy tale proportions. I enjoy but profoundly disbelieve most of it, but still would not have it otherwise, except for the fact that some creatures get damned with a grossly exaggerated reputation for villainy. I suspect a vested interest at work. If you get your 'jollies' by killing and maiming animals, public indignation may be averted by first labelling them vermin; so, many long standing slanders are perpetuated without their truths being questioned. Similarly, if you wish to destroy wild flowers you first label them weeds then spray them into oblivion.

In the role of defending advocate for wildlife, I would first demand recognition of the basic tenet: it is not a pre-requisite that wild creatures shall benefit man in order to qualify to be left unmolested. When man monopolises vast tracts of land that should support a properly proportioned balance of wildlife, then he should be prepared to pay the rent without turning murderously vengeful about it. A few cabbages and lettuce for the rabbits, grain for the birds and a few chicken dinners for the foxes.

If innocent means the defendent had no part in the deed, then my case is lost. If innocent means he did it in innocence, within the natural order of things, taking what he needed in a situation that has been forced upon him, taking without avarice, then my case is made, and if man still says guilty he sets a standard by which he is guiltier a billion billion times. If he says not guilty then he, himself, is still guilty of cruelly oppressing the innocent. From butterfly to bison, from tiger to turtle they have all learned of man's compassion.

I suspect man's treatment of his own kind is an extension of his treatment of the animals. The slip into barbarism is an insidious one, slowly, almost imperceptibly it erodes standards of decency.

As the threshold of what is tolerable slips backwards, that which once shocked and troubled the conscience becomes acceptable – the norm – and it takes even more savagery to shock, and this in turn is absorbed by the ever-retreating threshold until atrocities become commonplace. I make no distinction between the mentality that tortures the chained, defenceless prisoner; that tears apart the exhausted defenceless victim of the chase; that condemns the gunshot maimed escapee to die a lingering pain-racked death, whether it be the hare that has limped away from the firing line, or the goose broken in flight that has crashed out on the inaccessible mudflats. As if asking why, his weakening calls will haunt the tidal marsh for days, before a sad peace returns to the stiff reeds and the hump of feathers out on the cold mud.

How are the silent majority, who if they mobilised could bring all this to an abrupt end, kept silent? Mainly, as in all issues, because a sense of helplessness drapes a cloak of apathy over them. Their feelings need to be collected and directed. Partly because they are kept ignorant of what goes on, and partly because those who indulge in such practices vilify their victims in an attempt to lessen adverse reaction to their unholy fun. Man will massacre his fellow creatures for idle pleasure, just to see them fall; for profit, often to satisfy the utterly frivolous vanity of his fellow man. He will kill them that he may greedily occupy more land which he will often use in a wasteful destructive fashion for short term gain. He will use them as subjects in various scientific experiments that range from the perhaps justifiable medical research, through the trivial testing of cosmetics, to the diabolical testing of chemical and biological agents for war and the effects of various types of military and what is laughingly termed sporting ammunition on the living animal body. In all he will display a ruthless disregard for everything except self interest.

No other creature ever to walk this planet has conducted itself in this deplorable fashion, yet let a particularly horrific crime be committed – a baby raped and murdered, a frail old lady crippled – sobbing parents and stern-faced police chiefs are interviewed, and what do they say of the thugs concerned? They say, 'These aren't human beings, these are animals.' A convenient and amazing reversal of roles. An unfortunate and unfair comment that inadvertently complements the propaganda of the blood sporter, since

23

it appears to imply that animals are nasty vicious creatures for whom anything is good enough, from whom one can expect no better. It follows that those who maltreat them are doing nothing that's too bad.

The earliest supplements to Ferdi's rations were insects – easily obtained, just a matter of poking patiently through the undergrowth. The fox is a versatile chap, and the composition of his menu will vary from one area to another, depending on the density of various prey species. In Ferdi's part of the world there was still quite a lot of grassland. I think that generally the 'bread and butter' in the fox's larder is the small rodent, particularly the dwellers in and travellers through the galleries that vein the basement of grass meadows: voles, shrews and various mice. Plentiful and easy to obtain for most of the year, they are a food source that the young fox learns to tap to his great advantage. Predictably enough, Ferdi's first serious hunting efforts were directed at those plump little furries beneath the grass.

Firstly, there was the awareness that they were to be found in such places, this I think was merely through the functioning of keen senses, particularly hearing and smell. Once the presence of these interesting rustling creatures had been discovered, the technique for bringing them to the table quickly developed from an uncertain, doubt-filled inefficiency, with probably no better than a one-in-four or -five success rate, to a very confident, highly efficient, almost infallible technique.

It was very amusing to sit in the grasses on a warm summer's day and watch her. At first there was intense concentration: neck sloped backwards, head tipped down as though she were tucking her chin into her chest. She reminded me of a blackbird tracking an underground worm. A quick shift of the head, as the quarry moved, and a dab with one or both front feet. Her head would move again as she followed the rustle of the escaping creature, then there would be a hopeful poking about beneath her front feet with her nose, to discover nothing. She would relax, trot over to Sniff and begin to tantalise her – obviously explaining that she had not really been trying to catch a mouse.

Within a few days it was very different – sometimes an approach of such lightness of foot that she seemed to strive not to bend the grasses; instant transformation to perfect tableau, perhaps caught in mid-stride by the Witch's wand, raised paw turned to stone. 'Ah! Still alive.' The head tilts sideways, like a kitten on a birthday card. The victim is spotted. Sometimes, her quarry was located and pinpointed while she was on the move, but whichever, speed or stealth, the result was the same. A swift pace into position and up into the air she'd go, three feet high, almost vertically, she would come down stiff legged, all four feet bunched together, with a thump that collapsed the gallery on top of or around the victim. If she missed and he moved off, there was no time wasted exploring the first result; a swift movement and up again. It was rare for anything to escape, in plunged the sharp muzzle and out came a mouse, neatly as a winkle on a pin. These were no more than succulent snacks and would be flipped back and swallowed. Sometimes in a good twenty minute spell she would take a dozen little morsels. I used to think that were it not for foxes we should be knee deep in mousey creatures.

Rabbits were eventually to become, next to mice, Ferdi's most commonly taken prey, although she found them a far more difficult adversary and it was to take her much longer to acquire the necessary experience to make this important food source available to her. I like the old rabbit – part of everyone's childhood. *Brer Rabbit and Brer Fox, Brer Rabbit and the Tar Baby.* I've a lot of admiration for the resilience of a species that has been subjected to a scientifically orchestrated genocide and has made such a strong repost. It is reassuring to find that nature can occasionally prevail. Would that it could do so in response to all man's violations.

For Ferdi it was learn as you go, with no particular urgency about the learning. Life was still mainly for fun. Energy was only for burning and games were played at a hundred miles per hour. She had developed into the most beautiful runner, her speed and balance giving her an almost liquid progress. She had a furiously tight swerve (she was the only thing in the world to swerve sharper than my tee shot) and, linking a series of these moves together without noticeable loss of speed, she would thread her way through the chasing dogs. She could produce a huge leap sideways at near to full pace. Her ability was such that she would jump on to and off the back of a dog during the race. It was no longer a straight tail chase, she would pull out a comfortable lead then turn and run back into the pack jinking and swerving through them. It seemed she could do anything, but fly, and gloried in it. She would ease into a long loping gait until they were right on top of her, then, when it seemed she had left her escape too late, she would throw an incredibly tight turn with fierce acceleration, then ease her pace and let them come up to her again. Sometimes when she ran quite alone, for no better reason than sheer exuberance, she would curve her way in a series of absolutely regular lefts and rights, a racing metronome, her body swaying smoothly over her feet as she changed her weight, leaning far into the next curve like a racing motor cyclist. She could throw a glorious dummy – approaching the dogs at high speed she would dip her shoulders to the right, far outside the line of her feet, until it appeared that she must swerve hard right or fall over. At the last moment she would shift her head to the left, bringing enough weight back to restore balance, and with her legs and body in an exaggerated right-hand bank, she would hold a straight line or even move the other way. I don't think the dogs ever learnt to pick this one up – they always moved to intercept a swerve that never happened.

She was a glorious explosion of enthusiasm and the joy of living. It was contagious – after an hour in the presence of such unbounded zest and mischief I was invariably in a laughing mood, no matter how gloomily I may have started. The whole wild sky-larking pack provided a wonderful antedote to 'one of those days'.

It usually ended in the same fashion, when she, instead of attacking and rushing away, would worry at the hind legs of one of the dogs, it was usually Sniff, whose chunky build made her less agile than the rest. She would turn and grab the fox, and they would all pile into a tumbling, rolling confusion of teeth and paws. Then off to the bar for liquid refreshment, sometimes sharing the old stone trough with a couple of horses that lived in my field at that time. When playtime was over, the pack usually dispersed each about his own business. It was fairly unusual for them to tag along for a walk.

Rabbits were the source of greatest fun, whether pursued by the entire pack, as a pair with Sniff, or when Ferdi was alone. She chased them with great vigour and enjoyment, and for a long time, without any obvious attempts to increase her chances of catching them.

It was a very Corinthian attitude – the taking part was the important thing, not the winning. Ferdi was invariably the closest when the rabbit shot down a hole or under a pile of logs. Several times I saw her so close and borne away by the chase that her head actually plunged into a burrow and her shoulders thumped the soft rim. There was no careful locating of the quarry, no stalk into a position of advantage, no selectivity as to what was worth chasing and what had too great a start. It was all part of this great fun thing she'd discovered, called life. Although it wasn't getting her any rabbits, it was honing her fitness to an amazing edge.

Her speed of movement and reaction were demonstrated one evening while we were out walking. We had met someone else; as usually happened, at the distant approach of a stranger, Ferdi had melted away. A few minutes later, as Sniff and I approached my field, she reappeared again and came at a good pace along the hedgerow towards us. She startled a blackbird which shot from the hedge shrieking its alarm. With no warning and in full flow, Ferdi rose three or four feet and took the luckless bird out of the air. I have occasionally seen cats do this, using their claws to seize the victim, and I've seen dogs grab a pheasant, partridge or other ground bird that has crouched too long and allowed the dog to get right on top of it before it has attempted to rise, but never before or since have I seen a bird in full flight so neatly held.

About now Ferdi took her first rabbit. Whether her technique was improving or circumstances just happened to be advantageous, I don't know since I didn't witness the drama. She appeared through the hedge with a large rabbit. She was by now, I assumed, approaching three-quarters grown, although in fact she did not get much larger. She was to be quite a little lady. She was making awkward progress, head held high, neck strained back and still the rabbit's hind legs dragged on the ground. She was forced into mincing little steps to avoid treading on it. At first I thought she had picked up one with myxi', there were a few about again. She let me have a look at it, while she sat at my feet, giving me her undivided attention, obviously wanting it understood that I could take a look, but it belonged to her. It was, or rather had been until a few minutes earlier, a healthy rabbit. I returned the prize, and she did something I was to witness many times. She took it into the loose, fibrous soil at the hedge bottom and in remarkably short time cut it into two near equal parts. She used the specially evolved shearing teeth in the side of the typical vulpine jaw, but what I found remarkable was that although the large rabbit filled her mouth, hanging out on each side, she managed to cut it only in the one place.

She scraped a hole with her front feet, deposited half her rabbit and with nodding movements of her head pushed soil and leaves over it with her nose. I found this very amusing, laughed and called her an idiot, saying, 'use your feet you mutt' or something to that effect. She suspended work and raised a soiled muzzle to regard me. Any unusual noise was likely to elicit this response and it was very funny because it created the impression that she was giving very careful consideration to what had been said. It's fortunate that she wasn't, or she would have thought me the mutt, since the longer I knew Ferdi the more I realised that what she was doing is standard foxy practice. I have since observed wild foxes behave in exactly the same fashion.

The larder disguised to her satisfaction, she carried the now manageable other half over to her compound and buried it just outside the outer wire and next to a pile of horse muck with which she filled the scrape, poking her nose into it, quite unconcernedly. You would think that the sensitive moist nose would get sore when used as a scraper; why foxes prefer nose to feet for the operation I'm not sure. Perhaps it provides a progressive check on how well they are concealing the smell of the treasure they are burying. I could often get a good idea where she had buried a choice joint, by the debris that stuck to her nose, a particular giveaway being wet grass clippings. She would hide something in the garden by working round it, nosing clippings from a recent lawn mowing until it was concealed. When satisfied that her secret was safe, she'd turn up at the kitchen door with her face covered in green freckles.

5

The Big Search

Ever keen to give Ferdi more freedom, I experimented with a running line arrangement. The idea was to have her on a shortish line, say twelve feet or so, and to have this sliding on a long static line of whatever length I could brace taut enough to keep it from sagging to the ground. By way of experiment I ran a length of heavy, plastic-covered, electrical cable round three sides of the compound. Where it passed round the corner posts, it obviously lay against the timber, but it was slack enough for Ferdi to pull it clear and allow the running line to slide round the corner. This arrangement gave her freedom to roam within an area of twelve feet by one hundred feet, the compound measuring sixty feet by twenty feet. The running line was a thin cord of coarse, very strong hemp with a short light chain at each end carrying a spring snap, dog-collar-type, clip. One was clipped over the static line and one into the brass loop on her collar.

I watched Ferdi travel up and down the line a few times. The clip tended to jam at the corners but she just jerked it round, without problems. I left her and Sniff and went back to the cottage. After a considerable time Sniff wandered back into the garden. Sometime later still I went into the field. As I approached the compound I could not see the fox; she was evidently lying in the grass on the far side of the compound. She was not! Ferdi and the entire running line had vanished.

A few moments of disbelief.

The clip could not have come undone, therefore someone must have undone it. I am aware that I possess in full measure that typical human trait, the readiness to think the worst of one's fellow man, despite having been proved wrong in this assumption on numerous occasions. However, in this case there could be no doubt – unless the leaf-spring had broken, which was highly unlikely – that to detach the running line it would have to have been deliberately unclipped. The design purpose of the chain and clip was to prevent the safety cover tubes on agricultural equipment driveshafts from rotating when the shaft inside spins. They had been 'perked' from a recent engineering project I had carried out and were well made items.

Someone had either kidnapped Ferdi, still on the end of her line, or had unclipped her but, not daring to risk being bitten while releasing the clip at her collar, had undone the other end and let her, no doubt in considerable panic at his presence, trail a very dangerous handicap off across the countryside. Whatever his motives, personal gain or a misguided idea that he was liberating some unfortunate wild animal, I determined that when I caught the interfering 'gentleman', I would break at least one of his legs.

I sprinted to where a stark, tall elm stood in my hedge, sad victim of the Dutch disease, and climbed thirty or forty feet up its desecrated corpse. This gaunt leafless perch gave me good views all around, for a considerable distance. I could see neither man nor fox. I searched for five minutes in case either or both should emerge from cover into my view. Some movement excited my attention, but it was a man and dog bringing the Jersey ladies in for milking.

I climbed down, and yelled for Sniff. She appeared through the garden hedge, spotted me and trundled across.

'Find Ferdi,' I told her, 'Where's Ferdi?'

It was a fairly unreasonable request. The field must have been full of recent fox scent, crossing and recrossing in great confusion. But still, this was a game Sniff liked and was very good at. I displayed my open empty hands, palms towards her; this had, from very early days, been the signal for her to search; originally it had indicated that I wasn't pulling her leg, I really had thrown the stick and she was to go and fetch it. It developed into a general signal for her to track something. Away went Sniff, nose down, tail wagging furiously, well pleased with her task. She turned with the erratic, directionless gyrations of a wurlygig beetle on its pond. It was obvious that she was thoroughly confused by a plethora of good scent and was following the trails of Ferdi at play. I was impressed by her reaction. Her head came up and she began a steady patrol of the hedges, evidently continuing the search by sight and hearing. I walked with her as she worked along the hedge bottom. We had no luck.

When a fox is badly frightened, you don't need a sensitive organ like a dog's nose to detect its scent; it is pretty pungent. I hadn't noticed anything but I took Sniff over to the compound and again asked her to find Ferdi – there was a good chance that the scent of the frightened fox would overlay the general smells, and that Sniff would soon get us on the trail. Again we drew a blank – again she was spoilt for choice, with no one track recommending itself more than another.

Apparently Ferdi hadn't been frightened, which would certainly have been the case had a stranger approached her. I got another clip and, controlling it only from the free end of the chain, I experimented for a long while, but despite all my cunning it remained firmly attached. I was about to give up, concluding that Sniff had let me down, when I saw the clip rotate so that the leaf-spring came against the face of the corner post and, as I continued to pull, was forced away from the hook, leaving a gap. I reversed the direction of pull and the static line came to lie in that gap; a further jerk and the clip and chain dangled in my hand.

Now I knew how to do it I undid the clip half a dozen times in the next twenty attempts. 'Sorry little 'un.' I roughed the dog's ears.

She had no idea I was apologising, or why; but a bit of fuss was always acceptable and as I sat on the grass and indulged in a few profanities, she bundled into my legs and fell across my lap. Once again I had misjudged my fellow man. But the fact remained that Ferdi could get into a lot of trouble with that line and clip snarling every hedge she passed through.

It had taken me about twenty minutes to induce this trick to happen, but I am a great believer in 'Sod's Law', and I knew that the very first time that Ferdi had gone round the corner (after I'd left her), she might have sprung that clip. In which case she would have been free for over two hours and might be tangled up on any barbed wire fence, in any hedge or coppice within a radius of several miles. It suddenly seemed an awfully big country.

Sniff and I set out immediately, it was already late afternoon.

There seemed little reason to suppose Ferdi would take one of the regular tracks, but since it was all guesswork anyway, one direction was as likely as another. I decided to wander over to a place where she had recently chased rabbits on two or three occasions. Periodically I would call and whistle, and ask Sniff to 'find Ferdi'. I got no response and although the dog cast about over quite a wide track as we walked along, she only succeeded in putting up a few rabbits, which I discouraged her from chasing. The field where Ferdi had got used to finding rabbits, sloped steeply down to a railway cutting; it was the railway bank that was home for the rabbits. I approached this field until my head alone topped the rise and I could just see down to the railway. A dozen rabbits grazed steadily, well out into the field. Ferdi had certainly not been there recently. We continued along a track Ferdi had followed on several occasions, but we returned in darkness without having any suggestion of her whereabouts.

I went out into the fields around my cottage several times during the evening, whistling her. It seemed likely she'd come back at feeding time and as I walked along I could almost picture her sudden appearance, out of the hedge, out of the darkness, unseen until she was there with us, screeching her welcome, boisterous in her reunion. But it didn't happen and gradually it seemed less likely to happen.

That evening the topic that concerned us most was whether or not she was caught up by the line, and if she was, would she bite through it to release herself? There was a foot of light chain, closest to her, and I hoped she would not try to bite through that. The picture that haunted our thoughts was of that happy, vital little creature being casually slaughtered, or worse, cruelly treated by someone who knew nothing about her. Perhaps she was being baited by dogs – dogs she would not recognise as enemies, expecting them to behave like Sniff and Blackie.

Next day was Sunday and already life around the cottage seemed very flat, as if someone had turned off a catchy tune. It was the sort of quiet that we had come to recognise as a sign that she was in some mischief, that would prompt an apprehensive 'Oh, oh!' and set us trying to find out what she was up to. Her presence and personality had become so much a part of the place that we would still be surprised to look up and realise that she wasn't in the garden, or being chased out of the kitchen having eventually provoked Sniff beyond the rules of reasonable forbearance.

With Sniff, I wandered further afield to visit a large pit, the steep sides of which had crumbled to expose great webs of roots that dived back into the bank like worms trying to escape a giant blackbird. It was known locally as the 'Pit Hole' an apparently unnecessary duplication of terms, nevertheless that was how everyone in the area referred to it. It was very old and its origin uncertain, although it had most likely been dug out to produce the homemade bricks still evident in some of the older farms and cottages in the area. It was certainly several centuries old and had not been worked for much of that time, no one seemed to know when last clay had been taken out.

A good sized pool had formed in the bottom, willows and hawthorne had colonised its edge round to the steep end face, which sprouted some fine oaks, beech and sycamore, whose roots, thrust deep under the surrounding field on one side, arched and twisted in fresh air on the other, like mangroves left standing on fingertips when the tide empties their swamp.

At that time it was owned by an enlightened farmer, who regarded his acres both as livelihood and, wherever possible, a wildlife refuge. Shooting was absolutely banned, save for an occasional drive against rabbits and woodies if they became too numerous.

A hole in the ground is a valuable commodity, but Mr Jeffson had resisted the 'swift buck', easily earned by allowing the tipping lorries to regurgitate the wastes of industry upon his land. He had spared his hedgerows and left his bits of woodland standing. If I had charge of the matter, there would be changes in the way farmers qualify for subsidies. There would be no subsidies for ploughing back or pouring away the results of over production, over production stimulated by subsidies in the first place. There would be subsidies to encourage farmers of Mr Jefferson's philosophy.

The 'Pit Hole' was home for waterfowl, rabbit, rook, fox and badger, tawny and little owl, heron, roach and perch and much besides. There was so much to excite a keen nose that Sniff nearly wagged herself off her feet in her excitement as she tobogganed down the bank and threaded her way, nose to the ground, through the bowers of exposed roots and the holes beneath.

Earth and set had perhaps started as one large set and some holes on the flank had been usurped by foxes who, by deliberately scent-marking them with the pungent fox scent, induced the badgers to leave home. I climbed around the trees on that steep bank for a couple of interesting hours, but without having any reason to believe Ferdi was there. There was evidence that at least one earth was in use, neat paw marks in the finely crumbled clay around the mouth, and ruddy brown hair on a tangle of rusty barbed wire where an old fence had been undermined to hang part way down the bank.

The unmistakable five toes of the badger prints were everywhere, as were bundles of discarded bedding that had rolled like tumbleweed down to the water's edge. On a small loose bank at one end of the 'Pit Hole' we found the badgers' latrine – fastidious as cats in their toilet, they dig a shallow scoop, make their deposit, but, no doubt proud of what they have done, do not cover it over. Perhaps that's why cats do cover their work – there's nothing to be proud of about cat muck. The latrine bank was pock-marked with these shallow scrapes, each neatly centred with a white offering. I do not know what had been on the menu, whatever it was seemed to have been liberally garnished with whitewash.

We returned home by a different route, to cover as much ground as possible.

Since I had wandered fairly close to it, I made a diversion to take me into a small patch of woodland, part of an estate that leases out to a large shooting syndicate – keepered in the old mindless fashion – nothing being deemed to have any right to live on the estate except pheasants, and they only until the first of October. It was exactly the place where I dreaded Ferdi's getting caught up. The one full-time keeper and I had crossed swords before over the use of a pole trap. I considered him perfectly capable of setting his terriers to tear a trapped fox to pieces. The fact that she had got a collar with a name and telephone number on it would make no difference to him.

We had on that occasion come close to blows when, prowling where I should, strictly speaking, not have been, I discovered a pole trap set up in a woodland clearing. They are appallingly cruel devices, intended for birds of prey. Both the killing of birds of prey and the use of gin-type traps is illegal. The law depends on the goodwill of those concerned, since the places where it is likely to be broken are, by their very nature, places where the breaking is most unlikely to be observed; alas goodwill is not the strong suit of such people.

'Vermin' is this man's favourite word – he has a very simple zoological classification system. Pheasants and Vermin; goodness knows why the likes of Darwin wasted a lifetime when the matter is so straightforward. I consider the true vermin are my gamekeeping friend and his ilk. With Sniff called in close – I did not want to give him any excuse for shooting at her – we went through the wood pretty thoroughly; although I called and whistled I did not attract either the fox or the 'Vermin'. In fact, except for a few pheasants that scuttled off through the bracken, that beautiful little wood was almost devoid of animal life.

We went out into the field a few times that evening, but apart from a false alarm when Big Tom, one of our cats, came out of the hedge, we found nothing. With the working week starting next day, if Ferdi was caught up, her chances were slipping, since we would only be able to search in the evenings.

Monday dragged by with thoughts of the fox's fate regularly punctuating my working day. We arrived home with the usual escort, but their excitement dwindled on reaching the compound and finding that Ferdi was not in residence. They made the gesture of orbiting the compound a couple of times, then after hanging around looking rather lost for a few minutes, they began to disperse again.

After a quick snack, Sniff and I set out to use what daylight remained. We went round the field in case she had paid a visit home, but Sniff could find nothing by way of recent scent. There was no point in a long distance search, since by the time we had extended our previous radius it would be dark. So we kept it local, with our main hope resting on the possibility that if we got close she would come to us if she were free, or answer my calls if she were trapped.

With dusk well advanced, we turned back, having seen nothing to suggest that there was a single fox in the entire country.

The only positive thing to come from this trip was a plan of search for the following evening. We moved along a hedge that grew upon the lip of a railway cutting, swung left over a farm bridge and continued along the track, with the ground climbing on the right to a bristle of spruce trees that spiked the dark sky in a black frieze. Left, the field fell away in a gentle slope and over the hedge, wilting cabbages from a recent planting could be seen flacidly prostrate on the damp soil, their ranks trailing away until they vanished into the gloom.

I heard it before I saw it. I'd heard it several times before. When Ferdi ate a rabbit, virtually nothing was wasted, all that was ever left were the claws and pads at the very tips of those bony feet. The rest, including the head with its great chisels of incisor teeth, was consumed. When she crunched up a rabbit it sounded like someone very noisily eating crisps. Now, out there in the lowering dusk, something was noisily eating crisps.

I stared in the direction of the noise, it was an otherwise silent evening – breathless. Yes! There was something there, on the very periphery of my vision – larger than the sad cabbages, and it moved, or did it? It's so easy to imagine movement under these conditions – the crunching continued; I was sure a rabbit or something similar was being eaten – was it a dog or a fox? If a fox, was it Ferdi that was doing the eating? I tried the old trick of looking sideways; this arranges the optics so that the light-gathering power is increasing. I used to understand the biological explanation but it has long since escaped me; something to do with rods and cones, I seem to recall. Sure enough, the object did move. I had noticed that if I ever got very intense in my concentration, my attitude conveyed the tension to Sniff and she in turn became anxious. Now I felt the gentle tap of her fore-paw on my calf; she was either wanting to be let in 'to what was going on', or seeking reassurance that there was not anything really nasty on the other side of the hedge.

I called, 'Ferdi'. Realisation came simultaneously to Sniff and the fox. Sniff scampered off to find a way through the hedge. The fox rose and melted into the gloom. Sniff found the exact spot easily enough, well marked with a few tufts of rabbit fluff, then set off down the slope rapidly following the brand new scent. I was sure it hadn't been Ferdi, and I called her back. We wandered home through the still darkness.

1 A fox joins the family

2a First step – a playpen on the lawn

2b Friends from the start – Ferdi and Sniff

3a At home in the field – Ferdi hunting

3b At home in the lounge – Ferdi visiting

4a 'Psst! Have you heard the one about . . .?'

4b 'Sniff's love of sticks exceeded that of any other dog
I've ever known . . .' (This a mere twig)

On Tuesday evening, to win a bit more daylight, I dispensed with anything to eat, changed immediately, and headed Sniff back to the point on the stream bank, below the lake. From this place we had, the previous evening, searched downstream, to-ing and fro-ing across a half mile wide strip to take in virtually all the cover down as far as the river. This time we turned upstream to pass through the wooded gully that runs along the edge of the lake. It was getting dark when we reached a drain that emerged among the trees half way up the steep bank. This old drain had once helped to run water off the sloping land opposite, under a broad bank for about thirty yards and into the brook. It was not a pipe, but a tiny brick culvert – beautifully made in days when there had been time for such things – like the tunnel of an elaborate model railway.

In the past, when I had made my way along this bank with Sniff and Ferdi, they had both shown a keen interest in the drain, its mouth half concealed by a small mound of debris that had evidently come from inside. Now in the gathering gloom, more advanced beneath the trees, Sniff once again insisted that there was something interesting inside. The bank was very steep, and by stepping back a couple of paces, then leaning forward, I could lie against the slope with my face on a level with the hole. There was little to be seen. Looking at an angle over the small mound of sandy silt and leaf skeletons that had been shovelled from within, revealed a couple of feet of indistinct brick floor, before total darkness obscured all else, like a semi-circular patch of black paper pasted inside the hole. I could see nothing, but heard a soft scratch of movement from within.

Sniff, after scraping away some of the debris, was quite prepared to go inside and investigate. I watched her manoeuvre as she lined up with the tiny culvert; with legs extended so she was almost lying down, her deep-keeled, stocky figure filled the dark opening like a cork in a bottle. She might force her way in, but if there was no place to turn round and she had to back out, or if the section narrowed, there was an excellent chance of her getting stuck. It would then, with the culvert running deep into the bank, require a major excavation to free her, not to mention the destruction of part of the neat work of that old bricklayer, which although now quite dry, thanks to a modern land drainage system, might still perform its ancient function in time of winter floods.

I tugged the still exposed tail, and told her to come out before she got stuck. Judging by the struggle she had to retrace those few inches, it was a wise decision.

We returned home to get a torch. By the time I was once again stamping for a footing on that steep bank, it was quite dark.

On the rare occasions that it had been used recently, my torch, normally a powerful three battery job, had been giving a passable impersonation of a glow worm. Its sickly beam in the darkness reminded me once again that I had forgotten to purchase new batteries. I scraped away sufficient debris to permit me to look straight into the little tunnel; I lay the torch just inside, and slithered down the bank to get a sighting over the top of it. For a few yards the tired batteries revealed the neatly arched brickwork over a floor scattering of fine sand and leaf mould. Beyond this, an indeterminate region of increasingly gloomy twilight, before the black paper patch, which had retreated about four or five yards into the hole.

For half a minute there was nothing else, then suddenly beyond the black patch two small bright lights beamed back at me, and abruptly went out. They came on again and were joined by two more. These tiny headlights came and went with dramatic sudden-ness as their owners faced me or turned away. If it was fox cubs I was searching for, then I'd found them. How many, I could not be sure – there was probably not room for more than two cubs to stand together in that narrow arch – but the eyes that came and went, floating so fascinatingly, like stars in a black velvet sky, could have belonged to half a dozen or more. But not to the one we were seeking.

Sniff had made two or three attempts to push my head aside with her own, so that she could have another look into the culvert. I leant back, giving way to her.

'You were right, mate,' I told her, rubbing her back – her head had disappeared.

I replaced the mound of litter, and crumbled away my telltale foot holds from the bank. Then Sniff and I went home.

The rest of the evenings of that week were equally unproductive. By Friday we had put in a lot of cross-country dog/man hours since discovering Ferdi's absence on the previous Saturday afternoon. I could not go on looking for a fox for the rest of my life, and was beginning to feel that I'd largely discharged my responsibility towards the little brute. I would search hard through the coming weekend and after that I'd call off special search expeditions; if I found her in the course of being around and about all well and good, anything else would be up to her.

Friday evening, after another fruitless patrol, I came in for my belated meal. Over dinner, Carol and I considered the possibility of a different approach to our attempts to find Ferdi. We decided that I would sacrifice some search time during the weekend and make some traps that could be set and left around the field, in case she returned during the working day when only Sniff would be in residence. We developed this idea. It all depended upon her being free to roam, but if she were, and hungry, she might be drawn back to the kitchen, where she had, on dozens of occasions, stood with Sniff and the cats in head-tilting half-circle about my feet, while I doled out the night's rations.

She must associate the kitchen with food.

Here we had a trap ready built. The kitchen door opens inwards, and the kitchen, an extension to the very old original body of the cottage, protrudes at right angles to the lounge. So, by running a long cord from the outside door knob, through the shallow porch, round the corner and back along the outside face of the kitchen wall, and passing it through the lounge window, it became possible to slam the kitchen door from outside the lounge. That was the mechanism of the trap. The bait was simple enough – just the normal, familiar bowl of food – but how to know when to pull the cord?

In those days the kitchen floor was covered by one of those hard-wearing, non-absorbent modern linoleum-type variants, upon which the claws of both Sniff and Ferdi made a quiet scratching sound. If I were wide awake it might be sufficient to alert me to the fact that I had a victim in my trap, but it certainly would not rouse me from sleep. We had a formica-topped drop-leaf kitchen table; normally one leaf was raised and pushed against the end wall, and the other hung down to leave more room in the kitchen. When the animals stretched to get a preview of the night's offerings, they invariably placed their forepaws against the hanging leaf, causing it to rattle quite loudly against the centre table. That just might be enough to waken me.

With a plate of food set well away from the table's edge, and the communicating door to the lounge closed, I rolled out my sleeping bag on the lounge carpet, checked that the trip cord came easily to hand in the darkness, and settled down for the night. For obvious reasons, the cats and Sniff were shut in. Sniff thought it would be sociable to lie heavily against my side, and the cats to lie almost as heavily on top. They all received the same discouraging treatment.

Any fears I may have harboured, that I'd fall asleep and miss the warning tap-tap from the drop-leaf, soon evaporated. I have never been one of those possessed of the wonderful gift of instant sleep. I have always envied the dog who turns round two or three times, flops down and is asleep – like switching off a light. In many a tent, hostel, or sleeping bag beneath the stars, I've lain desperately trying to get to sleep before my mates began snoring, waiting for those first nasal rumblings, knowing with certainty that I was going to lose the race.

No matter what position I tried, the hard flat floor seemed to have a counter. I toyed with the idea of turning the convertible studio couch into a bed, but by then I was in that vicious circle situation when I was too tired to be bothered; in any case, I wanted to lie right up against the door.

As the hours dragged by I became more peevish; the chances of success seemed to diminish to the fringe of impossibility, and the lure of a warm, comfortable bed and a warm, comfortable wife were almost irresistible.

With a start I came out of a shallow doze. Sniff was sitting up beside me in the gloom, looking at the door, her head rotating in a series of jerky, flicking movements, as she tipped it first one way then the other, in keen listening concentration. Suddenly alert, I found myself imitating her. There was a sound from the kitchen. I groped for the nylon cord. I'd rolled the sleeping bag on top of it, and had to dig it out. I recovered slack cord through the window until I felt the first drag of resistance. More soft sounds, almost whispers, from the kitchen, more silence, then the noise I was waiting for – the unmistakable rattle of the drop-leaf. I hauled on the cord, the outside door closed with a great bang, following which there was continuity of sound for several seconds. As if the conductor's baton had fallen and a drug-crazed percussion section had run amok. Crashes and clanging, the unmistakable noise of tumbling, rolling saucepans, the clatter of crockery in the draining tray, the drop-leaf again, this time slamming into the table with a heavy thud. A sleepy voice from upstairs demanding to know what was happening: Sniff whining with frustration, scrabbling at the kitchen door.

I bounced out of the bag – what the hell had I caught?

The four-gang switch which controlled lounge and landing lights was mounted on the far wall – I did not bother with it, but hurriedly kicked the sleeping bag away from the door, thrust Sniff back into the room, and slipped through into the kitchen, closing the door behind me.

Pandemonium broke out again. In the dim light, the thing doing high speed circuits of my kitchen, weaving from floor level to table-top height, and accompanying its progress with a deafening cacophony, was obviously a cat. It sent the bowl of bait hurtling off the table. Down and up again in flying panic, it crossed the fridge and cooker, sending the frying pan clattering to join the saucepans about the kitchen floor.

The lighter patch, which was the window in the outside door, might be a way of escape; the cat jumped at it from the washing machine. Its claws hooked into the veil of net curtain that draped the window, bringing it down in its entirety, complete with curtain wire. The wraithlike object thrashed about on the floor, while the cat disentangled itself, and streaked across the sink unit, already cleared of obstructions. The main window in the kitchen is a three framed affair and runs almost the entire length of one wall, above the sink unit and washing machine; it is guarded by the colourful aluminium slats of a venetian blind, now in the closed position. The desperate cat tried to run up the tier of slender, curved aluminium, to a brittle clashing and rattling; the collapsing slats, now half of them turned inside out, gave way and the cat fell through the shaking confusion to find itself in a very narrow space between the blind and window pane, whereupon it came back the way it had gone with another deafening clatter.

At this moment, my wife opened the door from the lounge. I yelled at her to shut it, but Sniff was already through and entering into the spirit of the thing, adding further to the cat's panic. I collared Sniff and pushed her out again; trod barefoot, warily through the wreckage on the floor, with the cat whirling about me; opened the outside door, and while by the door, switched on the light to reveal a scene of devastation. A large dark tabby cat, ears laid back, mouth open, snarled his hate and fear from beneath the table. I moved towards him and he crossed the sink unit once more, leaped off down the wrong side of the kitchen door, to turn at bay in the narrow wedge of space between the back of the door and the wall. I had almost to lean over him as I again closed the door – such was his terror and savage demeanor that for a brief moment I wondered if he was going to attack me. With the door closed again I pressured him into bolting back beneath the table, then I reopened the door, wider this time, so that it lay against the wall with no room between.

This time as I approached, he sped like a greyhound through the opening and into the night. I hoped he had at least taken a few mouthfuls for his trouble. All lights were now blazing, and Carol once again stood in the doorway. She asked, 'What the hell was it?' Then made some very unladylike remarks about the state of her kitchen.

'A wildcat,' I replied. Of course it was not a wildcat, but it was definitely a wild cat. Probably a feral animal, but with its tabby livery, longish fur and savage aspect, it was probably the nearest thing to a wildcat that most people will ever see.

We went to bed. I'd had enough trapping for one night.

Saturday morning I visited several farms; no one had seen Ferdi but all promised to let me know if she appeared. This was good, since it meant that, in very casual fashion at least, a fairly large area was covered and it was always possible that someone quietly about his day's work might spot her. A naggingly frustrating idea persisted that one of those making the promises might have already shot her and on discovering that she wore a collar had decided to keep quiet about it. I had decided that in the afternoon I would go to see the gamekeeper of a large estate. I'd never met him but a neighbour knew him; he worked for one of the very old landed families from a nearby market town.

Down a tiny lane, off the main road, we wound our way behind a thick stand of mixed trees which contained a lot of yew. It looked exactly how one would imagine a gamekeeper's cottage to look: well weathered brick and heavy dark timber, standing near the wood, not built there to intrude like a bungalow or caravan, but grown there with the ancient trees. A few rabbit pelts were stretched on the side of a rough timbered shed; a cast iron pump stood by the kitchen door. In a large clearing in the wood, a high wire netting enclosure contained some well grown pheasant poults. They were late, presumably replacements; they'll be nice and tame for the guns when they are eventually turned out, the thought sneered in my mind.

I had bumped the half-open kitchen door several times without response. I looked over to where the hall showed between its avenue of chestnut trees a quarter mile off. There seemed to be no sign of life, the warm, mellow, sheltered, Hansel and Gretel spot had bewitched everything. The cottage was probably made of gingerbread. The impression was not so much broken as confirmed when a weepy-eyed, very ancient labrador shuffled up the hollyhocked path to lower its great grey head in ponderous greeting of Sniff, who had succumbed to this sleeping draught of a place and stretched out across the path. It only needed the murmur of a beehive to establish beyond doubt that this was where Rip Van Winkle got his head down.

I nosed about, took a look at the pheasants, found myself thinking unworthy thoughts for one who'd come seeking a favour. With an eye for the cover and the approach from the main road, I let myself in imagination idly follow a poacher moving through the wood to lift a few pheasants from the pen; or perhaps one of the commercially-minded city gangs who seem to make up in ruthless directness what they lack in finesse, relying more on force and intimidation than on guile, driving the whole lot into a portable cage, and away with them.

I gently roughened the old dog's ears and said, 'goodbye old 'un'. He responded with a few weary waves of his tail. We had just about cleared the small vegetable garden when a Land Rover rocked into view down the side of the wood. Mr Maylor looked as much the part as his cottage did: short and wiry, leather gaiters over stout boots sheathed bowed legs. Above the knees he wore ancient thorn-proof tweeds – judging by the frills and fringes, not as thorn-proof as I'm sure the makers must have claimed. Weathered, leathery, healthy, that was Mr Maylor.

I told him my story. He was very pleasant – No, he'd not seen a fox for sometime now.

As we talked, he headed us towards the shed with the rabbit skins. 'Best thing is to look out very early, see if you can spot any crows or magpies having a good shout,' he advised. 'They'll often give a good cussing to a fox if they catch him out in daylight.'

We entered the shed – it was what you would expect, a few skins, snares hanging up, a couple of traps for repair on a bench. No signs of gins I noticed with satisfaction. From a nail in the back of the door he took a dry hard leather ring and handed it to me; I realised it was a collar and knew what he was going to say. The cracked strap with its brass loop and plate dull and tarnished was probably less than two inches in diameter.

'A few years back I took that off a near fullgrown dog fox, that was how it was round his neck. I found the poor beast dead in Coneberry Wood. He was terribly emaciated but I couldn't find a mark on him. I examined him a couple of times before I realised he'd got that on, I felt the loose end poking up hard in the fur of his neck, the rest was so deeply embedded that his neck had virtually grown round it. He appeared to have a short piece of leather strap growing out of him. It is awful to contemplate, he must have grown inside that since he was a small cub while it progressively choked and starved him. I suspect that the poor creature eventually starved to death.'

He became silent and thoughtful, then shook his head sadly. 'He may have still been able to get enough air into his lungs to just about keep him alive, although it must have been a terrifying struggle; but by the end he certainly couldn't swallow anything solid, probably couldn't even drink.'

He was sadly quiet again, then shook himself out of the mood. 'I've shown it to a lot of people who've told me they've got pet foxes and badgers and other odd things. I always strongly deplore the use of collars on growing animals that might revert to the wild.'

I said a bit defensively that Ferdi was probably three-quarters grown and that I had been concerned about this very problem from the start and had always kept the collar as loose as possible. She might even slip it if she pulled very hard backwards, or push it over her head by getting both front feet behind it. I found myself hoping desperately that (as I turned that tiny collar in my hand) it was so, but having little faith in the theory.

Also, as I hung the cracked leather ring back on its nail, I was thinking of yet another in a long list of ideas I'd had, and done nothing about. When I'd been concerned about the collar problem, I'd thought of making collars of paper, perhaps a dozen layers of brown paper or rather less of tarred paper with the tar on the inside, stitched down the edges, wrapped around the buckle and stitched together like a normal collar. Metal eyelets would both provide holes for the buckle spike and crimp the layers together down the centre of the paper strap. It would be strong enough to hold young animals like fox cubs, would stand a limited amount of damp, but if subjected to long soakings, as would inevitably happen if the animal went back to the wild state, it would become soggy and fall to pieces, or be easily scratched off by the creature's claws. It would obviously have a limited market and the chance of selling the idea to a manufacturer seemed very slim. I'd not even got round to making one for Ferdi. As I considered the appalling story behind that collar, I'd willingly have gone into production and given the paper collars away if I'd any way of knowing who might be putting his pet at such risk. Just to have avoided one such incident would have been worth it.

I do not normally like gamekeepers but I was impressed by this caring man; what a contrast with the 'Vermin'. I wanted him to know that I cared and thought about these things too; I almost told him about the paper collars, but for some reason I didn't.

Yes, he said, he'd certainly keep a look out; if he saw or heard anything he'd let me know.

I thanked him and after a few words about the old labrador, which had shuffled up to welcome his return, I left, quite moved by the man who lived in the gingerbread cottage in this sleepy little place behind the wood. I changed my mind about that city gang: I'm sure he would have had some surprise waiting for them.

As we made our way back across country, it had been almost exactly one week since Ferdi had vanished. By now she must surely have either freed herself from the line and be making out well enough to have opted to stay away (although unless she did manage to slip her collar she would still have the lesser encumbrance of the chain hanging round her neck and even this would put her at a serious disadvantage, an extra burden that jangled warning of her presence); or have become hopelessly tangled, in which case she might well be dead from a variety of possible causes or even have been taken off captive, to spend her life in a cage. I hoped it was the former and that she had lost the collar and chain altogether.

I felt that the various visits I had made that day just about completed all that I could possibly do to help safeguard the cub. I could obviously continue to look for her, but I felt that after so long there was no way of improving the chances of success; she was no more or less likely to appear back in my field as five or ten miles away. The apparent hopelessness of the task and the haunting idea that I might be looking for something that no longer existed, made it difficult to maintain the original dedication to the search. To look for a needle in a haystack is a daunting prospect, but if you're not even sure the haystack contains a needle . . . !

It was well after tea and the light was beginning to smudge into dusk, when I wandered into the field with Sniff. I had no intention of going any farther, it was a fairly aimless exercise, just because I prefer to be out than in. I was just moving slowly, taking in the evening, when suddenly Sniff's whole attitude changed to one of high excitement, and nose vacuuming, tail whirling, she set off at a good pace and with great purpose. I gave her no commands at all, but dropped into a steady run behind her. Here were the first encouraging signs for days and it was entirely her show.

We crossed two fields before I had to check her progress. She went through a particularly dense and thorny hedge. I had to call her back, or at her rate of progress I would have lost her before I had found a way through. Off we went again, another field and a lane were crossed, then halfway along the next hedge and running downhill to the railway; it was next to the field where Ferdi had chased rabbits and where we had first gone to look for her over a week ago. Sniff checked for the first time, and proceeded to thread her way like a bobbin across a loom, back and forth through a bramble patch, knobbly with hard little green fruit, still smaller than the dried star of sepals that they centred.

While she explored and considered, I had time to reflect on the likelihood of her having got on to Ferdi's trail at last; and, if so, how close might the little fox be, for the scent was obviously good. It was strange to realise that whatever adventures and close calls may have been her experience for the last seven days, she might now be so close again, just out there in the slowly constricting circle of night. From Sniff's whole bearing I knew it was no rabbit; anyway we'd already travelled too far. My conjecture was interrupted when, having sorted out the confusion at the bramble patch, Sniff set off again at the same fast pace, which in the rapidly failing light was a bit hazardous for my ankles, as we ploughed on over rough country.

I had to yell hard to check Sniff's enthusiasm as we came to the railway line; I didn't want to take her a long way off the scent by using the official crossing where wooden steps descended the cutting, but I did want to continue the discipline I had established long ago, when every time we crossed the line she came in close and waited until I told her to go. It took some time to negotiate the hedge, descend the bank, bring her sternly to my side, then release her again. She bore the frustration of it all very well as she did anything I imposed on her, but was immediately on the scent and off again when I gave her the OK.

We crossed the lines and turned right to run parallel with the track until we reached the farm bridge, the same one near which we had seen the fox crunching a rabbit a few days before. We crossed back over the bridge and turned left into an absolute jungle of trees, bramble and briar that grew along the side of the cutting. The only clear space was occupied by eight or ten beehives; in this place I stood while she plunged into the thicket and could be heard, powerfully pushing her way about it.

Again I could consider the situation and look at the strengthening stars on this clear still night. Only the closest features still had three dimensions, all else had flattened into silhouette against the paler sky.

Sniff's excitement was now betrayed by little woofing noises, similar to those she utters when a rabbit is getting away from her. I called, 'Ferdi'; I whistled quietly; but I neither saw nor heard anything other than Sniff's now rather crude battering progress through the tight undergrowth. Such was her excitement, I knew that when we got back into the light I'd find her head full of thorns;

I was always concerned that she might tear her eyes, but she never seemed to.

At last she emerged and away we went again, her pale yellowish coat leading me on in the gloom. On down the farm track and into another lane; we were now going home. Up the lane towards my cottage – I was now running at quite a good pace to keep up with the yellow patch ahead of me in the dark.

We arrived home having completed a circuit of about two miles, but instead of entering the garden, Sniff led into the field again. We meandered about the field, moving towards the top hedge, where under an oak tree, she stopped and showed no inclination to go any farther. I was puzzled; she had tracked with such keenness, now suddenly she sat looking out past the tree into the darkness and went no farther. It was almost as if there was something fearsome out there in the dark.

Suddenly there was a screech that made me jump, and there was Ferdi coming towards us, belly to the ground, head down, ears laid flat, tail brushing the grass furiously. I could scarcely believe it after so much searching, but there she was.

I spoke to her quietly. 'Where have you been to, you little bugger? We've walked miles looking for you.'

She was now almost within touching distance. Sniff still held her position, tail thrashing. She seemed to know she'd done her part well. The fox touched noses with her, the screaming continued.

I could now see that the chain was still attached to her collar and to it about four inches of line, now so frayed that it looked like a fluffy ornament. I was suddenly aware that she could still vanish into the night, that the situation could revert to the hopelessness that it had held less than three-quarters of an hour ago.

She came to me, but it was at a maximum stretch that she leant to nose my fingertips, like a spring ready to shoot backwards at the release of a trigger. I failed to lure her any closer and after talking quietly to her for several minutes, while in a crouched position, I launched myself into a dive and to my relief grabbed the dangling chain with my right hand. I scooped her up in my arms, keeping a tight hold on the chain. As we walked back to the cottage she struggled briefly, then began to gently worry at my ear, a game she'd played many times before.

Sniff and I walked triumphantly into the cottage, where Carol took over welcoming the fox, while I roughed Sniff's head in a feeling of admiration and comradeship, and began to remove thorns.

So Ferdi came home from adventures that I can only guess at.

It was not to be the last time she would go about her foxy business, but never again was she to go with the handicap of chain and line. Never again would I doubt her abilities, and never again would I mount so intensive and prolonged a search for her.

After her week away she settled down into the home routine immediately, quite as though there had been no interruption. In retrospect I suppose this was the first sign of a growing ability to pass easily between the two lifestyles.

It took Blackie and his gang only a couple of days before the evening rendezvous were re-established.

Ferdi, after her week of practising what she'd already learnt and, no doubt, in the process adding considerably to this vital file on survival, still occasionally demonstrated a speed of assessment and conclusion that was quite impressive.

One gloriously sunny afternoon I was having a filming session. I was not attempting to set anything up, but merely following the fox and dogs around in an opportunist's role. We had strayed out of my field, and I had shot some footage, when they found a rabbit in a briar thicket and after giving me plenty of warning, by running around and poking into this barbed fortress, they induced the bunny to make a break for his burrow, which it transpired was amongst the roots of an oak tree some fifty yards away.

Ferdi and company all knew what would happen and were very keen, so that when the rabbit appeared out of the tangle, apparently already going at full speed, he gained little by way of surprise, and within ten yards they were all hard after him, going hell for leather towards the oak tree. All except Sniff that is. The tough little Sniff had done the hard work as usual; she had braved the spikes to push her way into the briars and flush out the rabbit. Like so many who work hard to set up life's exciting moments, she missed the fun herself. By the time she extricated herself, they were twenty yards on their way and flying.

Blackie and Butch did no more than hold station, perhaps even lost ground to the bouncing rabbit. But Ferdi closed so fast that as her head followed the rabbit into his burrow, I half expected her to pull him out by the scut or hind leg. But his clock had still some time to run, and she extracted her head and stood looking back at me empty jawed.

In turn all the dogs poked their heads into the hole just to check things out to their personal satisfaction.

I was provided with further subject matter when a herd of bullocks, inquisitive as ever, having closed on the activity under the oak, at a steady trot suddenly arrived in a rush, bucking, kicking, some bouncing along sideways, and began to chase the hunters of a few minutes earlier.

Ferdi and the dogs entered into the spirit of the thing and at little more than half their pace of the earlier chase, easily avoiding the clumsy trampling charges, allowed themselves to be chased through the hedge into the next field, where I found them waiting for me. Then, from a tuft of long grass, they disturbed another rabbit, a large one, which turned out to be a big hare.

Away they went again. This was a different chase, not the short blistering sprint after the rabbit. The field had been divided by a hawthorn hedge, but this had degenerated and was now a line of well spaced hawthorn 'trees', so that the field extended probably three hundred yards before sprouting a serious barrier.

Sniff lost ground so rapidly that she appeared to be running backwards; the two dogs never matched the hare's pace. Ferdi alone, once into her stride, stayed with the hare through the sparse hedge, then visibly began to fall back. The hare merely held the punishing pace with the beautifully fluid run of his kind. I've often watched hares on an airfield where I do some flying; at a distance they always remind me of balls of tumbleweed being blown along; so smooth is their passage it is hard to believe they progress in a series of leaps.

This one, now with a margin of speed and distance to spare, unaccountably turned back; perhaps there were people working in the next field. Whatever the reason, he turned in a long loop and came back parallel to his outward run. Ferdi saw his turn, cut across it and almost grabbed him, then he was past the danger point, and she was the one who had to make a turn while he ran on straight and the gap between them widened to twenty-five or thirty yards. Ferdi continued to follow but was now obviously not trying and the gap grew to fifty yards. The dogs came across but got nowhere near an interception.

Obligingly the hare ignored me completely, and now running back almost through the mark where the chase had started, came straight on to the camera, before passing me and going under a gate and across the bullocks' field at a comfortable pace, knowing he was no longer under threat.

Ferdi came up to me and stopped, little silver beads flicking off her tongue as she panted. When she did fail, she had a wonderful habit of putting on a show of complete indifference. This, obviously, was not what she was doing, but it leant itself easily to being translated into human terms.

Of course, she'd not really been trying to catch that hare – ridiculous suggestion. To emphasise the point, she had a roll on some dried horse muck – the hare already forgotten.

I used up the last few feet of film as the dogs straggled back, and we returned home.

I've little doubt that in those few high-speed seconds Ferdi learnt to distinguish between a hare and a rabbit and to come to a conclusion about misplaced endeavour in pursuing the former. She never missed the opportunity to chase a rabbit once she'd got to close quarters, yet I was to be with her on several occasions when a hare got up fifteen to twenty yards away and she merely watched it go. In fact I never saw her chase another one.

I'm sure hares are taken by foxes, but I think the fox would need the advantage of a near perfect ambush to do it.

Ferdi spent quite a lot of time in the cottage garden. Because I was uneasy about her wandering loose during the day, a fair proportion of this time she spent on a line. It allowed her the run of the lawn and was attached to an ancient plum tree that had been declining steadily for many years. A long low tack shed combined with a hedge to separate my garden from my neighbour's. The old tree grew hard against this and provided the cats with a route up on to the shed and then across the kitchen roof on to the main roof and through one of the turret windows into a bedroom.

It didn't take Ferdi long to perfect her own method of ascending this cat ladder. Lacking the sharp retractile claws of the cats, she merely took a few fast paces across the lawn, jumped up the trunk and in the half second that her momentum pressed her firmly against the rough old bark she put in another couple of kicks; her upward energy exhausted, she almost came to a standstill just as the level of the flat roof was reached. Fractionally before gravity sent her slithering back down the trunk, she stepped daintily on to the shed. It was a beautifully executed manoeuvre, with a very neat balance between all the forces involved.

One afternoon this trick was to prove near fatal. I couldn't spare the time to keep an eye on her, so she had been on the line most of the afternoon. I'd taken a look at her at regular intervals, everything was under control. She'd been romping with Sniff, stretched out in the sunshine or up on the shed roof. Late in the afternoon I was in the kitchen and heard a soft thump I couldn't account for. I stopped to listen, but it was not repeated. I almost dismissed it, but it remained an out-of-place intrusion into the afternoon. I told myself I ought to check on it.

The garden was empty. There was no sign of Ferdi on the shed roof. I called her and wandered towards the plum tree. Suddenly I was monkeying my way up into the shed. The line ran taut across the shed roof and out of sight over the far edge. I was looking down at Ferdi hanging by her neck; her hind legs did not reach the ground; she was quite still. I was horrified, grabbed the line and hauled her up. She plonked down on her feet and didn't even wobble. The recovery was instant. She was like a clockwork soft toy that had lain waiting to be switched on. She struggled briefly, seemed startled to find me on the roof holding her, then lapsed into her open-mouthed grin. The near disaster had occurred as a result of her having been up on to the roof and down again many times. On several occasions she had taken the line up one side of the old tree and down the other; eventually she'd wound so much line around the trunk that the remainder was too short to allow her to reach the ground when she'd jumped down on the far side of the shed.

By such fortunate happenstance are lives saved: had I not been in the kitchen and all else quiet at that precise moment, I should not have heard the tell-tale thud; had that soft noise not intruded into the afternoon and, because I could not account for it, niggled away like an irritant, I should not have gone into the garden to investigate. One should store such flukes of good fortune to set against the other sort and make them easier to bear.

As the year progressed, Ferdi became a virtual ever-present on our walks. There was never any guarantee that she would return with us, sometimes she would stay out when we returned. Sometimes she would slip away at the approach of other walkers, or if I went near farming activities. She might be back at the cottage, awaiting our return, or rejoin the walk, slipping from long grass, gliding from a thicket or snaking her way out of a stream bed. I would suddenly realise she had materialised. We were getting close to the association of free minds that I wanted to establish. She came along with us because she chose to, not because I dragged her on the end of a string. She evidently enjoyed my company and that of the dogs and Sniff's in particular.

It was getting to be exactly what, by my personal definition, a friendship should be: an association of completely free spirits, an undemanding coming together or staying apart as the mood dictated, without hurt or resentment on the other side; with no obligation, yet always welcome when the other's company was sought out. In honesty, I confess that it was not quite so idyllic as it sounds. The exception to complete freedom of choice was that I endeavoured to have Ferdi spend the daytime, when I was not at home, in her enclosure. Also, by not feeding her until late at night, I had got her into the habit of coming back to the cottage after any independent wanderings in the evenings. This was, in fact, a very tenuous hold, since she was not dependent on me for food, nevertheless she seemed quite willing to continue the routine. I guess an easy meal is always acceptable.

I hoped the arrangement would continue indefinitely because it was not totally unlike the activity pattern of a wild fox. It kept Ferdi from wandering abroad during the periods of greatest human activity and consequently periods of greatest danger and, perhaps most importantly, it was one with which she seemed totally happy.

This general pattern was certainly not invariable, for she was already developing an independence that would characterise the whole of our association: she would, quite unpredictably, vanish for a couple of days when there was always a prickle of anxiety, background to my thoughts, particularly if shooting was to be heard. She was still learning, and at times was acquiring her tuition in the academy of hard knocks. Occasional entries in a diary of that period read:

After two days away
– Ferdi returned, badly mauled, at 10.40 tonight . . .
– I think she had a 'run in' with an Alsatian which has been
  roaming Green's wood for several days now . . .
– spent all night on the studio couch: most unusual.

After one and a half days away
– found Ferdi in field, mid-morning, limping and cut about
  face.

There is also an entry indicating my concern that she may have picked up some poison, when for two days that bright shining spirit was replaced by a weary, dull-eyed creature without enthusiasm.

The only way to protect her was to confine her and that was unthinkable.

For the second time in this tale I'll quote a source anonymous to me: 'If you love it set it free. If it returns to you it's yours, if it does not, it never was.' It seems a commendable philosophy in a world where man spends so much time in his relationships with his fellows and particularly with the animal kingdom, demanding that they behave in the manner he prescribes, and often killing them if they do not.

6

The Fox and Vet

The fox and vet. It sounds like a public house. We were to take a week's holiday in South Wales and my parents were going to look after the fox. To have deliberately turned her loose for a week while I was three hundred miles away seemed to be pushing our luck unnecessarily. It was a busy week that preceded our departure. The arrangement was complicated because my parents could not come over to stay at the cottage until Tuesday, so Ferdi was going to have to put up with life in a cage for a couple of days. I made the cage, a timber frame covered in wire netting with a small door through which her usual sleeping box would pass. It was about six feet by eight and looked awfully small. Ferdi was going to be very bored.

Early in the week we had an invitation to supper with some friends who owned a black labrador. They thoughtlessly failed to tell us, until we had arrived complete with Sniff, that Jasper had only got over a bout of distemper a week earlier. So poor old Sniff spent the remainder of the evening shut in our car, although they assured us that the vet had said the labrador was now clear.

By the time Friday evening approached, Sniff had become very 'lack lustre'. With the dog and fox in the back of the car and the cage lashed to a roof rack, looking dangerously top heavy and probably illegal, we set off for my parents' home about fifteen miles away. Ferdi was promptly travel sick, but then settled down on the rear parcel shelf and kept an eye on the following traffic. This provoked an amusing incident as we queued at the crossroads of a local market town. Large soft toy animals were currently popular as car ornaments. It was a fad in which I would never indulge, but many people did. As we sat patiently waiting our turn to cross the High Street, several pedestrians were obviously admiring the amazingly lifelike toy fox decorating my rear window. When Ferdi, thoroughly bored by now, yawned her enormous gape, stood up, stretched, and lay down again, facing in the other direction, their reactions were worth watching.

A car makes an excellent hide, even a moving car – it is amazing how close you can get to wildlife by gently rolling up to it in a car, no matter how bright the body work. This insulating effect seemed to be reversible in Ferdi's case and she showed little of her normal anxiety at the presence of strangers, a fact for which we had good cause to be thankful.

On the second half of the trip Sniff also was the victim of travel sickness, an unheard of occurrence. When we got to my parents' home she was utterly listless, could manage only the feeblest flick of the tail by way of greeting and couldn't be bothered to get out of the car.

Dad and I were busy getting the cage sited and the sleeping box installed. On returning to the car to collect Ferdi I was surprised to find Sniff asleep on the front seat. She was obviously not very well. Normally an enthusiastic car traveller, she was now clearly most unhappy, and rather than subject her to another three hundred miles of misery, we decided that she too should stay with my folks.

About two hours into our journey, Carol suddenly exclaimed: 'That idiot Jill!' I looked at her, most surprised, since, when I'd made similar observations, she'd always flown to the defence of her friend.

'Bloody Jasper,' she continued, 'I bet Sniff has got distemper.'

I felt a touch inadequate and embarrassed that I, with my supposed empathy with animals, had not given it a thought. We stopped at the next phone box, told my parents of our suspicions and asked them to have a vet take a look at her. They were already considering just this action, because Sniff was showing signs of jaundice about the eyes and gums. A phone call the following day confirmed our fears. Sniff had probably got distemper and both she and the fox had been given injections. We were to hear the details of the story on our return.

The vet had come from the same practice that I had used on

several occasions and I knew him fairly well. He was the youngest of three who shared the practice. There had been no problems with Sniff, of placid nature and even more so now, being lowered by the effects of the disease. He finished with her very quickly. My folks then told him about Ferdi.

Yes, he'd confirmed, foxes were susceptible to distemper. 'She had also better have a shot.'

This time he was about to earn his fee.

It's hard to imagine a greater contrast in two animals of similar size than between a naturally friendly, cooperative and sick dog, and a badly scared, highly suspicious, extremely fit fox.

The cage was about three feet six inches high. Ferdi predictably backed off as far from the door as possible, so there was no difficulty in getting into the cage. My father closed the door after him. Now began what Dad described as the most one-sided contest since the All Blacks played the Women's Institute. Forced to sit on his heels and shuffle about like a clockwork toy, the vet tried to crowd her into a corner; charged hypodermic clutched in one hand, he tried to drive her back with the other. Even in the close confines of the cage she evaded him with ease, adding to his discomfort by giving off her pungent defensive scent.

Dad described an amusing scene. No matter what the vet did, Ferdi always seemed to be standing behind him so that he was forever waddling round to try to face her while she merely slipped round behind him again. The top of his head already sore from scraping the wire roof, his crouching posture eventually induced an attack of cramp in his thigh. With a yell he rolled on to his back and lay flat across the floor of the cage, bracing his leg out straight to pull the painful knots out of his muscles. Ferdi, made even more fearful by his yells, added insult to injury by jumping over his supine body. Gradually the cramp spasm released its grip and he sat up.

Since he was already rolling around the floor, which was also wire netting, with the grass of the lawn poking through it, and realised that in this position he could easily span the entire width of the cage, he began to edge his way towards Ferdi, by now every inch the hunted wild animal. Several times she jumped over him; each time he had to work his way back in the opposite direction. Eventually he managed to grab her brush as she attempted to pass him yet again. She promptly returned the compliment by grabbing his thumb and he let her go again.

That was enough. Round one was over, he crawled to the door and Dad let him out. There was no doubt that the fox was a long way ahead on points. He cleaned up his thumb, applied a plaster, had a cup of tea (what else in a crisis?) and they considered tactics very carefully.

Dad went to the garage and produced an old door almost exactly the right size, if placed sideways, to block off the full width of the cage.

To Mr Harrison the whole thing had now become a matter of professional pride. With a plea to my parents, 'Please don't ever tell my boss I wore gloves,' he donned a heavy leather gauntlet, a relic of my own or my brother's motor cycling days.

Fortunately, the door to the cage was right in one corner and so the other door could be slid across one end of the cage without trouble. It was difficult to manoeuvre, but advancing very slowly behind this barrier he forced Ferdi back until her only refuge was the sleeping box; into this she retreated. The fox was now trapped, with the door against the small entrance to the box, but Mr Harrison was on the other side of the door. He moved back, let the door fall towards him and scrambled over it to the box as fast as he could go. Luckily Ferdi made no attempt to leave the box.

He then readied his hypodermic, thrust the gauntleted hand into the box, grabbed a hind leg and pulled enough out to present her rump as a target for the needle. It only remained to extract vet and door from the cage and the operation was over.

Round two pretty convincingly to the vet, and an honourable draw declared.

During the conversation over another well-earned cup of tea, he learnt where the fox had come from, and he laughed and quite rightly forecast that I would be greatly amused to hear about the incident.

In the spring of the previous year, the two Welsh ponies and one very temperamental Arab mare that were kept in my field had required the attention of a vet. The tough little Welsh ponies had spent all winter in the field without shelter, many times I'd seen them on a crisp morning covered in hoar frost. The Arab had been taken away and pampered in a stable during the harsh nights. All three had lived on hay.

The coming of lush spring grass had provided a luxurious change of diet and they had gorged themselves, becoming not only thunderously flatulent, but also developing 'sweet itch' in the process.

As the name suggests, it is a condition that demands to be scratched. Any accessible scratching post, tree or sometimes barbed wire fence will be used to try and scrub away the irritation. So vigorously and persistently do the animals rub that the skin is soon removed and great raw patches develop; these attract flies which add to the irritation, until the horses are driven crazy.

Mr Harrison had turned up to give the horses an injection. I knew someone had gone into the field but had not taken much notice; after a few minutes he came into the garden. The owner of the horses had arranged to meet him but had failed to turn up. Would I give him a hand?

We decided to tackle the ponies first. They were lured with a bit of bread and we slipped a halter over Snowy's head. 'Hold tight,' he cautioned. His technique was to slap the pony's neck a series of rapid blows to dilate a vein. He then deftly flipped the needle of his hypodermic into this thick cord. It reminded me of someone playing darts.

Snowy didn't appreciate the role of dartboard and the reason for the warning to hold tight was suddenly apparent. Short, stocky, despite its diminutive size, the Welsh pony is a powerful beast. He pulled me along for several yards before I eventually contained him.

'Well done,' said Mr Harrison as he screwed the body of the syringe to the needle and administered the injection.

I had been regarding Tecko the Arab with growing concern: she was twice the size of the Taffies and of unstable temperament. I'd been extended by the ponies. I secretly admitted that I had not a snowball in hell's chance of holding Tecko.

Mr Harrison read my thoughts. 'We use a different technique for larger horses,' he said cheerfully. 'We hold one front leg in the air and they won't try to run.' He spoke very confidently, without looking up, as he busied about his case of vials and instruments. 'We'll give her a bit more.'

We took a long time getting Tecko into position. Eventually we were ready. I was standing under her towering head, with her right foreleg lifted and held with the hoof turned back and upwards, as if I were going to fit a shoe. It seemed far too simple a ploy to prevent so much horse from moving. With my back arched as I bent to the task, I was feeling very small by the side of this chestnut monster.

'OK?'

I grunted something non-committal.

Mr Harrison started slapping. Tecko trembled all over and tossed her head, thumping me heavily on the back with her muzzle. I felt that things were getting out of control. The vein grew like a small snake, while she continued to tremble and fidget nervously. I felt that it wouldn't have been out of place if I had begun to do the same.

Mr Harrison flipped his dart and suddenly I was trying to contain forces far too powerful for me. A great weight came unto my back and arms as she tried to put her foot down. I was propping up one corner of a horse. I hung on grimly. 'She won't run if you keep that leg up.' Those casual words came back to me. The vet knew it. I doubted it, but unfortunately Tecko had no doubts at all. She, having failed to get her foot to the ground, merely took off on five legs, two of them being mine. I went trundling backwards desperately holding up the right front corner. For a few seconds, that seemed like a couple of months, it was all very hairy. I was in grave danger of falling backwards and being run over, yet I daren't let go and attempt to bale out. From my position virtually underneath the horse, if I released the front foot it would come down on my legs. Once on the ground I should be lucky to avoid the hind hoof. I continued to rush backwards, muscles at bursting point and a painful conclusion likely if the brute did not stop. A real tiger-by-the-tail situation.

She did stop.

I dropped that foot and stepped clear, blowing hard. I put hands on hips and gave Mr Harrison a look which I think explained my opinion of his theory. He grinned sheepishly as he walked the twenty yards to my new position. 'Well,' he said, 'I've never seen that happen before. They usually stand still.'

I said, 'I don't think I'd like to be your assistant on a permanent basis.'

Tecko cooperated during the rest of the operation.

As we walked out of the field together the incident had already assumed the highly amusing quality that scarey situations invariably do when viewed in retrospect – we had a good laugh about it.

So, I was much amused to hear the story of the vet and the fox. I felt Ferdi had repaid an old score.

7

Chicken on the Menu

The distemper crisis passed without causing lasting harm. Sniff, once she began to recover, did so very quickly and Ferdi showed no symptoms at all. The year had rolled into late autumn. It was dark by the time Sniff and I were back at the cottage after one of our evening walks.

An hour or so later the phone chirruped and a neighbour explained that she found the matter embarrassing to mention, but 'Could my fox have been knocking off her chickens?' The lady couched the question much more diplomatically, of course, but that's what she meant.

I had often seen the wheel-about hen coop in their fields and knew well that half the time they forgot or didn't bother to shut up their free range biddies for the night. Apparently the fowl were now non-producers, of great age and were pensioned off because they had been with the family for so long and no one could face ringing their ancient necks.

They all had names, and had lived out their retirement until one by one they had popped off to scratch around in the great celestial farmyard. Of the dozen or so that remained, Snowball, a particular favourite with the children, she explained, had disappeared a few nights before. The children had all left home, but I guess to a mother, once a child always a child.

'Our fault of course, for not shutting them up; we always mean to, but it gets late and so we decide to risk it, just for one night. When we went to lock them up tonight another one was missing. I didn't think you would mind if we mentioned it. Has the fox been loose this evening?'

I assured her that I didn't mind in the least, that I'd never seen Ferdi take any interest in the fowl (both true) and that she hadn't been loose that evening (grossly untrue).

After she had rung off, with further apologies for even mentioning the matter – they are very nice people – I gave Sniff the nod and we slipped into the field. It was a quiet night; my neighbour of the recent telephone call lived about two hundred and fifty yards away so I daren't whistle or call Ferdi. We moved through the field to the enclosure, where I chanced a low voiced call, without response. I had patrolled the boundary hedge between my patch and my neighbour's without detecting any signs. Halfway down the same hedge on the return journey I made one of my frequent pauses to listen to the night. This time I heard something. Sharp but quiet; I couldn't identify it, but it undoubtedly came from across my neighbour's fields. By the time we'd crossed the adjacent field to the far hedge and paused again, I *could* identify it – something was eating crisps again!

Please don't let it be Ferdi with a chicken supper. The noise emanated a long distance from the hen coop, over against another hedge. We crossed stealthily in that direction, and suddenly flitting about us, her colour beautifully suited to night time camouflage, was Ferdi, drifting in and out of view. What glimpses I caught showed that she was carrying something.

I eventually persuaded her to come to me; hanging from her jaws was a red-feathered chicken. At least this one was not Snowball. She allowed me to look at her prize, as usual, but this was one time when I betrayed her simple trust. The last thing I wanted was tell-tale feathers scattered around my field and her compound. Circumstantial evidence was heavily against her, and my futile attempt to come to some conclusion about the mode of demise was really academic since providing Ferdi with an alibi would be my first consideration.

The chicken was partially eaten, cold enough to have been dead an hour or more and stiffening. It could have died of its venerable condition; it could have been killed by something that did not eat it or carry it off. There was a boxer dog that had recently got itself a final warning and cost its owner a few pound notes when it slaughtered a dozen fowl after jumping into their open pen in a nearby garden. Or, and I had to admit I reluctantly favoured this alternative, Ferdi might have chopped it.

I carefully pulled out all loose feathers and left them behind, before turning back to my field. Ferdi, now a close and very attentive escort, awaited the return of her prize. I left her looking out of the compound, with that hurt uncomprehending look of one who's complete faith and trust have been betrayed. The corpse was interred at the top of my garden: 'We buried him darkly at dead of night, the sod with our bayonets turning.' To steal a quotation that used to afford us much amusement at school.

Knowing how quickly Ferdi learnt a lesson and not wanting to lose her trust and cooperation, I took a rabbit that was intended for our own table and walked back across the field to make a peace offering, which seemed to be accepted in the spirit in which it was offered. I just hoped that she wasn't smart enough to conclude that if you wanted a nice plump rabbit all you had to do was knock off one of the neighbour's stringy old biddies.

Ferdi and the remaining fowl were to be involved in an amusing incident some time later, but this was to end happily and merely place my heart in my mouth for a few high-speed seconds and provide some slight evidence to suggest that she may not have killed the red biddy after all.

This incident occurred one day when I wandered into the field to see if Ferdi felt inclined to come walking with us. She was not in her compound, nor could I see her about the field. I whistled a couple of times and she appeared close to where she had been with the dead chicken. She was travelling very fast on a bee-line towards me, when I realised that a straggle of geriatric biddies was scraping about right across her track and apparently quite unaware of her approach. She passed straight through the middle of them; belatedly they scattered in squawking confusion, but there is no doubt that had she wished, she could have taken her choice.

On the list of Ferdi's dietary items, perhaps I should add the Rhode-Island Red.

8

Crumbs Under the Carpet

Ferdi had increasingly been paying social visits to the cottage, during her independent evening activities. She would often come into the garden and scratch at the kitchen door exactly as Sniff did, from whom she'd presumably learnt this 'open sesame'.

One sharp, bright night in winter I was to miss the opportunity of a splendid photograph. It was, like most good compositions, absolutely natural and uncontrived.

Well after dark, the familiar scraping had sounded on the kitchen door. It was obviously Ferdi, since Sniff was twitching away in front of the blazing logs, as she pursued some dreamland rabbits. We were both preoccupied, and it was ten minutes or so before I went to the door; there was no sign of the fox. I walked into the chilled air. With the door closed behind me, I soon realised that it was a beautiful winter's night – brilliant, with a near full moon low and huge in the sky, with a touch of blood in it. Under the play of moonlight an early evening frost gave the garden an ethereal, almost irridescent look. I couldn't see Ferdi and turned back towards the cottage, looking up at the moon floating so low that it looked like a great luminous ball balanced on the ridge tiles. In my star-gazing I spotted the fox, sitting quite still and very erect, right on the ridge, rather like one of those rangy guardians of the Pharaohs on their final journey. She sat, no doubt watching me, but no movement of her head betrayed the fact. As I moved down the path, the moon, the fox and I drifted into alignment, and there in sharp-edged relief Ferdi and the cottage stood in perfect silhouette.

It was such a strikingly dramatic composition that I went back into the cottage to get camera and tripod, hoping that she would oblige me by holding her pose while I set the camera up, and through a lengthy exposure. As usual it took a few minutes to find things and before I'd got myself organised, she was knocking the door again and the chance of an unusual photograph had been lost. It was the first time I had seen her on that lofty unexpected perch, but certainly not the last. I was to watch her mount to the same vantage point in broad daylight. She made it look very easy. Up the plum tree on to the tack shed, jump off that on to the slope of the low kitchen roof, cross this and casually walk up the main roof to the ridge.

Ferdi came into the cottage; she had very quickly picked up the house trained discipline and, after the inevitable few disasters, we could now relax without any fear of her using the cottage as a latrine. Nevertheless, she needed watching when she was indoors. Full of mischief as usual, she promptly started provoking the very peaceful Sniff. She countered Sniff's tendency to try to ignore such childish behaviour by, apparently accidentally, walking all over the recumbent figure roasting contentedly in front of the fire. Ferdi in tantalising mood was about as difficult to ignore as a disturbed wasps' nest.

The deterioration in Sniff's temper was almost visible; her reactions rapidly went from low grumblings with eyes still closed, as she desperately tried not to abandon those dreamtime rabbits, to a sudden explosion of thrashing legs as she sought the quickest way to get her powerful little body into a position to destroy this unbearable pest. She came to her feet with jaws clashing. Ferdi nimbly hopped out of harm's way. Sniff's spell of temper was very short, but while it lasted she was determined to create sufficient mayhem to discourage the fox from such insolence in future.

Ferdi's ability to move I have already described in detail. Contained within the walls of our lounge it could be devastating. Anything that wasn't fastened down was likely to be sent flying by two pairs of powerful hard working legs.

We already had a conversation piece in the lounge, which usually amused visitors. The only furniture that the animals were allowed upon, was an old studio couch with a cover on it. That all should be seen to be treated equally, this rule applied to the cats as well, although they had to be evicted from other sticks of furniture fairly frequently.

One night Ferdi had come in with muddy feet, a fact that had gone unnoticed until in escaping one of Sniff's lunges she had skipped on to the studio couch up the back, and taken a couple of strides across the white wall above, like a fairground 'wall of death' rider. We were left with a neat set of prints, three feet six inches up a vertical wall; we decided to leave them there. How long we tolerated these wild antics depended upon how long it took the chaos that was being created to outweigh its amusement value. This particular night it wasn't long before I roared at them, sending the fox scampering out into the kitchen and Sniff to resume her place in front of the fire. Peace descended and we got engrossed in some television. So engrossed that the usual prickling sixth sense, that gently nags away – 'it's too quiet, it's too quiet' – went unheeded. Perhaps an hour later, the programme ended and we stirred ourselves, Carol into the kitchen to make a cup of tea. Now the truth began to dawn. The pantry door had been left unlatched.

'You little bugger!' The kitchen door opened and closed again as Ferdi was evicted.

'She's eaten a whole packet of chocolate biscuits,' the voice accused. The tone if not the words said 'your bloody fox'. Ferdi always seemed to be mine when she did anything of this sort.

She had reached a sealed cellophane pack of biscuits off a shelf, opened it and disposed of the lot. The wrapper and a very few crumbs remained. It had, like most things she did, been a neat operation.

With Ferdi fed and shut up for the night, we headed for bed. Earlier I said the truth began to dawn, now the rest was revealed. As we went upstairs, an occasional soft crunching noise came from underfoot. I stopped and dabbed about on another tread and sure enough 'crunch' went the stair carpet.

Realisation dawned on us simultaneously and we started laughing. I lifted the edge of the carpet and beneath were the crumbled remains of the chocolate biscuit upon which I had just trodden. Examination revealed that neatly inserted, two per step, one on each side, choccy biscuits were hidden away under the carpet on nearly every step. Most were still whole, a few had been crushed as we had climbed the stairs. Ferdi in fact could have eaten only one or two, but her instinct to store food against less bounteous times had got the better of her.

Our kitchen leads off one corner of the lounge. The stairs climb up from another corner. How many biscuits she carried at a time I've no idea, but to convey them unbroken must have required several trips across the width of the lounge. The lower half of the stairs would also be in view from our sitting position. It must have been an amazing feat of stealth or we must have been very deeply into that television programme.

9

It Takes a Thief . . .

I am now, I think, the ultimate conservator. I even attempt to avoid hitting moths when driving on the lanes at night, a luxury one dare not indulge in the roaring impatience of the main roads. At that time, however, there was one exception to this creed.

Earlier that night, we had walked by one end of the lake. On the return journey Ferdi had slipped away, and now as I crossed my field at 10 pm, she had still not come home. It was a dappled night, with rags of cloud blowing across a half moon. The sky was littered with these rags, so that the times of light and shade were about equal.

The lake, like so many others, had been adapted to serve man's purpose, and although still known as a lake it was, in fact, a domestic water supply reservoir. The holding capacity of the natural lake had been greatly increased by the piling up of a great earthen bank across the downstream end and the raising of one side where the land fell away. The material for this bank had been dredged up from the bed of a small stream that had meandered down the length of the lakeside. This dredging operation had both provided material for the bank and produced a deep steepside gulley and watercourse through which the river could be diverted in times of spate, when the water was too dirty to be allowed into the reservoir.

This had all happened a long time ago and had been achieved by teeming gangs of labourers, with spade, barrow and muscle power – a scene that must have resembled a disturbed ants' nest, from which, miraculously, came order.

The deep wide gulley is now a fairy grotto of a place, well tree'd and densely undergrown, home to a multitude of furred, feathered and finned creatures. Sufficient water is allowed to escape to keep the stream alive, even in the severest droughts. When in spate, the angry tawny torrent has scoured away, until the stream runs over bedrock and gravel bank so that at quieter times the water is tap clear, so shallow that the shingle over which it chuckles its way, bumps and dimples the surface. There are a few smooth glides of deeper water, perhaps a foot to eighteen inches, enough to fill the wellies of the unwary. Through these runs, alarmed fish shoot with the current, to turn and sink into the few deeper holes.

Trout, escapees from the lake, the very few that find their way through the labyrinth of control sluices, culverts and underground pipelines, live happily in this beautiful stream. They hold station in the current, fit and brilliant under the dappling sunlight that penetrates the fidgeting canopy of leaves. They only achieve a fraction of the size of their cousins, still in the great water on the other side of the bank, but their waters are not lashed to a froth by flylines or cleaved by the lee boards of sailing dinghies.

I moved downhill towards the lake, the webbing of an ex-RAF large pack patting my back as I walked through fields chased over by patches of silverlight and shadows, like the floor beneath the rotating lantern at a gigantic disco. I reached the steep wooded gulley that barred my way to the lake; a larger cloud turned the night dark as I descended the slippery steep side. Deeper under the trees it darkened still, until by the time I stood beside the stream, it was almost black.

I found a noisy place, where the water rattled shallow over shingle bed. I had no wish to find one of the few deep quiet holes.

On the far side, the process was reversed and I climbed into improving light. As I emerged, so the cloud cleared the moon, and to my eyes, wide-pupilled from the gloomy cutting, the light seemed alarmingly bright and revealing. I searched briefly, crouching low to silhouette as much as possible against the sky, before moving out of the fringe of trees and away from the gulley's edge, in order to escape the gurgling of the brook down below.

The surface wind was a mere caress compared to that bullying blast that panicked the high clouds, but it was still enough to have the trees leaning their heads together to whisper and sigh over sad news. The autumn brittle leaves fidgeted drily or scratched their way down to earth through the canopy. As the year settled to its tired end, the fall had not yet arrived, despite what the calendar had to say.

It had the makings of one of those instant autumns, when in a few hours the seasons are brought up to date. So far frost and wind had stayed their hand, and trees still had their summer fullness as the leaf stalks' weakening grip kept them respectable. One sharp frost, one big blow, and within hours they would be exposed, naked and stark. Then every step would noisily stir and swirl the drifts of scratchy curling leaves, and that sweet, sad, musty perfume of autumn would hang on the moist air to pervade the countryside.

The trees' nervous whisperings were most irritating to one keenly trying to listen to the night about him. Be cautious and concentrate, but not over cautious or you will become jumpy, unwilling to move, nervous of every footstep. It's a fine balance that comes with experience and instinct. When you can almost automatically monitor and account for the normal patterns, then it is much easier to detect the sound or smell that intrudes, for it is out of place and it jars. Then that prickling sensation crawls like an insect along the hairline, and with the persistence of a nagging wife, something insists you take some action – investigate or melt away.

All seemed well and I moved steadily, quietly, along the base of the bank. My goal was beside the concrete race through which the river is led into the lake.

On the corner, where river meets lakeshore, was an excellent place for hand lining, the inflowing water making it easy to drift the baited hook, supported by a large buoyant float, well out into the lake. Even more attractive was the fact that the new water brought with it a fresh food supply, and fish were usually to be found working through and along the edges of the rip.

As with most good things in life there was a 'but'; but it was also an obvious place for a bailiff to lay his ambush. He was unlikely to keep random vigil, since that way lies long cold fruitless nights, but if his suspicions were roused by someone's incompetence, then you might be putting your head into a noose of someone else's making. I sometimes leave the pack near some prominent land-

71

mark and do a very stealthy recce before finally settling to the purpose of my visit. That chance, that fluke of coincidence, is always a possibility. Had someone recently been at the same game and attracted attention, or left tell-tale evidence for the dawning light to reveal? If a watcher is already in hiding, no matter how good one's bush craft it will require a lot of luck to detect his presence, unless he does something particularly silly.

This night I settled to the fishing quite quickly; by now, had those on the side of the angels been in waiting, I'd already shown them all they needed to make their snatch. I was relaxing after that first fidgety few minutes while the line is stripped off the wrapper and layered on the bank; here the concrete side of the reservoir is a godsend, since it reduces tangles to a fraction of what would be experienced working off a grassy bank – another reason that this is a prime spot.

The line at this stage is upside down, the hook end is at the bottom of the bale; if it were cast, the lower layers would drag the upper layers out with them causing the inevitable 'birds nest', which in the dark is sometimes impossible to undo. I now layered the line onto another patch of concrete, so that when the float and hook came to my fingers, the line was ready to cast with the lead end on top and, in theory at least, free to strip line progressively off the bale without snags. It is a wearing few minutes, because the preparation requires concentration if one is to avoid wasting an awful lot of time on tangles; this occurs when one is highly keyed up, having just arrived, and trying to watch the skyline to the rear at the same time. If the river is noisy, that is another fidget factor, for it means that you cannot hear anything else. You just have to hope your approach has been good. When the river is noisy it always takes me a long time to settle. The first couple of minutes are quite an exercise in self discipline: one wants to complete the job as quickly as possible, but it has to be done steadily and methodically. It is the couple of minutes when I always feel most vulnerable.

Hold the shank of the hook up to the sky and by a combination of sight and touch impale the bait. Take the baited hook in one hand and the heavy float in the other, and make the first cast. A false start. I have inadvertently put my foot on a loop of loose line, there is a snatch, and the elasticity of the nylon brings the float and hook back on to the concrete with a thud; luckily they miss the layers of line, otherwise, the expedition would probably end there and then in an almighty bale-up. Check that the worm is still attached – I have occasionally wasted a lot of time fishing without bait.

With the line swimming out nicely in the current I needed only my fingertips to tell me what was happening in the water, and I could again turn most of my attention to the darkness behind me. Now feeling much less vulnerable – relaxing nicely but not yet completely – if there were watchers in the darkness they might still wait to catch the villain with a fish in his possession. They would not have long to wait. I took a nice fat rainbow on the first pass. It pulled hard in the current and I knew it was going to weigh about two pounds. The retrieved line I layered, ready for the next cast, until the last few yards. Then I walked well clear and hauled my breakfast up the bank. I have had fish thrash their way through my nicely baled line before. It would be difficult to deliberately create a greater tangle. I swiftly dispatched him with a small hide hammer, before unhooking him. I see no reason for subjecting the unfortunate creature to the discomfort of being unhooked, only to be banged on the head when that ordeal is over.

I was at ease, thoroughly enjoying the night. A further two fish lay in the nettles just beyond the concrete. Another had been plucking at the line held between finger and thumb and was now, I suspected, drifting with the fat worm held in its mouth, for I had not felt anything for several seconds. I began to cautiously recover the line in order to re-establish contact. I was concentrating on the fish.

Suddenly, very close to my right and slightly behind me, a soft scuffing sound, and a movement on the very periphery of my vision, registered simultaneously.

At rest, I have a very slow heartbeat; it must have accelerated to a couple of hundred beats per minute. I was caught redhanded! I spun and reared up from my crouched position. There was Ferdi, tail fanning the concrete, in her turn as startled by my reaction as I had been by her sudden materialisation at my side.

'Yuck-yuck-yuck,' she chuckled at the joke she had played. She stretched up and touched my hand with her nose.

'You barmy bugger, I nearly jumped into the bloody lake,' I told her.

There were no secrets, she went directly to the nettles and had a disinterested sniff at the trout. If bailiffs were like foxes, there would be no poachers.

The trout had in the meantime taken his worm and gone.

I decided three was enough, and we started for home. On the journey, Ferdi drifted in and out of my company. I never quite knew whether she was there or not, so perfectly a part of the night was she. We arrived in my field together, and I made the ritual gesture of giving her a titbit before shutting her in the compound.

It was 2.00 am when I got into bed. I lay reflecting upon an interesting expedition. It was the only time I had been caught.

10

Ferdi and Friend

The Indian summer stretched daringly on and on, but like most who take too many liberties with a powerful adversary, found that retribution, when it came, was ruthless. For two days the wind-raked sky was a whirling confusion of flying leaves, piling in deep wind-teased ridges, clogging guttering so that rain spilled down the cottage walls and windows, blocking drains so that the soap-slippery overspill bubbled its way across the yard and down the steep drive to join the stream that was once our lane. Wet leaves stuck like tattered labels to windows and motors cars.

After the first punch of autumn/winter had been delivered, in this year of confused seasons when nature had again demonstrated its complete independence of such utter trivia as man's neat calendar with its beautiful seasonal pictures, a dramatic change had been completed. Stark branches sang in the chill blast, even the rich harvest of hawthorn berries had been decimated by the hammering rain. They now lay, a rash of dark pimples beneath the naked spikes.

Having experienced some alternatives, I regard the British climate as one of the worst in the world. I perhaps cope better than most with its vagaries, but it is the sheer frustration of having events spoilt by its spiteful behaviour that leads me to a love/hate affair with it. There are exceptions of course, but generally wet cold summers and wet raw winters, neither able to achieve a useful consistency of heat or cold, are the fate of those who live out their lives under the gloomy grey shroud of this bronchitis-blighted island. I sometimes think this green and pleasant land demands too much in return for its green pleasantness.

The few wild days of transition from summer to winter did not make much impression on our wanderings. The changing seasons did nothing to reduce the enthusiasm of Ferdi and Sniff. The shifting drifts of leaves were just another plaything for that happy pair. Providing yet another variation on the basic game, it mattered not to them whether they were rolling each other in the long grass of summer, the leaves of autumn, the snows of winter or even on occasions belly-deep water, although Ferdi was not so keen on water and since she always came off worse at that particular sport, the contests were usually very brief. The main thing was to be alive, to keep it simple and play it with enthusiasm. An excellent philosophy. The beauty of it was that their whole attitude was infectious.

It had been a miserable day – grey, windy, with occasional wild moments that tugged furiously at coats and brollies in street corner ambushes, while icy rain streaked for the exposed gaps. These at least had broken up the otherwise unrelieved even weight of the rain.

By teatime things had begun to improve, and when, suitably clad, I crossed the field with Sniff to liberate Ferdi, there had been a dramatic change. The apparently endless supply of soggy grey candyfloss had at last been exhausted and now the wind blustered through clear air between the bowing tree tops and the cold clear prickles of light in the vast black ceiling. I headed off downhill, while from the darkness behind me an occasional burst of snarling suggested that Sniff was being tormented while she was trying to concentrate on some serious matter.

I wandered on through the darkness, enjoying the sense of great open spaces after the close damp confinement of the day, while dog and fox weaved about me in the gloom. It was a very ordinary leisurely walk with nothing unusual to mark the memory, until we were close to home on the return journey. I had dropped down off the fields about a quarter of a mile below my cottage; Sniff had come in close but Ferdi was not with us, although she had been when we first hit the lane. I gave her a whistle, to no avail, and had walked about another hundred yards when, from the far side of the field on my left, came Ferdi's scream of excitement. After the first rending of the night, she began to screech away almost continuously, the awful sound rapidly diminishing as it traced her progress downhill in the direction from which we had just come. She was travelling very fast. I stopped and listened until the cry, now very faint, was drifting up from somewhere in the valley bottom near the river, where it stopped altogether, or was lost in the wind's own lament.

I'd reached the top of our hill where the lane changes its bearing from east/west to north/south in a very tight blind bend; a hundred yards further on is my cottage. As I reached the corner the scream sounded again, then again, louder, and louder still. She was coming back up the hill and must have been flowing at her best.

The next scream seemed no more than ten seconds later and she was in the corner field, and close enough for Sniff to consider it worth while taking a look at the cause of so much excitement.

A single ice-blue light guards the dangerous corner; it sometimes actually works, although usually only in the daytime – by some vagary of the timing mechanism it normally turns itself off at night. I think it's afraid of the dark. It happened to be working and as Sniff slipped through the hedge, thirty yards down the north/south arm at the extreme range of the blue glow, a pair of slim shapes flitted between the hedges and into my field. Ferdi and friend!

She called again from out of the darkness. Sniff bundled through the hedge, also on the fringe of the blue light, crossed the lane and went off into my field to play gooseberry.

The speed at which they'd covered the half mile or so between the river and the hilltop, up the slope and in the dark had been quite impressive. I left them to it and went into the cottage. I told Carol, 'I think our youngest daughter has eloped with a handsome highwayman.'

A quarter of an hour later Sniff was scratching the door, but all alone.

I was convinced that such a powerful influence as meeting a wild dog fox at a time when she might well be coming into her first season would awaken her innate instinct to mate. Her life weaved a fascinating pattern across the border between domesticity and the wild way. There was evidence to suggest that she was already an individual well adjusted to and comfortable on either side. This experience would surely drop an irresistible weight on to the wild side of the balance. I did not expect her to return.

Perhaps it was an hour later when scratching on the kitchen door surprised me. 'She's back,' I said and went into the kitchen and picked up a torch. I opened the door and Ferdi grinned up at me with her open-mouthed grin and walked in.

'Have you brought your boyfriend home?' I said to her as I shone the torch around the garden, but there was no sign.

We amused ourselves with a series of pretend dressings down, talking to her as though she were a wayward daughter, caught out on a dirty weekend. All very silly, and she responded in a thoroughly modern fashion, taking not the slightest notice.

11

The Wife Swap

Two significant events occurred within a few weeks of one another towards the end of Ferdi's second year. One was a sort of wife swap, although not the result of one of those racy parties one reads about. By lunchtime on a particular day in September, I was in need of a change of scenery from that of the office: it had been yet another of those mornings. I'd do a quick scoot through the local supermarket and then get into the park for half an hour. I left the office, walked down the factory side to my car and drove along a dual carriageway towards the shop. The traffic slowed to a mere crawl; for some minutes the reason was not apparent, but as I slowly grew nearer to the site of the hold up, there was a big handsome dog – an Alsatian on first impression – escorting an electric delivery vehicle belonging to the Co-op Dairy.

The pottering electric truck was itself a considerable handicap to drivers trying to compress into their lunchbreak twice as much as there was actually time for. With a large dog weaving about the main road and orbiting the truck as it trundled along, the situation was both annoying and dangerous.

I took my turn to slip past.

I made my purchases and drove up to the next traffic island to get into the other carriageway for my return journey. There in front of me, now working the houses on the other side of the road, was the milk truck, with the large wolf-like figure still running rings round it, and in considerable danger of getting itself squashed. Annoyed that anyone should think so little of his dog, I pulled ahead of the truck and caught the milkman as he emerged from a front garden.

'If you must take your dog on your rounds, for God's sake keep him in the cab – if you let him follow you like this he'll get himself killed and maybe someone else as well,' I told him bluntly.

He looked quite hurt. 'It's not my dog,' he told me, 'I can't get rid of him.'

From the dog's behaviour, it was hard to believe.

The dog had joined us as we talked. A lot of Alsatian, rather dark flanks shading to almost black along his back, a good Alsatian's head and body; medium size for that breed. His handsome appearance was enhanced for me by his rear end, where dropping all pretentions of being some snooty blueblood, his tail curled over his back and appeared to have put a series of little waves in his coat as it swished enthusiastically in response to my thumping him about the shoulders. He was a fit, hard-muscled brute, certainly no sign of neglect, but he had no collar.

I said, 'If he's from around these parts he'll almost certainly know the park and the golf course; I'll take him there and see if I can lose him, or if anyone recognises him.'

He didn't need inviting twice to jump into my car, where he was completely at home. In the park he behaved as if he had never known another master; although ready to explore every inch he showed no sign of recognising any landmarks and was always back alongside every fifty yards or so. On returning to the car park he picked out the correct car and sat by the passenger door waiting for me to open it; then without needing to be invited, he hopped in, pushed his way between the front seats and took up a position on the rear seat where he sat, in what I was to learn was a very characteristic posture – very erect, front legs straight and vertical, head held high and back sloping steeply and straight to his haunches.

During afternoon teabreak I wandered down to the car. He was perfectly happy, greeted me with enthusiasm, irrigated a couple of clumps of willowherb, then as soon as I told him, jumped back into the car for the remainder of the afternoon.

Carol had some after-school activity to attend and would be an hour later than usual at the rendezvous where I picked her up each evening for the run home. I had undertaken to do the shopping while I was waiting, and had been duly armed with a list of requirements.

Since I had completed this chore at lunchtime, I spent the hour touring three local police stations, leaving a description of the dog and my phone number but, with the very willing agreement of the police, keeping the dog with me.

Carol was less than enthusiastic when she saw him and heard the story. Which rather surprised me, particularly since she was as fond of animals as I was, and it was she in fact who had rescued Sniff, one of those sad Christmas presents that lose their charm in June, when a licence becomes due.

'And what if no one claims him?' she challenged.

'Then you've got yourself a handsome bodyguard, for those dark winter nights in the country when I'm not there,' I answered, closing the subject, for I knew that for whatever reason she was choosing to be scratchy, it was nothing to do with the dog.

A few weeks later all became clear. Carol left to bestow her charms upon someone else.

So the wife swap was complete. I swapped mine for a large dog, a quite amazing character of steadfast devotion, and infinite faithfulness . . .

Mr Big got his name from the baddy who was currently trying to make unpleasant things happen to James Bond, or some other super hero. It certainly had no significance as far as his character was concerned and was arrived at after he failed to register any preference for one of hundreds of possible doggy titles with which I tried him.

Usually known as Big or Biggy, he was ever popular and earned from various subsequent girlfriends such pet labels as Biggington, Bigness, Big Enough and from one smutty little blonde, referring to the punch line of a dirty joke – Not Big Enough.

So Mr Big joined the team.

The introduction of a character like Mr Big, a powerful influence both physically and through his personality, was like dropping a brick into a calm pool. It was bound to take some time before the ripples subsided and a new calm returned. He was the first newcomer for a very long time with sufficient import to disturb the established order. The domestic repercussions were soon settled. Sniff showed an initial few flashes of jealous resentment, and made a noble attempt to show this oversize newcomer that she out-ranked him in the household; in order to make these points, she had to stand on her hind legs, propping herself up with her front paws thrust against his chest in an attempt to look him squarely in the eye. He accepted it all with good humour and in no time they were great mates.

If Sniff had been slightly overwhelmed by his size, Ferdi had no such problem – he was immediately accepted. Here was another playmate for her to run rings around. When she found that he could give her a much closer chase than the rest of her friends, they became almost inseparable. In fact there were times when his enthusiasm for the game outlasted hers, then the tables were turned and while she tried to concentrate on other business, he would bait her, lunging towards her, front legs thrust forward, as he barked downhill at her. Then, just as Sniff would snarl and snap at the tormenting fox, so now it was Ferdi who became so exasperated that she would yak-yak and snarl at the dog, rushing at him with ears laid flat, mouth wide and tilted up at him, all teeth and aggression. Biggy would go skipping backwards before her charge, only to return to his baiting the moment she turned away. If she made a determined effort to ignore his boisterous tormenting, he would pat her firmly with a large front paw, and round she would spin to drive him off again. It was all quite harmless and merely provided additional exercise for all concerned.

Sometimes Ferdi and Sniff would combine to try to bring him down. He would cooperate and flop over on to his side with a hollow thump. Then they would pile on to him, worrying at his ears and paws, tugging at the heavy loose pelt about his neck. He was much gentler with them than they were with him.

After the first startled flight up the plum tree, to consider things from the safety of the kitchen roof, both cats were completely at ease with him inside a couple of days. Little Elsa in particular made a great fuss of him, rubbing against him and walking between his legs. The big one took it all in his stride with great confidence and good humour. So he was easily absorbed into the immediate menagerie, to add his own character to an already interesting mix.

Unfortunately his assimilation into the wider order was to be less happy.

He was never claimed and so his origin and how he came to be where I found him, apparently a complete stranger to the area, is purely conjecture, but there were one or two clues. In the early days he would run after lorries, not in the lunatic suicidal fashion of some dogs, but suddenly alert and interested he would follow a certain type of vehicle, usually a large van or lorry with a covered back, for fifty yards or so. When it did not stop he would merely trot back to me. There are few enough lorries around the lanes, but when he came into town with me, it happened quite frequently during the first week or two.

I believe that he had been a driver's companion and guard dog and had probably been travelling with the freight in the back of a covered lorry. The lorry had stopped, Biggy had hopped over the tail board either thinking the journey at an end or to water a roadside tree. Unknowing, his master had driven off and had perhaps travelled several hundred miles before discovering that the dog was missing. The search would have been a pretty hopeless task. If this theory is accurate, why he subsequently became so attached to the milkman and how long he had been lost before doing so, I've no idea.

I've always been very lucky with dogs; here as with most other things in life you tend largely to make your own luck. There have been four dogs in my life, they have all been mates rather than pets, or some subservient object to gratify my ego. There has never been one who conformed to some ludicrous kennel club specification. How dare people impose their own personal whims and preference upon an animal? Ask that symbol of British courage and tenacity, the Bulldog. Originally bred for the thoroughly unpleasant business of bull baiting, the British Bulldog is today still a fighting dog; it has been bred to such grotesque distortions that it spends its life fighting for breath.

The old joyous evening assemblies in my field had largely ceased; Blackie and Butch were still likely to pop in and always got an enthusiastic welcome from Ferdi, but only rarely did they indulge in the old wild energy extravaganza. Perhaps the king was slowing down and, almost as an act of respect, Butch didn't seem inclined to chase about without him.

The sudden arrival of Biggy, age unknown, but certainly a mature dog, smack in the middle of Blackie's kingdom, was a cause for some anxiety to someone as fond of both dogs as was I. Biggy

had already demonstrated his capabilities when rightly disciplin-
ing a neighbour's labrador. Their first few meetings were very
tense affairs. Despite stern voiced warning from me to the pair,
they took their face-out to finest possible limits, to a degree where
neither could turn away or make any sudden movement for fear of
triggering the other. Ridged with bristles, stiff leggedly, so close
that they were almost touching, they circled shoulder to shoulder,
heads in opposite directions, slowly turning on carefully placed
feet, each denying the other an advantageous position.

Speaking quietly and sternly, I would slowly walk away; so
delicately were they poised that I would not risk approaching
them. Several times, although it seemed impossible that they could
withdraw from the brink, they did so and went their separate
ways.

Perhaps for some reason known only to the dogs, the matter HAD
to be decided. It seemed to me that Big was not really a rival for
leadership, since he was never to be one of Blackie's pack. But the
situation of two dominant animals in such close proximity was
apparently not acceptable to either.

Possibly I, as common denominator, was the problem.

Blackie, the old despot, was certainly not ready to step down and
Big was not prepared to be other than top dog on his own property.

The eventual eruption came in my field. I was with Big, Sniff and
Ferdi, when Blackie brought Butch to visit. Ferdi rushed off to greet
them, while I called Big in close to me and held his collar. Ferdi with
the two newcomers, rejoined us, and after a few minutes everything seemed to have settled down. Perhaps Blackie had come on
to Big's domain to make a point, perhaps it was merely one of his
social visits which he intended to continue, Big or no Big.

This time there was no brinkmanship, they just stormed into
each other. Similar in size, Blackie was slightly outweighed. Big
came out the better, and after being pinned a couple of times,
Blackie, obviously tiring, seemed prepared to accept the outcome.
He tried to disengage with some dignity still intact, but Big had
decided that the matter was going to be settled beyond any
possibility of a need to repeat the contest, and would allow him
none. I managed to get between them and Blackie began to move
off towards the field gate. Big, despite my fiercely shouted order to
come to me, swept past and hurled off in pursuit. Blackie had been

top dog too long for his pride to let him run, but he made an obvious gesture of acceptance by not turning to face the attack. Big, not to be placated, hit him in the side of the neck from behind at full tilt, knocking him off his feet. He wrenched and tore at the unresisting Blackie, while I punched, booted and tried to choke him off by twisting his collar, all to no avail.

By the time he did loose, I had, for one of the very rare occasions in my life, completely lost my temper with an animal. After a few seconds, Blackie got to his feet and without a backward look, headed for the gate. I didn't have a chance to examine him, but despite his rough coat being glossy smooth with saliver, I think the heavy loose pelt that, fortunately, both dogs had about the neck, had saved Blackie from serious damage. It was very sad to see that grand old bandit, our first visitor and consistent friend, deprived of all dignity. One could almost see his shame, he seemed to shrink visibly as he slipped away.

I should not make excuses for what happened next, it was inexcusable. Perhaps my personal traumas of the time had some influence. I gave Biggy a savage beating, using only my hand, I should like to explain, which he accepted without any attempt to avoid it, or to defend himself, looking all the time uncomprehend-ing, hurt, betrayed. I roared at him to go away, which he did as sadly as Blackie had gone in the other direction. He would stop and look back with that great sad question mark hanging over him, then when he received no recall he moved on again, until he lay down out by the compound, confused, betrayed, but still with a sad resigned dignity.

That evening I was full of remorse and quite disgusted with myself, but Biggy had gone. I had little sleep that night, and damn well serve me right. I'd driven that super dog away, for doing no more than nature decreed, no more than Blackie had done to many another in his time. Hurt, sad, confused, had he gone off to the nearest main road to look for his lorry? God, if he got run down because of me, I'd never forgive myself.

Next morning I was up as soon as it was fully daylight. Sniff and I would go and find him. I was prepared to be out all day. He was back outside Ferdi's compound, lying, ears down, uncertain, watching me approach. He didn't attempt to come to me, unsure of what reception to expect. I called him and he shot up and rushed to me; I patted and towsled and hugged him. I foolishly explained it all to him. He didn't care about my gibberish; he was just amazingly happy that we were friends again. He would get a very occasional thump from me during the years, but never again would I hurt his feelings and bewilder him like that. We all three celebrated by taking the anticipated long hike anyway. Big bounding along as happily as ever.

Fortunately this was the final upheaval. Mr Big was now an established factor on the local scene, and although he and Blackie never became friends, they never again did anything more than make threatening postures.

Blackie was forced to make the concession of staying away from our property, which was unfortunate. Big showed no interest in running with the local pack. So an uneasy truce was observed.

12

In Good Company

I tried to adhere to a pattern of practice that had evolved about Ferdi. It seemed to give her the best chance of avoiding unnecessary dangers without restricting her to a degree that limited her experience and competence. It was no great cause for anxiety if she broke the pattern, but generally I preferred her not to range free during the day unless I was there, and to shut her up last thing at night. At other times she could please herself whether she went about her own foxy business or kept company with the dogs and, or, me. This in no way guaranteed her safety; but it did reduce her exposure to what I considered the most dangerous circumstances. No matter how long it went on, I knew that this fascinating relationship could end in the time it takes to squeeze a trigger. There are plenty of trigger-happy gunmen about, who would see her merely as a target.

Why the dogs were not with me, I cannot remember, but I was crossing the fields behind my cottage with Ferdi ranging along the hedgerows and every now and then returning to see how I was getting along. I had no particular destination in mind and was content to follow the direction the fox took. She'd had several nights away recently and I thought it might be possible to get a few clues as to where her interest lay just at the moment. However, either that interest had waned or she wasn't prepared to share it with me, for it became obvious each was waiting for the other to lead and consequently we wandered erratically about the fields. We came to a lane with a row of houses on the far side. As I reached the top of the bank and looked over the hedge down into the long front gardens opposite, a powerful stocky dog, with a lot of bull-terrier in him, was advancing very menacingly down the drive towards the lane. I think his other parent had probably been a collie, but the weight of bull-terrier jaw and neck made him look very formidable. The reason for this threatening advance was not immediately apparent, and I quickly looked about to fix Ferdi's position. She was nowhere to be seen. I had no fears for her as long as she stayed clear of him, for he'd about as much chance of catching her as of catching pigeons.

Suddenly Ferdi appeared in the lane, right opposite the drive down which the dog was advancing. She was still in no danger, but this was, I thought, being a bit silly. I called her but she ignored me and walked towards the dog, who quickened his advance. Her touching faith that all dogs were playmates looked likely to get her into trouble, and if he fastened on to her with his great jaw power she might be badly mauled before I could negotiate the thorn hedge and go to her aid.

I turned my attention to the dog, ordering it back with all the venom I could muster. It continued its stiff menacing advance, it was now dangerously close. I cast around for suitable missiles, but as is usual when one needs such a thing, there was nothing about.

Ferdi, dusting furiously with her brush, walked up and sniffed at his muzzle. The change in him was quite visible; Ferdi had, quite unconsciously, played a psychologically devastating card. Her absolute confidence and disarmingly friendly disposition so confused the dog that his aggressive posture began to melt. He turned away back towards his house, his head flicking round in quick nervous movement to keep an eye on her as she came alongside him. He stopped, turning to face her, watching her uneasily as she walked around him. Finally his tail went down and he walked on up the drive, twitching his head to look back at her. I last saw him as he rounded the corner of his house and disappeared.

Ferdi, evidently deciding that he wasn't much fun after all, turned and came back up the bank and through the hedge.

'You cocky little bugger,' I told her. 'You'll come unstuck one of these days if you make a habit of that sort of thing.'

If the dog knew anything at all about foxes he would have known that they didn't behave like that. Nor, under such obvious threat, did other dogs. I'm sure that it was not fear of physical harm that had so unsettled the dog; he was much more powerful than Ferdi. I think it was anxiety at what he did not understand that so completely demoralised him. Fear of the unknown, that which makes a man's senses prickle when he's alone in a house he has been told is haunted.

It was some time later, after we returned home, that I gave consideration to the idea that in the entire world Ferdi was one of the very few foxes, conceivably the only one, who still had a claim to be a self-reliant wild animal, and could have so confused that dog.

Like the rest of the menagerie, our cats had not been sought, but had just happened. An old bachelor schoolmaster, who taught with my wife, lived with his cat, and, it seemed, required no other company. It was a she cat – to steal a line from an old joke, 'There was nothing strange about this gentleman'.

He would not have his friend spayed, and so, with utterly dependable regularity, she presented him with a basketful of kittens. Mr Jackson, as a matter of personal honour and duty, always found good homes for the kittens. To have done otherwise would, to his caring old head, have been to let down his friend and companion, and such a thing was unthinkable. In order to give the kittens the best chance of being cherished as he wanted, he housetrained them to the point of brainwashing, before allowing them to go to new homes. (Whatever his technique, I'm sure the CIA would welcome him.) No kitten of his would ever be kicked out because the new owner couldn't put up with the mess it made.

Carol had brought home a cardboard box with two identical, amazingly symmetrically marked, fine lined tabbies. They were like a pair of book ends. We were acting as a clearing house for one of them, but the friend who was supposed to have him was slow to collect, and so we kept both. The training to which they'd been subjected had been so intense that it had eliminated all discretion. They would interrupt play in the garden to rush into the cottage and use a box of soil that was placed in the kitchen.

It took some time to persuade them that the box was for

emergencies and that the great big world outside was the real loo. It was achieved by a slow progression. The first step in deprogramming these feline computers was to place the box of soil in the garden. When nature made her demands, they would approach the evicted box of soil in some confusion, go into the kitchen to make sure there was not another one in the correct place. They then returned to the box in the garden and, in a state of some embarrassment, it seemed, did the necessary out there in the fresh air where everyone could see them. After several days, we removed the box and shut the doors and windows of the cottage. Now, when the need was felt, there was enormous consternation as they sought and failed either to find the box or get back into the house. Eventually, internal pressures forced them to the disgusting practice of using the flower border. No matter how fastidiously they covered things up, so that no one should know what they'd done, it was evidently a thoroughly embarrassing and humiliating experience.

There was an amusing sequel to this brain washing and de-washing. During the few days it took to re-educate the little brutes, we, one evening, forgot to bring the box of soil back into the kitchen. We were settled down in front of the TV and quite engrossed in the programme, when a dreadfully wet raspberry sounded close behind us. We whirled about, expecting to be faced by a major carpet cleaning job.

It is probable that caught in such circumstances, of the entire animal kingdom, only a cat could look dignified and aloof. We were apparently the ones who had betrayed our lack of breeding by turning to stare. Big Tom, already beginning to show as the larger of the pair, was poised with enormous dignity and superb balance, his feet bunched in neat alignment on the thin edge of a bowl of hyacinths which stood atop a china cabinet. Above this very cramped footing, shoulders and head angled forward into the room while, with gymnastic elegance, his balance was maintained rock steady by the hind quarters and tail, angled towards the wall. He had neatly scooped the leaf mould for the centre of the six hyacinths, and with legs extended to give him the necessary height to clear the blooms, had done what he'd had to do in the centre cavity.

'A cat's got to do, what a cat's got to do!'

We hooted with laughter as he perched there, full of contempt for our bad manners.

The hyacinths did very well, although they spent the rest of their lives outside in a greenhouse.

As the cats grew up, they remained virtually identical except for their size, the one a miniature replica of the other. Big Tom and Little Elsa (one of millions of she cats to share the name, thanks to the fame of Joy Adamson's lioness, she was sometimes known as No Sense and Little Else, which was very unfair) were both neutered the same afternoon. Little Else took almost literally no notice. Big Tom, like the big brave male he was, spent all evening perched on the arm of the chair with his back end overhanging in fresh air, and at about one minute intervals let out the most mournful, dejected yowl in an unspeakably gloom laden voice that was about twice as deep as normal, it seemed that the castrato idea worked in reverse for Big Tom. The cats, like all our animals, provided one or two lively moments. They very soon established a regular route up the plum tree and over the roof to the bedroom window. By the time they were half grown there was a fine crop of that year's rabbits, scampering along the hedgerows of my field. We would be awakened in the middle of the night by a firm soft thump – scuttle, scuttle. The cats had delivered another present. They would catch rabbits up to three-quarters grown, and nearly as big as themselves. In quite an impressive feat of strength, especially for Little Else, they would climb the plum tree with a rabbit in their jaws, cross the roof, haul themselves up onto the window ledge and drop the rabbit, quite unharmed, into the bedroom. We had a double divan bed with about three inches of ground clearance, an obvious bolt hole for a frightened rabbit. Carol and I spent long sleepy minutes lying one either side of the bed, she with a broom trying to push the rabbit within range of my arm thrust beneath the bed from the other side. It was a very one-sided contest – the rabbit was wide awake.

We soon learned that once we'd caught him it was pointless to turn him loose in the garden again, because, no doubt thinking us churlishly ungrateful, the cats would re-deliver their present within twenty minutes. So we kept a large box in the kitchen – some mornings it would have three rabbits in it.

I've mentioned the cats because it was about now that Little Elsa earned her other name – Walking Cat. She had always been an incredibly friendly little soul, rolling on her back in the lane if a stranger so much as spoke to her. Whether this bears translating into human terms I do not know; if it does, she was a very fast cat indeed. She began to accompany us on our walks, not just the few hundred yards into the field that they'd always done, but for cross-country miles.

I doubt if many have walked along with two dogs, a cat and a fox for company, and all completely free to make up their own minds about it.

Sometimes Elsa would keep close, sometimes, like Ferdi, she'd slip off on her own account and rejoin us later, so that, again like the fox, I was not sure whether she was still with us or not. We'd once followed a stream, Sniff as ever splashing along in water, Big, Elsa and I on the bank above; Ferdi had spotted someone approaching in the distance and slipped over the stream and faded into the undergrowth beyond.

The man came up with us, stopped for a chat and expressed surprise at the presence of the cat. I said we'd walked about a couple of miles so far. To add to his surprise I added, there's a fox over there waiting to rejoin us as soon as you've gone. His grin said 'You're pulling my leg.' I assured him I wasn't and he said he'd sit quietly and watch. He could have saved his time. Ferdi was far too cagey for that and didn't rejoin us until he was well out of sight.

I don't suppose the guy ever did believe me.

Mr Big, now a firmly established member of the team, took over responsibility for discipline. The evening feed had become quite a major operation. I had become friendly with a local man who counted among his duties the collection and disposal of condemned meat from slaughter houses. This, depending upon its condition, became pet food or fertilizer. Now that I was feeding two dogs, two cats and a fox, I had recommissioned a large old pressure cooker, and some of the more wholesome cuts used to find their way inside.

My practice of feeding late to encourage Ferdi to return from her evening's roaming so that I could shut her up before turning in myself, meant that towards dusk in the long summer days there would be a gathering in the garden about the big pressure cooker like boy scouts around a camp fire.

In the dark winter evenings it was quite probable that all five had been stretched across each other on the studio couch for the last hour or so before feeding time arrived, and they would tangle in a confusion of heads, tails and legs, all apparently quite contented, like some fabulous multi-coloured composite creature escaped from the verses of 'Jabberwocky'. Then when I said 'grub time', there would be one furry eruption as all those interlocking pieces attempted to get up at once, dived into the kitchen and waited facing the door ready to pile out into the garden.

In summer they were fed by the last daylight. In winter by the light from the kitchen windows. The five bowls were set out. The two dogs sat behind a bowl, the other three manoeuvred continually.

The menu was usually the same – liver, lights, tripe and meat plus biscuit meal. I endeavoured to fill all the bowls before letting any of them get tucked in, to avoid having them grabbing food as fast as I doled it out, so that I'd have no idea how much each had taken. The dogs were no trouble, the chief offenders were Ferdi and Big Tom.

After observing my method a few times, Mr Big assumed the role of dinner monitor. As the bowls began to fill, he would begin to rumble a caution to the cats and fox on the opposite side of the circle of bowls, letting his lips curl to show a glimpse of teeth. If this was ignored, which it usually was, he would get up, cross to the offending cat, lower his head bringing the top firmly against the cat and, still growling, walk forward, pushing the offender away from the bowl of food. There was something of the ponderous dignity of the law about the way he did it. Like the old village bobby wagging his finger at the kids he'd caught scrumping. He was very effective against the cats, but never managed to prevent Ferdi from making a lightening snatch and skipping off up the garden with her prize.

Once all was ready and I gave the word, the race was on. The cats, despite having much less than the others, were always last to finish and yet were never robbed. The other three, if I'd got the handicapping right, finished at the same time. They seemed to have an understanding that once the original owner had left his plate the other two could give it a final licking. They always rotated round the empty plates at least once. But if such liberties were taken prematurely there would be a great curling of lips, and stern warnings growled. When they fed together there was always something to chuckle about.

13

Winter Sport and Hard Times

After a raw, soggy prelude, winter suddenly decided to get interesting, becoming progressively colder from shortly before Christmas. Tracks which had for so long smudged and smeared, sending my boots skidding exasperatingly, so that every now and then I came to a halt at the end of two long smoothly planed slicks in the well lubricated clay, while the dogs and Ferdi spread their toes to leave huge prints behind them, now quickly stiffened and a few evenings later we were making our way home, a stinging north wind firing my face, the underfoot nobbly and ridged, fanning into needles of ice and making an enduring record of those huge paw prints. Within a few days, sports fixtures began to be cancelled; a couple of weeks later we were dragging old pairs of hockey skates, long forgotten, from the backs of cupboards, and Saturday afternoons were being passed, not romping about rugby pitches, but rasping over the surface of frozen lakes. These had long since ceased their ominous creakings and cracklings. That cold deadly water lay beneath an armoured crust eight inches thick.

The satellite weather photographs had shown the approaching snow clouds; for several days the crystal alpine air had become smudgy with soft grey clouds that scattered confetti to the hill farmers in warning handfulls. Then the great grey, horizon-to-horizon blanket was drawn up, and from the vast winter vistas visibility closed to a restless tumbling confusion of twenty-five yards. In two days an almost continuous snowfall laid a soft even moulding, twelve inches thick over city and countryside alike. The rubbish tip and coal yard, sports field and railway siding, were suddenly the subjects for artist and photographer.

The city was beautiful. Even the major roads, salted and sanded, for a long while became no more objectionable than tracts of demerara sugar. Aerial photographs showed them like great dark veins converging at the heart of the beautiful pale corpse that was the city. It stirred memories of Keats's line: 'St Agnes' Eve – Ah, bitter chill it was! etc., etc.'! inflicted upon me, and thousands of other Philistines, at grammar school. If the city was beautiful, the countryside, already enchanted by the petrifying finger of frost, now became a fairyland. There had been no wind during the snowfall and the slimmest twig bowed beneath a thick white sausage. The spruce and fir had been deeply thatched into sloping white rooves. The deep blurred tracks and tumble of displaced snow showed that life was going on.

Perfect delicate prints of wings with beautifully spread pinions showed where birds had lifted from or landed in deep snow. The drama of a hawk strike put on record. Probably a kestrel, had taken a small bird, perhaps struggling to get out of the snow. When times are hard one takes what one can get. In the depressed snow, flecks of crimson, in startling contrast, diluting to pink at the margins, and feathers to suggest the victim had been a chaffinch, born deep into the yielding layer by the thumping arrival of the hawk. And the hawk's own wide slender pinions, spanning beyond into the still smooth snow, as it lifted off for a better plucking site.

The cats were not overly enthusiastic about this sudden change in decor, lifting each foot very daintily from the neat small hole it had made, and shaking loose snow off with a deft flick before putting it down once again. The other three were, predictably, like kids let out of school. Before the snow came we had enjoyed a lot of fun on the frozen worked-out gravel excavations that are plentiful along the line of the river valley. Several of these are deep and the ice needs checking carefully before one takes too many liberties, but some are very shallow pans of rainwater, no more than a couple of feet deep and ideal for skating. I got into the habit of hanging my skates over my shoulder when we set out for a walk, and after a few times, as the knack returned, I had discovered a game in which I could compete, perhaps had the advantage, over Messrs Sniff, Ferdi and Big.

On one of the shallow pans it was possible to skate for a quarter of a mile without having to turn round. I would work up a good pace with the pack bounding along beside me, then throw the tightest turn I could muster and hare off in the other direction. Sometimes I'd have all three of them, legs shooting away, rolling and slithering on across the ice, paws working furiously on the uncooperative surface as they fought to regain a standing posture. Heads turned towards my retreating figure, while they, like ships careened, slithered on in the original direction.

Sniff, weighty, stocky, shorter in the leg, was worst affected by sudden directional changes, and by far the most amusing to watch. As soon as she lost control her face wrinkled into what, in a human being, would be a very worried look. To see her, front legs gone away, chin on the ice, hind legs still standing, furrowed countenance, staring in one direction while she continued to progress in the other, was like the Walt Disney sequence when Bambi first discovered that 'the water was stiff'.

Ferdi and Big rarely did more than momentarily lose balance, then increased their turning circle a little, but I did have my moment of triumph when all three would go down in a swirling, gyrating heap. Then I would sprint like mad to be first back to the starting point. Sniff was almost as funny when retrieving sticks from the ice. Full of enthusiasm as usual, she would pound up to a gently slithering stick, scoop it up in full flight, then bang on her brakes. Resembling a tightrope walker with a balancing pole, she'd slide along on braced legs, sometimes slowly rotating in a drunken ice ballet.

The snow brought an end to these icecapades. It muted the tinkling chandeliers that flanked the waterfall. For weeks these had grown in magnificence. The willows and alders dipped their branches into the stream and bobbed in never ending dance to the tug of the current. Ever moist with spray, they had become encrusted with an extravagance of jewellery. Orbs and peardrops, needle clusters, bridges and veils. The vainest Hollywood superstar was never so bejewelled. Beside them a pallisade of reeds, glass-rodded, chaffed and rattled in accompaniment. Just as in summer, leaves meeting overhead made a green bower to frame the sparkling water, so now a rich white cape enclosed the Ice Queen's Palace and quieted the brittle tinklings.

In a haze of flying snow, they progressed around the field. Ferdi spread her paws and lightfooted across the snow, her progress least affected. Mr Big, heavy but long-legged, kept his body clear and bounded along with little trouble. But little Sniff, already at a great disadvantage in their games of chase, now had an additional serious handicap. Her weight bore her through the snow until either her feet hit solid ground or sufficient of her body was embedded to support her weight; if by then her feet hadn't found a solid object from which to propel herself, she was virtually staked out. While the other two continued their tail chases with a dramatic plume of snow drifting behind them, poor Sniff burrowed along like a maggot in a corpse.

Snow is always a good photographic subject, and with a supporting cast of such star quality I exposed both ciné and still film in some quantity.

The wind came and although it quickly spoilt the breathlessly balanced filigree of the woodland decoration, it scooped and sculptured civil engineering feats of great beauty. It stole snow from the fields to fill the sunken lanes; a gently rising bank hid the hedges and eight feet beneath its smooth crest lay the icy tarmac.

For days the only way in or out was on foot. Many of the fields were easily walkable, the snow had been blown off them. Arches, cornices, impossible cantilevers, waves curling to give the surfer his tube to 'shoot', but never breaking. It was all moulded with the magician's touch.

And now it was not only Sniff that thrashed and struggled like a fish caught in the mud, for she was often joined in this fun by Big and sometimes with much laughter by me, when I walked over an invisible bank and plunged armpit deep. Ferdi alone, the superb all-rounder, seemed to skip over the deeps with rarely more than half a leg below the surface. Until, that is, their rough and tumble took them into a deeply filled hollow, when the dogs seemed to combine, and take great delight in burying her, and themselves in the process. When it finally became too exhausting, they would lie in the hole, covered in snow, sharply contrasting pink tongues flicked to their panting, as jets of steam coned from their mouths.

Sniff's life became largely preoccupied with her own version of mountain rescue, not that what she rescued was very important to anyone but Sniff. I could keep her amused for hours by hurling sticks deep into snowdrifts. The thin entry slot often collapsed leaving no obvious mark to show where the stick had gone. She'd seen it go, could probably smell its presence; and no matter how long it took she was going to find it. She tunnelled away, often the drift collapsing on top of her. Every so often she'd emerge in a minor eruption, just to see if I was still there. She appeared to be laughing, mouth open, a pancake of snow between her ears like a white fur cap. Dusted white all over she looked like one of commercial TV's flour graders. She poked her head out of her snow cave just to be sure that we'd not been deceitful enough to slip off and leave her mining away in the bowels of this floury mountain. Reassured, she'd turn and dive back down the tunnel. It was evidently unbelievably good fun.

Her efforts were continually hampered by the other two. Neither Big nor Ferdi shared her passion for sticks and in a very human reaction to that which does not interest one personally, seemed to regard Sniff as some zany eccentric, with much sport to be had by generally poking fun at and hampering her endeavours. When she was deep into a drift, Ferdi would follow her down the tunnel and grasp her hind feet. Sniff's struggle to turn round and the subsequent fight invariably brought the drift down on top of them. This process was sometimes abetted by Big barking encouragement and taking a great leap on to the drift above the tunnel. For a brief moment it was possible that nothing lived within the snow tumble, then the surface would begin to move, like water coming to the boil and, collapsing in upon itself, the fine snow poured into unseen cavities like sand in an hourglass. Up would pop two heads, like dynamic spring bulbs, one pointed face and pointed ears, one blunt muzzle and half-pricked ears, both open-mouthed, bright eyed, insubstantial, like the cheshire cat; just a face in a drift of white smoke, as they shook to clear the snow.

All these interruptions meant that retrieving a stick could take a long while, and by the time she was proudly offering it for me to throw again, that beautifully smooth white wave would resemble an arctic battle field. Sniff's love of sticks exceeded that of any other dog I've ever known. She was a strong little dog and big sticks were merely a bigger challenge, the bigger the better seemed to be her motto. She stole fence posts when the horsey people were repairing the fence about my field, these were of roughly trimmed pine, five feet long and varying between four inches and six inches in diameter. She would experiment until she'd found the centre of balance, then stagger away with the load jamming her chin hard against her chest, and swinging her ponderously off course each time it hit a tuft of grass.

With amazing single mindedness she never gave up on sticks, to the point, one hot summer, of very nearly drowning rather than lose a great waterlogged bough of a thing, which as she pushed it through the water had scooped up a huge mass of blanket weed. The effort of propelling the ever increasing weight of that raft had so exhausted her that by the time it formed a firm buffer against the bank and she was still several yards out into the pond, she was about finished. The idea of giving up the precious log never occurred to her, and her attempts to wrest it from the dead weight drag of that great soggy mattress, drained the last of her considerable reserves. She rolled beneath the log and weed, and all was still.

Lucky I'd been watching her carefully as she struggled, lower jaw under the water, so large was the log, she gurgled and sprayed at each breath. I leapt in, parted the thick layer of weed, and grabbed her by the collar. I beached her, losing one of my 'jandles' deep in the mud. I held her upside down and gave her a good thumping; she wretched up some water and blinked her eyes. I planted her right way up and for twenty seconds she sat absolutely motionless. Then she stood up, shook water all over me, and made for that damned log. I told her in no uncertain terms to leave it alone.

Such was little Sniff's affinity for sticks, and she had developed a very efficient manner of communicating with the stick thrower. She would wait for what she considered a reasonable period of time, during which she would offer the stick to hand, then, if this were ignored, she would place it across the boots of the thrower. She would tire of the ill mannered treatment she was receiving, pick up the stick and with a quick flick of her head, give you a sharp wrap on the shins, usually enough to start you from your daydreaming.

My abiding recollection of that winter is of Sniff laboriously working her way through a drift cut sheer on one face by the wind. Eventually she'd reach the brink and the collapsing snow would dump her at the bottom on firm ground, and her furrowed, worried look would change to a laugh as she panted, open-mouthed. She was like a kid having a lot of fun.

We could now walk briskly, picking our route through the wind swept shallows, or lark about in the deep drifts as we chose. While it remained very cold and the snow light, one could remain dry after being completely submerged, for it brushed off like that beautiful alpine powder that allows the good skier to smoke his way down hill in spectacular style.

These conditions continued for six weeks.

During this time we were out one weekend afternoon when we met a party from a rambling club. Like so many other similar parties, they were keen to convey the joy of being afoot in the 'great outdoors'. They had beamed and all greeted me as they came up in Indian file. By the time the last one passed me, I had said, 'Hello! Yes, it's great to be out,' about a dozen times.

A ripple of excitement ran through their ranks; some of them had spotted a fox, and were indicating to the others, who hastily gathered around to see where it had gone.

Ferdi had slipped away, and been quite conspicuous against the revealing white landscape. As she went up the rising ground it seemed she would remain so until the horizon. But already she had vanished, using the ridges and hollows in what at that distance appeared an even, unrelieved white plain.

I headed for quieter parts so that Ferdi might rejoin us. On our way downhill to look at the waterfalls, we crossed the old disused branch line that used, when the century was young, to serve a now equally disused mine. Both had been spared nationalisation, but the latter had, if one could believe reports from the local environ-mental vigilantes, suffered an even more disturbing fate: its deepest shafts now contain some very unpleasant substances indeed. These will no doubt in some form or other eventually find a geological fault and reemerge to cries of, 'Who'd have thought it? It seemed a good idea at the time!'

The old track is in parts a jungle of broom bushes. These were, according to the vagaries of the wind, either stripped naked or wearily bowed under concealing mounds of snow. Those that had been relieved of their burden were providing an emergency ration for rabbits and no doubt other gnawing creatures that weren't in a chilled coma awaiting spring's 'early call'. The height a rabbit could reach when stretching on its hind legs was marked by the clean white wood before the bark began again. The crushing weight of snow had lain some bushes almost flat and the rabbits had tunnelled into the drifts to take advantage of this.

I had seen few since the heavy fall but here was evidence of great rabbit activity, everywhere paw marks and droppings mottled the flattened snow. As I looked at the ground I spotted an almost straight line of dimples; there was no detail, they were merely small depressions into which the floury snow had fallen. As I slowly followed this track I fancied that I could see very shallow scallops where a tail had occasionally brushed the surface. I was fairly sure it was the track of a fox or cat moving slowly and very deliberately, for there was only the briefest scuff mark at the tail of each depression. The thought had barely occurred to me when Big and Sniff bounced off excitedly, sending snow cascading from the buried bushes so that some of them managed to stagger upright again, like weary swimmers rising from the sea as the beach shelves up beneath their feet.

I'd seen the dogs react like that so many times before, I felt sure Ferdi was close. I expected to hear her greet them as they were lost behind another dome of white.

Then I could see Big, punching his front legs forward into the snow bobbing his head down, barking as he did when he was baiting Ferdi. Still no foxy sounds. A flicker of concern crossed my mind, was she dead, trapped, shot, poisoned? I charged through the snow to Mr B. There she was, not speaking because she had her mouth full. Legs stiffly straight, neck held back, head high, chin tucked in under the weight. She was tip-toeing along trying to hold the trailing legs of a large rabbit clear of the snow. She held him by the shoulders and he drooped down on either side of her jaw. I called Big away. Ferdi stirred the snow furiously with her tail when she saw me.

'Are you staying with us, or off on your own?' I asked her. She seemed undecided; the dogs sniffed at her rabbit very interestedly, but neither attempted to take it from her, they never did except in fun, when a tug of war would develop. The same could not be said when the positions were reversed: if either of the dogs had a desirable prize, Ferdi was very likely to try to pinch it. I crouched in the snow and slowly reached out for the rabbit. 'I'll carry it for you,' I volunteered. These exchanges I had with my animals were partly one-sided conversations and partly the speaking aloud of my thoughts to the only audience available. Nevertheless, I believe that tone and voice modulation convey some meaning and that the bond is strengthened by this practice. It is also my experience, after spending some time alone in remote parts of the world, confirmed by others with similar experience, that any object, animate or inanimate, is likely to be engaged in conversation. Even if one does not need the company, it seems one does need the exercise in communication, to remain 'half way' articulate.

Ferdi entrusted her supper to my keeping, confident, no doubt based on previous experience, that it would be returned to her. Thereafter she mooched along with the dogs, but frequently returned to my side where she held station like a well trained dog brought to heel. She trotted neatly along looking up at the rabbit dangling from my hand, occasionally lifting her muzzle to take a sniff at it. Then she'd skip off again to join the dogs, only to return a few minutes later for a further check. It was always the same when I carried her kill. I got the impression that she'd have been happier carrying it for herself, but weighed carefully against this the consideration that it would be a nuisance; that she'd need to take it straight home or bury it, rather than walk it for miles round the countryside; it would be a great handicap when she was trying to keep involved with whatever the dogs were up to. This was her usual compromise. I think she considered me basically honest and to be trusted not to sit down and eat it myself.

It was a hard time for prey and predator alike, and that no doubt explained the obvious concentrations of rabbits at the broom bushes. I thought it likely that it would also be a focal point for those that live off rabbits, but I could find no more of those aligned tracks that crossed the snow like the perforations on a sheet of white paper.

Freed by the wind from their muffling snowy burden the trees and bushes of the riverside were again jangling merrily. Since the snow belt had passed, the days had rarely crept above freezing point and more often than not frosts had persisted day and night. I had recently had a milk bottle cracked after a night on my kitchen draining board, when the milk had frozen inside it.

The waterfall marks the start of the wooded gully, mentioned earlier, down which the stream flows to bypass the reservoir. From a sluice gate beneath a stone bridge the stream descends in three great steps formed by breakwaters built across it, to reduce bank erosion when the gate has to be raised in time of flood. Only a narrow race down the centre showed that the stream was still moving, both sides had petrified into a glass stairway like a pantomime set.

Below the last breakwater lay the real waterfall over which the stream tumbled to its bed in the gully. Here the more violent action of the six foot cascade had prevented ice from forming on the surface, but the spume had frozen to encrust all it touched.

The snow-muffled sounds of our approach were completely masked by the noisy tinkling of the ice. Reeds and nettle straw supporting a screen of snow concealed us from view, and as we came to the waterfall we surprised about a couple of dozen coots out on the ice. Not the most accomplished aviators; in a drumming of wings they panicked into the air and labouring hard, skimmed away a few feet above the ice. It took Sniff no time at all to get into the free water, and with the rest of us watching from the warm comfort of solid ground, she happily swam about in the race. I was a bit concerned that when she did eventually tire of her frigid bath she'd have difficulty getting back on to the ice, with a possibility of getting swept underneath it. For both our sakes I hoped she wouldn't, for as I looked at that noisy glittering scene the thought of deliberately jumping on to the sheet of ice in order to smash it and let her out held no appeal at all. After a couple of attempts to hook herself up on to the ice, during one of which her body did swing beneath the sheet, leaving exposed only her head and front paws hooked over the broken edge, she solved the problem by, apparently quite calmly and deliberately, swimming over the waterfall and landing with a fine splash in the deep hole that had been hollowed out six feet below. She then swam to the side and walked ashore. I let her finish shaking before I bent to congratulate her; I'd been caught like that before. I called her a brainless bugger, but she really was very confident and competent in the water.

By the time we returned home that evening it was freezing very hard again and Sniff carried, in the words of the highway code, an audible warning of approach. Her wet coat had formed a series of spikes of fur that had become tipped with ice so that she clattered quietly as she trotted along.

14

Water Sport and Easy Times

The year progressed and at last a vast volume of warm air moved in off the Atlantic; as it slipped over the chilled surface it draped pale wisps over the land, and the snow began to slink away. The dazzlingly beautiful snow drifts turned to dull banks of soggy cotton wool and then to dirt-crusted grey slush.

The ground beneath was still hard frozen, so the melt water set off across the surface; ditches and lanes alike became chuckling waterways, gathering momentum as they headed down hill for the rivers and pools; everything that could contain water overflowed, the river was half a mile wide and all the flat fields along its course became lake-land, as pools, gravel pits, rivers, roads and fields became one.

In no time those weeks of perpetual ice and snow had slipped into the realms of the unbelievable. It required the odd, sad, soggy, grubby patch of snow, cowering in some sheltering place, to remind us that it had indeed been so.

As the flood eventually receded, damn great fish were to be found churning the ever retreating waters in the bottoms of ditches and other small depressions. The clumsy, bulky carp from a couple of pools well flushed by the food, seemed to have been least able to resist the rush of water. Some of these great finned piglets turned up a half mile from their original home, trapped in the rapidly draining shallows. Fortunately, the big carp is a resilient fish able to survive out of water for quite some time. Many were returned to the pools, but inevitably some died and an unknown number were washed away with the river.

With it seemed, half the world turned into a swirling brown

soup, Sniff was literally in her element; the other two pressed on happily enough, but without quite capturing her enthusiasm. The roles were reversed and now she often had the advantage. She would trail the vee of her wake over this world that slipped past so steadily; chin resting on the waters, nose pointing into the stream, tail streaming along the surface, she crossed the flood, visited the islands. Making instinctive allowance for the current, always aiming well up stream, she traversed with little loss of ground; rarely was she swept past her target.

Not so Ferdi or Big – on the few occasions when they did get into the flood they would swim strongly enough, but only to the nearest point at which they could scramble out again. So while Ferdi, Big and I squelched and slopped our way around the edge, Sniff often paddled her way across a narrow tongue of water and would be waiting for us on the next headland. Fox and dog together would spot her intention and rush ahead in showers of spray to get to her or beat her to her land fall.

Eventually the rivers slipped back between their banks and a sediment dried powdery grey to encrust the lowlands in drab uniformity. Successive winds and rains combined to clean up the countryside until all was back to normal and one suddenly realised with that perpetual surprise that winter had slipped away and spring was with us.

It usually takes early nests of shining eggs to make me realise that while I've still been thinking winter, the year has moved on. Soon there was real warmth in the sunshine when it found its way between the clouds; no longer the thin pale yellow wash of watercolour that had occasionally brought an anaemic brightness to the floodlands of a few weeks before. The land responded to this kind treatment and soon it was burgeoning with busy purposeful creatures. Energy overflowed – territorial squabbles, courtship, mating, hatching, rearing, feeding. The season geared the food supply to support all this industry.

Then the easy days came, just in time as always, just when earth and set contain half a dozen vigorous, tumbling playful cubs with fine appetites, so the fields, woods and hedgerows are full of young inexperienced rabbits, squirrels, rats and mice.

With fledglings making their first under-powered solo flights

Free Spirit

and the chicks of running birds getting waterlogged in the wet grass. With ducks, like the mallard that nested in my field, faced with marshalling her delightful, fluffy dozen, that scuttled around like clockwork balls of wool, across country for half a mile to the nearest water large enough to provide them with comparative safety.

We became aware that they'd hatched and were on the move one afternoon when her anxious persistent quacking eventually prompted me, and a neighbour, to investigate. We walked quietly up the lane; when we were quite close to her we stood and waited. From our lowly position we could not see into the field over the high bank and hedge. She seemed quite agitated and once we heard her become airborne. Eventually there was movement in the base of the hedge and down the steep bank she came, her big flat feet and low slung hull flattening the grass. She quacked again and down the steep chute of flattened grasses came, slipping and tumbling, six bustling ducklings. Once they'd untangled them-selves at the bottom of the slide she lead them in good order across the lane to the opposite bank which was less steep but had longer grass; into this they disappeared and their progress was marked by twitching, fidgeting grasses which spread slowly up to the hedge bottom when all became still again, as presumably the last one scrambled through into the field beyond.

'Only six, she's lost a lot,' I said. I had kept an eye on the nest ever since she had started flighting into the field regularly and I'd realised that she had honoured me by taking up temporary residence.

I had eventually pin-pointed the nest site, while the terrible trio were amusing themselves by taking it in turns to try to dig a rabbit out of a small warren system in one of my hedgerows while the two non-diggers, keen as coiled springs, stood apart watching the other exits. For the unlikely combination of two dogs and a fox, they had become a remarkable team. Although he insisted on having a go, Big's excavations resembled more a mine shaft than a fox hole and it was amusing to see the other two impatiently push past him to take over the digging, their tunnelling commencing from where they'd left off last time, well forward of the face Biggy was working. So, although he showed a willing spirit, his actual contribution to the progress of the tunnel was nil.

After a while I left them and climbed on to the stable roof where I sat idly scanning around with my binoculars.

The duck came over and flew a couple of fast circuits. She dropped her great air brake feet, side slipped wildly in both directions on half closed wings, then in a final flurry of wing beats dropped into the grass.

Such an exhilarating display always leaves me feeling slightly envious and deprived. Why couldn't *homo erectus* have decided to fly instead of messing about trying to balance on his hind legs; we might have learnt the trick by now! I kept the glass on her, knowing she'd be hard to pick up again if I once lost her position. I had to be patient, she was not about to show all and sundry where her precious nest was hidden.

Eventually, after much checking and listening and moving away and moving back, she led the sly spy on the stable-top to a bramble curtain draped over the lower stand of the barbed wire fence, with plenty of last year's dead nettle stalks still threaded through it.

I later carefully removed the leaves and grass with which she had covered the eggs during her absence, counted fourteen and re-placed the camouflage. I'd kept the animals away from that part of the field, as best I could, and fortunately neither Ferdi or the cats had discovered the nest.

After several loud quackings the grass began to shake again and the duck reappeared at the bottom of the bank on her own; the ducklings had evidently been given their orders and had no doubt frozen into invisibility among the grasses beyond the hedge.

She quacked away again, while slowly patrolling up and down at the base of the hedge. From as far as twenty-five yards apart, over the next few minutes, ducklings struggled out of the grass and scuttled to join her; when she had another five gathered up she headed once again across the lane and through the swaying grass.

The field into which they'd passed was of half grown mowing grass and would probably be a serious barrier to the little adven-turers; after that the fields sloped steadily down to the pools beside the river a half mile away. I reflected upon how long the journey would take and how many would complete it. I assumed that whatever had scattered them, and I suspected magpies since there had been three of those bully boys in that corner of the field earlier on, had already accounted for three of their number. Magpies also have to eat. In this I was wrong, on taking another look at the abandoned nest I discovered that three eggs had not hatched.

With all the places one would have imagined a duck to consider highly desirable and convenient nest sites along the miles of water margin, why she should choose my field so far from water, I cannot imagine. But then ducks will occasionally nest in most unusual sites. Of the dozens, perhaps even hundreds, of nests I've found, usually with the help of the dogs, the vast majority have been where one would expect, along the banks of streams and near edges of pools. But I have also found them on railway embankments and once a mallard's nest about fifteen feet up a tree on a branch that overhung a stream. The ducklings from that high-rise accommodation must have started life in a very exciting fashion, with a fifteen-foot drop into the water. It was a fairly narrow stream at that and had there been a strong crosswind blowing at the time they might very easily have missed it; although they're so light and fluffy that they would have probably come to no harm.

This was the season of glut, as the year drifted on into high summer. There was a meadow, two fields away from mine, a natural grass meadow – not the boring unrelieved even green of a carefully selected, highly nutritious grass strain, into which let one wild flower trespass at its peril. This was a beautiful place, like an alpine meadow, full of a variety of delicate trembling grass heads, some that it's impossible to hold still, locally known as 'quiverum-quakem', of an abundance of wild flowers, of fragrance and busy insects.

It always gave a heavy crop of hay, which I doubt was any the worse for its variety. This meadow became a favourite place to idle away an hour; hummingbird hawks hung stationary on the blurred wedges that were their wings, before the black and purple bombs of the knapweed flower heads, sipping nectar like their namesakes; only their hair-spring tongues unrolling to make contact with the flower and delicately probe for that sweet sip. Does their fascinatingly gentle feeding habit contribute towards pollenating their host? Or unlike their fellow nectar seekers who wade knee deep in pollen to reach the precious draft, do they slyly steal and slip away without paying the bill?

Fritillaries, walls, meadow browns, skippers and common blues restlessly bejewelled the meadow. Grasshoppers scraped and launched themselves off great reversed hind legs, like roman seige machines, high over the stirring ocean of flower and grass heads. Burnet moths in their plastic reflective safety tunics fluttered to explore the bobbing flowers. It was a warm, humming, lazy place with always something to catch the attention.

In serious mood Ferdi, lost to sight, would rear like a polaris above the grasses and drop stiff legged, heavily to trap some small snack. She would toss her head back so her face was just seen, disembodied, hazed in grass, and gulp the morsel down. When she hunted and fed like this she reminded me of a gourmet with his plate of oysters, one nip to release the flavour and swallow.

In more frivolous, exuberant mood she raced through the waving patchwork ocean, porpoising into view, over the grasses in a long flat arc, often joined in this sport by Mr B, so that at high speed they popped up and were swallowed, popped up and vanished sometimes in the air simultaneously, sometimes independently as they rose to get another bearing. Like friendly dolphins sporting around the bows of an ocean liner.

The natural meadow, the real meadow by my terms of reference, was a pleasant place. A small brook trickled along the ditch down one side; it sported nice patches of watercress and the blue-flowered water mint that grew at its margins added to the aromatic excellence of the meadow, until on a warm still summer evening it was like walking through a herb garden.

At dusk on such an evening, after a good walk, I often contrived to return via my favourite meadow. There was an amazing sense of peace and stillness; beneath the larger trees the canopy had trapped the heat of the day like a soft warm blanket, into which one walked, suddenly, from the delicious cool of the evening. Through the fragrant grassland I dawdled, with Ferdi skipping along, jumping to snap at the ghostly silver white moths, almost phosphorescent in the gloom that drifted through the grass heads like brief puffs of smoke.

That splendid little creature the hedgehog left very discernible tracks where he trundled his low slung bulk through the tightly packed vegetation, in quest of slugs and the other thousand items that supply his universal diet.

Hedgehogs were often to be found at this time of night. The prehistoric little beasts never failed to provide a source of great interest to Messrs Ferdi, Sniff and Big; the tightly curled spiky footballs would be scrimmaged around from one scraping paw to another. Big would pick them up and toss them into the air, whether for fun or because they were too spiky for comfort I know not.

A hungry fox can open up a hedgehog, not with the efficiency of a badger, for that fellow comes equipped with his own personal tin openers; nevertheless if he's hungry enough to ignore a few prickles, he can take a meal off Hotchi.

I kept an eye on matters the first few times but no harm came to the hedgehogs that the trio found. Their spikes made excellent shock absorbers and they were well able to take the tumbling around. Never to my knowledge did Ferdi make any serious attempt to put one on the menu.

I think, of all the times I was privileged to spend with Ferdi and her chums, perhaps those gentle walks through the balmy summer dusk are remembered with the greatest sense of loss.

In those days there was always a feeling of disappointment when the mowing machine chattered its way to and fro, and the real meadow was gone until next year.

Alas that herb garden has been sprayed into submission by its new hedge grubbing, tree-felling owner. The mint-scented brook now skulks three feet underground through a concrete pipe, the mint long gone. It's now possible to get in one extra furrow with the plough.

The mini jungle gone for ever, and destined it seems to be rapidly followed by its full scale counterpart. Unless man's heel is removed from this, once beautiful, ravaged world.

We are quite unnecessary, probably the only species ever whose absence would not affect the interdependance of the exquisitely balanced system. There seems every chance that we will do the world the great favour of removing ourselves from it. Unfortunately we will probably remove the vast majority of our fellow creatures in the same rolling dust cloud, and those that remain will have little to look forward to. Why? Because there are too many of us, and dogma, superstition and vested interest, usually masquerading under the names of religion or progress, prevent the implementation of any sensible worldwide programme to deal with this base cause of all our troubles.

15

The Rat Strikes Back

I do not share the traditional hatred and revulsion of the rat; that's not to say I'd ever welcome him about my house or garden, mainly because he might be carrying Weil's disease. The situation never arose while there were so many predators in residence.

Sniff, in most respects a gentle creature, was sudden death to rats. This had been the case from very early days and had initially been a matter of great surprise. Where this instinctive animosity had come from, I have no idea; she did her best to catch rabbits and would always scamper after water voles; one would have expected a creature so similar in general appearance and often found in the same riverside environment to stimulate the same reaction in the dog, but this was observably not so. Sniff seemed to have an extra gear into which she changed on sighting a rat; everything about her seemed to go up scale, she became hair-sprung – vitally alert and very quick.

Sniff was less than a year old when this strangely misplaced assassin's instinct first showed. Into the old stock compound had been dumped a ramshackle hen coop and several cages. I had on occasions seen a rat scuttle about the place, but never seen where he vanished to. He was a clean, fat, furry chap, let down like all his kind by that tapering knurled rod of a tail, that has a raw appearance and gives the impression that the unfortunate creature has mange which has, so far, only stripped off the fur as far as his bum. If he'd been blessed with a fluffy tail that curled over his back, he'd probably be a popular character in nursery books and a model for cuddly toys. Instead of being subjected to all manner of unspeakable barbarisms, without it seems one voice raised in dissent.

With no thought of rats on my mind, I moved the coop by walking it on its corners; as it shuffled along, a football size bundle of dry grass was exposed. A dormitory, but was anyone at home?

Sniff had followed me into the compound and was very interested in the whole procedure and particularly in the ball of grass. I poked it with a stick and out shot ratty in a hurry. The poor little bugger never knew what hit him; before he'd cleared the marks left by the base of the coop, Sniff had snapped him up, shaken him in a blurr of movement and dropped him quite dead, still within the yellowed patch of grass.

I was flabbergasted, gentle Sniffy had killed her first rat with the professional efficiency of a champion bull-terrier. It had probably not taken three seconds and I'm sure it was the violence of the shaking and not the bite that had despatched him, probably rupturing internal organs and scrambling the brains.

Ferdi would sometimes take a rat when she hunted in the proper meadow, thumping down to enfold it in a mat of grasses and snapping it while it struggled to free itself from the entanglement. The net and trident technique from the Roman games. I don't remember seeing the actual kill; instead of flicking her head back and swallowing, which was her habit with the usual tit-bits she snatched from the meadow, she would, after a short delay, emerge at the field's edge with the rat already limp in her jaws. Her technique was quite different to Sniff's – there was no shaking, the fatal injuries were delivered by biting. When I saw them, most of her victims had crushed heads.

Both Ferdi and the cats ate rats. Ferdi following her usual formula of burying what she did not require at the moment. I don't think either of the dogs ever ate a whole rat, although they sometimes cleaned up squidgy bits left on the lawn by the others. Ferdi's attitude towards the dogs, in this respect, was interesting. She never got possessive or minded their interested sniffing over what she'd caught, whether rat or rabbit, probably because they'd never made any serious attempts to take her prize from her, and she'd now got faith in this fact. But she'd never bury food in their presence. If Sniff or Big followed her when she slipped away with half a rabbit, she'd return still carrying it. Not until she managed to drift away unnoticed would she return without her meat. Perhaps we would pass close to the spot a few days on, when again she'd slyly drift away, to rejoin us later, whiskers full of dust and leaf litter, having finished off her meal.

During the melt, when flotillas of polystyrene and plastic bottles had swept unopposed over the drowned land, an ancient bridge, that bestrode the river in four gracefully arched paces, had finally submitted in dreadful weariness, to the power of the berserk torrent which filled its arches and rose still to burst like ocean combers over the ancient sandstone parapet.

The two centre spans had been devoured by the raging tawny monster, broken and strewn over hundreds of yards of river bed. It was sad – there was romance in the old bridge that had stood long enough to have conveyed both stage-coach and juggernaut safely across the stream, before it was bypassed by a modern dual carriageway and a youthful meccano bridge sporting an acne-rash of rivets and bolt heads. In its retirement, in gentle contrast, it continued to serve, transporting cattle, hikers and dogs dry footed over the river.

Big, Sniff, Ferdi and I were mooching about by this ruin. I was standing on one of the remaining arches looking over the parapet whose sandstone was deeply scarred by ancient initials, hearts transfixed by arrows, edges vague and rounded by the weather, mellow and interesting in contrast to the mindless aerosol graffiti that over-sprayed it proclaiming, 'Punk rules OK!' and 'Man United!'

Big and Ferdi had followed me on to the bridge and stood with me at the ragged edge where the old road ended abruptly, where one could look into the rubble-filled heart that had given the old bridge its massive dead weight to resist the pushing river for so long.

Sniff had gone down the bank to get on with important matters, like swimming, disturbing water vole and waiting for a stick to come floating past. I looked down on her, as belly-deep in muddy water she poked along the bottom of a well-ventilated bank of clay, where the riverside troglodytes had been busy. Suddenly a rat scuttled up the bank and set off along the brink. Sniff lunged after him in a shower of muddy water, scrabbling wildly up the steep face.

By running along the edge of the bank, the rat had wasted

5a 'The fare of a wild fox is very varied . . .'

5b 'Grub time'

Ferdi gets the better of Big

6a 'Hello Biggy!'

6c 'Oh, go on!'

6e 'Well, I'll just have to fight you for one, then!'

6b 'What about a kiss?'

6d 'Don't be a spoilsport!'

6f 'Gotcha!'

7a 'With her mouth partly open, she always appeared to be grinning . . .'

7b 'Ferdi seemed to skip over the deeps with rarely more than half a leg below the surface . . .'

precious seconds in which he might have found cover. She came up on him rapidly and just as she closed, he dived over the edge, they hit a small shingle beach within a half second of each other, and Sniff snapped him up before he'd made another five yards. He squealed briefly then blurred to silence. She shook him so violently that from on the bridge I could hear her ears crack softly against her head.

She carried his limp body back up the bank and dropped it at the top. She shook herself radiating water and then did something I'd never seen her do before. She scraped him over with her paw and sniffed at him. The corpse miraculously returned to life and fastened on to her nose; the slender chisels of his lower incisors entered the left nostril and sliced through to slide their angled cutting edges against those of the upper jaw, cutting in from the top.

Now it was Sniff's turn to cry, she gave a great yelp and jumped back with the rat dangling from her nose. She tried to shake him free and he whirled and flayed about her face until she generated sufficient centrifugal force for his body to tear itself away cutting a slot through the soft lobe of her nose as it went. She fell on the rat in a fury, biting three audibly crunching bites, before shaking him again, showering blood from her own nose as she did so. Whether she deliberately threw him or the shaking merely tore him from her grip, he spun away to splash into the river which bore him off, waterlogged and still. If there had been anything unpleasant on the rat's teeth the copious flow of crimson that dribbled off her muzzle would have washed it out of the wound.

The parapet had obscured the view of Ferdi and Mr Big, and it was not until Sniff's yelp that they had dashed off to investigate. By the time I joined them down on the river bank, Sniff was being treated to a pretty intensive valeting service. In delivering the *coup de grâce*, she had liberally streaked herself with blood, particularly about the head.

While her own pink face flannel sought to clean her nose and lap the blood that ran down her muzzle, a self supplied tranfusion, Ferdi and Big, stationed on either side were cleaning her ears and cheeks. She accepted their administrations very patiently, only muttering an ungrateful warning when Ferdi attempted to help with her sore nose.

How much of this was prompted by concern for a wounded comrade and how much because they liked the rich packet of crisps taste I do not know. But it made a touching scene, there with the battle ruins of the old bridge behind them. Alas my camera was several miles away, a fairly usual situation!

Already the dribble of crimson had slowed to a sluggish film which she cleaned off as fast as it oozed from the loose rubbery nugget that was the lobe of her left nostril. This was flapping loose but still attached to the centre by a slender but gristly tough section. When she stopped licking it for a moment it appeared to assume approximately its correct position and I decided that the application of stitches, super glue or rivets was not necessary.

The obvious moral to this tale will be regarded as quite unnecessary by most folk. It is, 'Never sniff a dead rat, in case he ain't!' Sniff carries a permanent reminder of it, for her nose is slightly lopsided with a distinct groove tracing the line left by the teeth of the rat that fought back.

16

The Rabbit Hunt

We topped the rise and looked down the slope of well-grazed field that fell away to a thick hedge on the brink of the disused railway cutting. As was often the case, a fact well-known to the trio, rabbits from the embankment had fed well out into the field and were scattered, a series of brown bumps, slowly bobbing and feeding, bobbing and feeding, through straggling ranks of fluffy blonde thistles. Just on the edge of the thistle patch were two that did not bob and feed. Sitting up, ears straight to the sky, still as porcelain, they flanked the feeding area, alert, on duty.

As my eyes came level with the brow of the field I checked to survey the scene below. My attitude of concentration told the trio that there was something to be seen. As I have mentioned before, when Sniff and I were alone such frozen concentration would bring her to my side; anxious, sensing danger, she would tap my calf with her paw asking for reassurance. It had often happened when I was concentrating to critically focus my binoculars.

The three had to advance well ahead of my position before they could see the sweep of the field where the rabbits bobbed. I stood still and watched them. They reached a fringe of long grass, which, ironically enough in this cattle-mowed field, marked the line of a bridle path that rarely felt the hiker's boot and whose coarse grass the cattle had spared. They stood still. I could see their heads, floating in a haze of grass. They did not emerge into the open field, but slipped back down the gentle curve of the ground, and out of the line of sight of both the rabbits and myself.

The field fell away in two directions, before me to the old railway, and sideways, down the slope they had taken, where the path followed a hedgerow to the cutting. The fall away was considerable and I could see only the top of the tall hedge.

For a long time nothing happened, then suddenly there was a burst of racing rabbits. The quietly feeding brown bundles shot away, criss-crossing in all directions. Normally, when disturbed, they nearly all streaked downhill and vanished into the thick undergrowth that flanks the cutting. But that was the direction from which the danger threatened.

Breaking cover in the bottom hedge, Big was moving fast into the confusion of scattering rabbits. Sniff, farther over and being left behind, was pounding up the slope as fast as she could go, not close enough to be a threat to their safety, but still sending half a dozen of them swerving away from the hedge back towards the patch of thistles.

In what proportion the elements of thought, innate instinct and pure chance influenced Ferdi's tactics, it is impossible to confidently appraise. I certainly believe that the first two contributed most, for she seemed to anticipate that as the dogs came on to them, some of the rabbits would turn back and run through the thistle patch.

I spotted Ferdi a lot farther over, flying through the straggle of thistles that ran up the slope, and into which probably a dozen rabbits were now heading with Big in hot pursuit. He and Ferdi were by now running almost at right angles to each other, he going across the slope and she straight up it. Sniff, having made her humble contribution, was now so far behind as to be virtually out of the chase.

The bounding collection reached a dense patch of thistles, with the far hedge and safety only twenty yards beyond. I thought Ferdi had picked one up. She swerved wildly, and stopped so abruptly that she almost performed a handstand, head down and brush waving briefly above the screen of thistles. A faint squeal reached me and a drift of white parachutes floated like smoke above the place.

All the drama was over – those that were to escape had escaped. I saw Ferdi, seemingly on tiptoe, as usual, head held high as she sought to prevent the dangling rabbit from tangling between her own front legs. She trotted across the intervening space and vanished through the hedge.

I had not moved for several minutes while this fascinating ancient pageant, in one form or another as old as life itself, had been performed before me. I now wandered down the slope. Sniff and Mr Big emerged from the dense thistles. To my surprise, Big was carrying a rabbit. They trotted up to me, very pleased with themselves. Presumably Big had been close enough to take advantage of the confusion caused by Ferdi's sudden appearance in the thistle patch, and had snapped up an unfortunate rabbit that had perhaps turned on sighting the fox.

I crouched down in our traditional greeting, while they came up and leant against me. Big presented me with the rabbit, but evidently only to admire, for as I stood up to continue our walk, he picked it up again and trotted ahead. The pride and novelty soon wore off, and I suddenly realised that he no longer had his rabbit, he'd put it down while about some other business and forgotten it. I pointed back the way we had come and sent them off. This was a game Sniff loved, and tail wagging furiously she led Big back down the trail. There was always the possibility that she would decide to bring me a damn great stick instead of the rabbit, but I dangled my feet over the bank of the stream and sat and waited. Five minutes later they returned complete with rabbit. This time I took charge of it.

We'd been back home a half hour before Ferdi slipped into the garden, muzzle caked in soil. She settled down to some serious face washing; she had evidently put a joint in the larder for a rainy day. At mealtime that evening I negotiated with Big and Sniff on the basis that while they liked both rabbit and condemned lights, livers, steaks etc., I much preferred rabbit, and so I'd do them a swap. They didn't seem to have any objections.

During the evening, I looked at the trio collapsed before a non-existent fire. That was when the thought first occurred to me, and I began to consider the differences between the old helter skelter pursuit of rabbits, and that afternoon's hunt with, what had at least appeared to be, elements of organisation and even teamwork. I thought about the early days when the chase had usually been led by old Blackie; it had all been rollicking good fun, with the cub, Ferdi, as likely to be leaping to worry at one of the dogs as they careered along, as to be concentrating on the fleeing rabbit. By the time Big arrived there was purpose in Ferdi's hunting. It was divided into two distinct areas, one of which was still a fun romp, an excuse for rushing about with her pals, when rabbits were pursued with great enthusiasm without, it seemed, any serious intention of catching one. They were chased when they had a fifty yard start and only the same distance to reach safety. In private, Ferdi was responding to an instinct to practise, to learn, to perfect innate hunting skills, even though she was not dependent on the fruits of those skills.

I think much of the basic technique is inherent; by that I mean the cub, even in the absence of its parents, does not have to discover by a long process of elimination by trial and hungry error, which is the best method of catching those mice buried in the basement of the grass meadow. I choose this example again, because it is such an obviously specialised technique with a very high success rate. There was probably a time many thousands of years ago when foxes had tried to dig out the wee creatures, scrabbling down into the gallery with their paws, then following along exhaustingly exposing yards of passageway, while the mouse skipped off twice as fast as the fox could dig. Then presumably, by normal evolutionary process, those individuals that found better hunting techniques thrived and passed on those advantages.

Ferdi tried no other hunting methods than the obviously correct one of collapsing the galleries and isolating the victim in a very small section. I have already recorded the speed with which she polished her initially clumsy, uncertain performance, into a slick, highly efficient one, like a gymnast progressing from his first ragged, nervous flick-flacks, to the smooth, controlled beauty of a championship display. I draw fairly confident conclusion from watching Ferdi hunt mice, because it was all so easily observable. Much less obvious, because of its greater scale, and because much of it was done away from my viewing, was her hunting practice for rabbit and other food. But I suspect that the idea, that she honed to perfection a basically innate technique, still applies. She rapidly concluded that when hunting seriously, the company of myself and the dogs was a major handicap. Consequently, it was on comparatively rare occasions that I managed to observe her early attempts at rabbits. The first time I noticed a shift from the frivolous helter skelter was one evening when, having located several rabbits well out from the sheltering hedge, she had stalked belly to the ground, very much as a cat stalks, and using the grass and cow parsley to mask her approach, she greatly reduced the distance between them before running out of cover. Later, and by then she had managed to catch the occasional rabbit, I saw signs of consider- able progress when, again spotting some feeding rabbits without being seen herself, she had not stalked directly towards them but had moved stealthily away until she had gained the shelter of a hedge that ran much closer to the feeding rabbits than any cover out in the open field. This may also have been a deliberate attempt to gain a position between the rabbits and their burrows. In neither of these incidents did she succeed in getting her supper, but she was definitely becoming a much more dangerous opponent.

I think she had done remarkably well to have achieved what I now considered to be the complete fox's repertoire, for I now believed her to be as fit and competent as any wild fox. It had taken longer than the wild cub would have been allowed, but she had achieved it without the obvious benefits of parental coaching and example.

To digress slightly. It had not occurred to me until this moment of writing, that I could at this stage, while congratulating Ferdi, perhaps have accorded myself a pat on the back, for it seemed that all those goals, decreed while we had anxiously waited to see if that wobbly ball of fluff would take solid food, had been achieved.

It had suddenly turned unseasonably cold. I considered lighting the fire, but the wooden cradles that flank my fireplace, and in wintertime contain kindling wood and split logs, were both empty, and at that stage of the evening I could not be bothered to go outside and organise these things. I kicked off my moccasins and buried my feet in the tangle of fox and dog fur that littered my hearth. It was warm as toast, and as I wriggled my cold plates deeper, three heads lifted wearily and turned to regard me with a look that clearly said 'Oi – what the hell's the game?'

I continued to let my thoughts drift, idly considering the effect that Ferdi's company had upon Mr Big and Miss Sniff. Unlike Ferdi they were, obviously, too far removed from the natural order to have the same compelling drive to be self-sufficient. Scatter- brained, frivolous, full of fun, they chased rabbits, they even, very occasionally, caught one. It was usually due to some very bad luck for a young inexperienced rabbit, rather than hunting expertise on the part of the dogs. Even Sniff, who had no chance of catching a bunny in a straight chase, had been known to pick one up. It had happened when a luckless young rabbit had been panicked by the exuberant bustling of Blackie and Butch into fleeing through its bramble hideaway. It emerged via its escape tunnel in the long grass that grew about the bramble patch, and had the appallingly bad luck to collide with Sniff who, either by low cunning or more likely sheer fluke, was waiting on a path right in front of the run. There was only one other time that I could remember her getting a rabbit, and I have no explanation for that unlikely event. She merely appeared out of a thicket, with a freshly killed rabbit; again I can only assume he was a most unlucky creature.

So casual in fact had Sniff's approach to rabbit hunting been, that I'd often had a good laugh at her; when, while carrying a large stick that she was trying to persuade me to throw, we had disturbed a rabbit, Sniff, not the fastest quadruped even with everything in her favour, had bumped off in pursuit without even bothering to drop the precious stick. Her plan was, presumably, to cause the rabbit to collapse with laughter, then beat it to death with her stick. You've got to get your priorities right, and to little Sniff sticks were a lot more important than rabbits.

When either of the dogs had got a rabbit, it was a fairly safe bet that they had picked it up in one of the lanes, a victim of a motoring accident. Rabbits were definitely more for fun than for food.

What, then, was the explanation of the afternoon's remarkable performance. I had little doubt that they had been influenced by that beautiful little professional, young Ferdi. But how? Had there really been some form of communication between them?

It had seemed so dramatic to me, because I had only just noticed it, but perhaps she had exerted a gradually increasing influence by their close association over a long period. I recalled them working together at the rabbit warren in my hedge on the day that I had discovered the mallard's nest. Perhaps she, now mistress of her craft, had quite unwittingly subjected them to a mild form of the coaching by example which, under different circumstances, she herself would have received.

In human activities, those who are athletically inclined will generally agree that there is something admirable, enviable, about the performer who is the smooth, confident master of his chosen discipline. He may not be coaching, may not even say a word, but others are induced to slip away and quietly try one or two of the manoeuvres they have admired.

Is it possible, at a different level, that Ferdi's confidence and efficiency had in some way reached the dogs, had prompted them to accept her as leader of the hunt, and that by close and long association they had picked up some of her habits, learnt simple tactics, to manoeuvre for a position that would increase the chances of success, instead of launching off on a wild chase with the rabbits hopelessly out of range? Whatever the explanation, and I personally believe my theory of quite accidentally achieved leadership by sheer confidence, and coaching by example, was probably correct, I still found that what I witnessed that afternoon was unbelievable, unless some form of communication took place. Many gregarious animals have a system of leadership, but that a group comprising two domesticated dogs and one virtually wild fox should accept the little vixen as leader, I found remarkable.

From an admittedly very biased point of view, I considered my dogs the two best in the world, and therefore quite capable of learning under the correct stimulus. I can accept that they let Ferdi lead them away from the brow of that field, and unseen down to the cutting. What happened after that has either to be left unexplained, and accepted as a pure coincidence – a thousand to one fluke happening – or must surely have involved some sort of fairly sophisticated sensing of what the other two were going to do. Having watched it, I could not go for the idea that it was the product of a purely mindless fluke. That fate played a considerable hand in the outcome was obvious, but the start was more contrived. They started from a good position between the feeding rabbits and their burrows; they did not charge out in an excited bounding group, but broke cover from three different positions; indeed the vixen had probably been forty yards away from Sniff, who had the middle position. I did not spot her immediately, but knowing her capabilities and the position she'd reach when I did pick her up, I believe that Ferdi did not break cover until the dogs were well into their run.

That they picked up two rabbits was good luck. That they were in a position to do so, I firmly believe was not. I found the whole incident fascinating, and the possibilities it suggests absolutely intriguing. Whatever the advantages and disadvantages of Ferdi's experience versus that of the normal wild fox, there was no doubting the remarkable development from her cuddly toy days, when Sniff's maternal instincts had prompted her to enfold the orphan cub in a caring protective blanket, even to the degree of suffering the indignity of allowing the needle-toothed waif to try to suckle her and, in its frustration, bringing yelps of protest from the long suffering Sniff.

From those distant days things had changed radically, until Ferdi, quite inadvertently, had repaid some of the care and protection she had received from Sniff and later from Big. His willingness to serve in this role had never been called upon but was very apparent and continuing. As for me, I had been repaid a thousand fold, through the sheer enjoyment of her company, the interest, the education and eventually the material and inspiration for a very nervous excursion into authorship.

17

Myxomatosis, a Gunman and Foxy Mischief

Myxomatosis raised its obscene head again in a brief outbreak. The attitudes of Ferdi and the dogs towards those tragic victims of biological warfare, the myxomatosed rabbits, were markedly different from each other. To Ferdi, they were just a bonus, easy pickings. She performed one of the important functions of the predator in imposing nature's ruthless quality control system. The weak, sick and injured are taken, while the fit and fast escape and thus the perfection of wild creatures is maintained; only the fittest, fastest, most cunning prey animals survive and this decrees that only the fittest, fastest, most cunning predators get a meal. So the more efficient the meat eater, the higher performance is demanded of the meat and consequently of himself. The higher the standard he achieves, the higher becomes the standard that is necessary. A ruthless system but one which eliminates all the tragedies of the subnormal.

With all they shared, with all the interflow of influences from one to another, in some respects they were still as far apart as the wild and the domesticated can be. Ferdi was about her own affairs; as the dogs and I moved along a path that was the centre parting for a thirty-acre field which lay across the ridge above the old railway. As we went downhill I spotted the rabbit fifty yards ahead, right beside the path. Even at that range, there was obviously something wrong with it. That intangible difference that distinguishes the sick, injured or dead from the fit and well. Perhaps it is to do with what I've just been saying. The standards of the fit and healthy wild creature are so high, that anything less is noticeable.

Myxomatosis, was the first thought – probably quite advanced. My fears were borne out.

Sniff and Big spotted it when it moved, a weary slow motion, stretch with the front feet and hop the hind legs up to them. They rushed off; the rabbit heard them approach and turned its sightless head up the slope. That it was a myxi victim was confirmed for me when the dogs slowed down, all zest for the chase gone. They slowly approached it and I saw the rabbit start as they sniffed at it. The whole aura of something awfully wrong reached even the dogs. I'd seen them behave like this before – predators themselves, but so far removed from Ferdi – perhaps influenced by my own sad mood in the presence of these pathetic creatures, resigned and helpless, feeding quietly in the open, blind and seemingly uncaring about what dangers might threaten. I find a tragic, quiet dignity in these blighted victims as they patiently wait for slow-footed dawdling death to rescue them.

I came up to where the dogs gently explored the rabbit. After the first nervous starts it now fed quietly, cropping the short grass and moving with the infinite weariness of one whose sole wish is to lay down a ponderous burden. It did not react to the presence of me or the dogs in any way. The flattened, dull fur, brailed where the vertebrae poked into it, hung like a skirt with its emptiness. The draped bones seemed barely able to support the grossly deformed head, as emaciated as the body, save for the eyes. Great bulging orbs crusted and superating, dribbling a pussy discharge that dried and cracked into fine biscuit crumbs on the cheeks. Sightless eyes deep buried in these obscene living volcanoes.

I picked up the stick that Sniff had dropped and performed a tiny kindness for the weary little brute. It was pitifully inadequate to compensate him for what my fellow man had done for him. That, and things like it, make me seethe with frustration at my impotence to make everyone see the issues as I see them. That nothing at all can justify deliberately subjecting an animal to the experience that rabbit had endured.

The dreadful pathos threatened to hang over the afternoon's walk like a dark cloud, and it required a considerable effort to shake it off. I headed towards the river, intending to sink the body complete with its fleas, a rather futile gesture I guess, but it's always possible that, if left lying around, fleas carrying the virus might migrate to a healthy new host, should one happen to feed nearby. I was lucky to be distracted from my gloomy mood when I got the chance to watch three kingfishers falling in among the stickleback shoals, where a small brook joins the river.

Every thinking creature is influenced by its experiences. Ferdi, the wild creature that made friends with and learnt to trust one man and some dogs, reacted in a dramatically different way to certain situations from a totally wild fox lacking the basis upon which to make a judgment that it was safe to trust one individual amidst the thousands in whom such trust would be fatally misplaced. So, with good reason, he trusts no man. Ferdi trusted only me, retaining her instinctive suspicion of all other men, and so her association with me did not undermine her security, for I would never betray her, and while she remained close enough, she would receive whatever protection the dogs and I could provide. In turn, there were circumstances in which she appeared to have an influence on the dogs; the rabbit hunt had been the most dramatic example I had yet observed. This influence had not been exerted through physical dominance, as is usually the case in animal societies, but by some much less tangible means. I guess it was not possible to keep such company without each being influenced, at least slightly, by the others. Nor was I immune to that mischievous little charmer. A long time lover and, when the opportunity arose, protector of wildlife, I would, by now, have gone to war for her; I was reminded anew what a miraculously beautiful thing the natural order is. Good pals the dogs and Ferdi were. Co-operative team-mates they could be. Yet in some respects the gulf between me and the dogs and Ferdi was as enormous as the gulf between the tame and the wild will always be.

Time tripped on into a mellow rich autumn, without the extravagant over-abundance of a really good year. Nothing seemed to have done badly. A disturbing factor intruded into the pattern of practices that had evolved to help Ferdi avoid unnecessary hazards.

The fields around my own patch had only occasionally rung to the crash of the 12 bore as one or other farmer's lad picked up a couple of rabbits for the pot. Most of them had heard about Ferdi and, hopefully, would not be tempted to shoot at a fox, particularly one close to my place.

One day a van stopped outside my cottage and two rather grubby looking, unshaven types asked if there was any shooting to be had. I told them they would get no shooting around here and they drove on. Shortly after that incident the blast of shot guns became much more frequent, and one day I found a couple of spent cartridges lying in the field close by one of my hedges. A van, which I thought to be the same, was regularly to be seen parked in a field gateway. It transpired that a farmer who has already appeared between the covers of this book, had let them have permission to shoot over his land. What he charged for the privilege, I do not know, but the gunman seemed determined to get his money's worth – as he no doubt saw the matter – by slaughtering the maximum possible. What he did for his living I've no idea, but sometimes at the crack of dawn, sometimes at dusk, and any time in between, he was likely to be banging away. His enthusiasm for killing things seemed unquenchable. My first exchange with him came one afternoon. A few shots had sounded from way beyond my top hedge. Some twenty minutes later, I shut the dogs in the kitchen and slipped into the field. Ferdi was in her compound and, aware as ever, spotted me immediately and hopped on top of her 'kennel', for a better view over the grasses, some of which the horses refused to eat, and these now stood to near shoulder height, dry and polished by the sun.

Ferdi had been free all morning and was not feeling starved of company, or keen for exercise, and although I could see her brush swishing about, she did not scream her greeting. It may have been that she was aware of the presence of a stranger, although the field is L-shaped and the compound is not visible from the leg bounded by the further hedge. Using the patches of long grass and the overhang of the hedge, it was easy enough to move undetected towards the end of the field. My hedges are towering thickets of hawthorn, hazel, bramble and briar, with a few mature oak, ash and crab apple interspersed. In a landscape that is increasingly assuming a skinhead look, they attract a rewarding variety of wildlife. It is precisely for this purpose that my hedges are un-kempt, and field margins wild. A matter over which I exchange fairly strong opinions with one neighbour in particular. The prospect of having some trigger-happy bastard use my mini sanctuary as an ambush site, was, to coin the euphemism of the year, not amusing.

I was about thirty yards away when I spotted him. He was not easy to see, wearing sensible clothing – camouflage smock and trousers, courtesy of his local Ex. WD store; the broken line pattern of the camouflage and the coarse crinkle of the deeply grooved bark blended admirably.

He was tucked tight into the hedge, quite still, leaning against the huge bole of an ash tree. I would have spotted him anyway, before starting across the next open bit of ground; evidently this patch provided the flavour of the month, for the horses and rabbits had combined to produce a bowling green. But what betrayed his position so quickly was the stark harsh straight lines of the gun barrel, contradicting the natural curve and sway of bough and grass.

I watched him for a couple of minutes, I picked out a spaniel lying at his feet. He barely moved, he had that passive alertness about him. His head turned a couple of times, a quick anxious movement as he scanned back down the field towards me and the cottage.

His intentions were obvious, to ambush any rabbit, pigeon, or probably anything else that was stupid enough to show itself. As I moved out, the last fringe of the tall grass that had hidden my approach so well, now let me down. It concealed a litter of brittle ash twigs left over from a wind blown branch, long since cut up to warm my cottage. Carelessly I trod into the middle of these, lost my balance and set off a series of crackles like an exploding jumping jack. The figure whirled to face me, then as I walked up he began scuffing his boots to disturb the undergrowth and telling the dog, 'Find it. Find it.' He'd shot a rabbit in the other field and it had staggered into my hedge, he explained.

I expressed myself in terms that left no room for ambiguity or misunderstanding, including in there somewhere a judicious reference to the local bobby, to whom I referred by Christian name as though he were a close personal friend. The nasty man and his very nice little spaniel departed, he with very ill grace.

My second run in with the gentleman came about a week later when I was in the garden on a warm, still afternoon, concentrating on sewing up a badger that I was mounting – I do a little amateur taxidermy. This unfortunate old brock had been killed on the main road a few miles off. He was a magnificent old boar of well over two stones in weight, but he'd been badly battered and was requiring some careful restoration. Giving my full attention to the work, I scarcely registered the bang, bangs from the nearby fields. Then several seconds after one report, I found myself in the middle of a fall of spent shot. None of it hit me, the dogs or fox, all of whom were sitting around, mighty interested in what I was doing. But it pattered down all over the roof of the cottage, the small yard and the drive. It did absolutely no damage, but had someone been looking up at the time and taken a piece in the eye, it might have been a very different story.

I was very annoyed and dashed into the field with dogs and fox streaming along with me. It was the same guy just beyond my hedge; he started to walk away when he saw me coming; I yelled at him, but he kept going. Ferdi sheared off as the dogs and I scrambled through the hedge and went after him. We caught up with him and while Big, Sniff and the spaniel socialised, he and I did not.

I told him I'd had a belly full of him. I quoted the registration number of his van and said the police would be calling on him as soon as I could lodge a complaint and I hoped he lost his gun licence, assuming he had one. He was bigger than I, but as the saying goes, 'It isn't the size of the dog in the fight; it's the size of the fight in the dog that counts'. At that moment, the fight in this particular dog was too big for him. His defence, such as it was, was sulky and resentful, rather than aggressive.

He went off, leaving me with an uneasy gut feeling. I was pretty sure he had seen the fox, and he'd probably be vindictive enough to shoot her if he came across her on his side of the hedge. If this happened, I knew perfectly well that there was nothing within the law that I could do about it. I decided not to dwell on what I might do outside the law, fervently hoping that the situation would never arise.

My fears were groundless: I never saw the man again. Not that my hollow threats had anything to do with his departure. He apparently seemed to think that he had purchased the rights to shoot over the entire county. Several people complained to the farmer in question and the arrangement was terminated. However, it was a fortnight before all this came to light and in the meantime it provided the background to a bit of Ferdi's mischief, and a joke on me.

I tried to reduce the amount of time she spent on her own, and to compensate, encouraged her to accompany the dogs and me on more of our wanderings. Normally this was left entirely to her, she either fell in with us or she did not. I now began to start the walk with Ferdi on a line; there was no guarantee that she'd stay with us once I released her, but it worked to a degree and she probably spent more time with us than she would have done normally. An Indian Summer had set in, we had returned from an evening stroll as details were starting to get lost in silhouette.

Back in my field, Ferdi decided that she had matters to attend to along the hedgerows and ignored all my attempts to persuade her to come back to the cottage or into her compound. There was no immediate danger, but I did not want her to be loose all night, in case we were due for a dawn barrage. The prospect of getting up at the crack of dawn to try to find her held no appeal.

A half hour later I went back into the field to try again. We found her easily enough, despite the advanced dusk, still messing about in the top hedge. Whatever it was, it was very interesting and the dogs joined her in nose down investigations that took them threading back and forth through the broad base of the hedge. When I coaxed her in sugary tones she merely looked at me through the tangle, waved her brush and yucked softly. I patiently followed along as she made her way exasperatingly slowly through the length of my hedge, then tantalisingly, just out of reach of my fingertips as we crossed an open space and into the continuation of the hedge down the next field. This hedge, much lower than mine but still quite wild, had pushed out dog rose and blackberry thickets into the field so that something of a maze had formed. A mixed herd of Herefords and British Friesians grazing this field had cropped the tongues of grassland that had been isolated but not yet engulfed by the encroaching thickets. What residual daylight remained was just sufficient to show that numerous cattle were camping for the night amongst these thickets.

As I crouched to lift or part the tangle to see where Ferdi had gone, I was continually disturbing these ladies, some lurched to their feet and blundered off a few yards, others turned their great placid faces towards me and refused to get out of bed. I was at times literally climbing over or pushing aside a great weight of beef which yielded with a quiescent reluctance as this thoughtless little intruder stumbled through the dormitory.

By now Ferdi's neutral tones rendered her nigh invisible in the twilight. Big and Sniff, who confined themselves to the far side of the hedge, giving the cattle a wide berth, were comparatively conspicuous as a large dark and small light patch. But the vixen had melted into the night. I heard her digging inside a patch of briar, and at almost full crouch I thumped yet another hairy leg and ordered the owner 'move over Daisy'. Daisy did not move, so I thumped her again and straightening up I pushed her hard with my shoulder. A huge patient head swung round to regard me, we were almost literally eyeball to eyeball. In the gloom a triangular white blaze showed conspicuously, as did the large silver ring to which it pointed. I quietly thanked the patron saint of good fortune that the farmer had not preferred a Jersey bull to this gentle placid Hereford, whose acquaintance I'd already made on several occasions in daylight. However, I thought I'd not push my luck too hard, so I gave his great curly forehead a rub with my knuckles, apologised and moved away directing a few well chosen words at Ferdi for having led me into that situation. I might have been forgiven had I thought it a deliberate prank when, prank over, Ferdi joined the dogs and me as we walked back to the cottage.

18

Big Solves a Problem

I have earlier claimed to have a great affection for all animals. Although I believe this generalisation holds good for wild creatures there are certain individual exceptions among the ranks of the domesticated tribe. The Jack Russell terrier is something of a *bête noire* as far as I'm concerned. I've never owned one and certainly have no ambition to do so; my experience with these little brutes is, with only two exceptions wholly disagreeable. I will not cite a boring list of anti-social to criminal behaviour that has led me to feel as I do, suffice it to say that in my experience the following incident is not atypical. I witnessed one pampered creature, suddenly and apparently without the slightest provocation, remove a large piece from the back of the hand of its doting owner, exposing bone and tendon, and showering with blood a new carpet in the Rugby Club lounge, to the chagrin of the general committee but amazingly not of the owner and his wife; their doting seemed to falter not one jot. Personally I don't care what mayhem the JR perpetrates upon anyone daft enough to own one – it comes into that court martial offence category: self-inflicted injury.

It has just occurred to me that the nasty guy from the popular soap opera, the man whom the devotees love to hate, appropriately enough shares the same initials – it can't be coincidence! Perhaps I should say, for the sake of a balanced opinion, that the two exceptions were both grand little chaps.

The Jack Russell population in my vicinity had, at about this time, reached epidemic proportions – I was half expecting some agro-chemical company to bring out a handy size aerosol spray for controlling them. One in particular seemed to have declared war on me personally – it had bitten me on two occasions, once through my Wellington boot, quite harmlessly, merely pinching my calf slightly; the second time was both more annoying and more painful. I was leaning out of my kitchen window talking to the dog's owner who was standing in my yard. Suddenly the dog, taking advantage of the launch platform provided by a plastic sack of sand which lay just below the window, jumped up and bit me in the chest. I was only wearing a thin shirt and although fortunately he did not break the skin, he pinched me sufficiently to produce a horse shoe of blood blisters. Both incidents were in the presence of his master, yet earned him virtually no admonition at all. This again, in my experience, is typical.

With the idiot courage of his kind, he would occasionally make what I can only describe as raids into my garden. Courage is a quality I admire, but not the mindless, fanatical, suicidal kind. He would bundle in on his bowed and bumpy joints, that gave him the appearance of suffering from chronic arthritis, aggressive and challenging to everything he met from Little Elsa up through the range to me. He was no serious threat to the cats who merely popped up a handy tree. Sniff, being a bitch, did not get involved in any serious exchanges although she certainly did not like him. She peeled back her lips and trembled with menace when he came nosing round her. Big, I think, was puzzled. I don't believe he could take the challenge seriously, and couldn't quite understand why JR blustered around making so much disturbance.

He usually went for Ferdi, if she happened to be in the garden, like a berserker. She could make rings round him while bouncing on her brush if she wished, but she knew he was not playing as the others played, and she'd usually drift off into the field. In any case, after his first pass, Biggy would come up alongside him muttering stern warnings. He would then turn all his attention on to the big fellow and rave away, while Big lifted his head well out of the way, looked down with chin tucked into his chest, wrinkling his face as though he was frowning thoughtfully, and wagging his tail in that sort of stiff trembling way dogs have when they are prepared to be friendly but have serious reservations about the whole matter. It reminded me of someone comfortable in the knowledge of his own abilities, telling a young tearaway not to be a silly boy. I did not want to tell Big to see him off, nor to be too hostile myself in case he interpreted that as licence to take matters into his own teeth. JR was a damn nuisance, and it was obvious that if he persisted, sooner or later Biggy, who had shown amazing forbearance – perhaps remembering the Blackie incident and not appreciating the difference – would take serious exception to his noisy impudence.

For my part, I had pulled back one of my two-goal deficit when he attempted to repeat his window trick. This time as he raged away, I counted his leaps – one, two, three – he reached up for me like a bouncing rubber ball. A nice easy rhythm to anticipate and on four I shut the window on his head. It must have made his ears sing, but he was back within a few days laying siege to the place again. Whether taking his example from me, or making a unilateral decision that enough was enough, Big now took a hand. Perhaps, like so many of his human counterparts, JR had mistaken tolerance and peaceful disposition for timidity and even cowardice. He had got so used to shouting abuse and threatening violence with impunity, it must have been a nasty surprise when Big, without any preliminaries, grabbed him by the head and lifted him clear of the ground. The terrier's head lay across Big's own so that his nose protruded on one side and his ears showed on the other side of Big's jaws. The powerful little body swung and thrashed about causing Big's head to rotate slightly, like one of those toys that sit in the back of motor cars.

I called, 'Good lad Biggy, bring him along,' and I started towards the lane. Big followed rather unsteadily, his gyrating burden disturbing his balance. I suppose to thrash around against the restraint of a large set of teeth must get quite painful; in any event, by the time we reached the lane JR was hanging quite still and Big made better progress. At the corner, I stopped and Mr B dropped him. He scuttled off a few yards, turned and started his furious abuse again. I restrained Biggy with a word, and dropped my hand on his collar. For a few seconds it seemed that, completely un-cowed by his experience, the suicidal little idiot would attack Big or me or both, but he slowly moved away, turning to growl and bark in a face-saving show of defiance as he went. His spirit seemed unquenchable, but he did not come back again, and that was the end of that little episode – peace returned to the cottage. I considered a score of 2–2 to be a satisfactory result.

Ferdi had had her third night away within a week, but she joined us as we moved through the 'real meadow', now sporting a mere 7 o'clock shadow of its former glory. Since the hay had been harvested, its crew cut had been maintained by continual grazing.

I expect she had watched our approach for long enough to satisfy herself that no one else was about. As usual, she was not seen to arrive, but was suddenly there, calling to us. She swung towards us, swishing her brush and yuck-yucking loudly. The dogs pounded off to meet her and they all set off on a chase away down the hedge before, turning at the far corner, Ferdi led them back to say hello to me. Brush sweeping vigorously, she sniffed at my fingers, but it took several attempts before she let me get hold of her collar. I fussed her and scooped her up in my arms, while asking where she had been getting to recently. She worried gently at my ear, then decided I hadn't washed behind it and proceeded to remedy this omission.

I knew she'd tolerate this treatment only for a brief period. Sitting on my forearm, she put her front paws on to my shoulder and, taking advantage of extra height, she was content, for a few minutes longer, to have a good look around. Then she hopped up on to my shoulder and jumped down behind me.

The dogs were waiting for this and grabbed her to start a wild rough-house. The fun of reunion subsided and our walk continued. Suddenly Ferdi appeared in the middle of the path I was following looking for all the world as if she had an enormous black cigar in her mouth. Five or six inches long and two and a half inches in diameter, the mole, held only by its rear end, protruded from the side of her mouth. She was obviously waiting on the path to ask a passerby for a light. Had she been a Bulldog, she would have looked very Churchillian indeed. With her sharp slender features she had more of the unpractised appearance of a schoolboy having an illicit drag. Like several others I'd seen her with, I did not know if she'd caught it, or found it already dead. I suspect the latter.

When talking about her diet, I said that she had a virtually universal pallet, and that nothing, save the odd toenail, was ever wasted. Hedgehogs apart, which she regarded more as sports equipment than as food, moles were the only exception to this rule. I never saw her show any inclination to eat a mole; she would carry them around for a while but never, to the best of my knowledge, did she eat one or bury one for posterity. I never formed any firm idea why this should be. Perhaps the texture of the velvety fur put her off, although she did not mind holding them. Perhaps the mole has a protective taint to its flesh, but I've seen kestrels take them. Perhaps the ones she found had been poisoned by cyanide-dipped worms placed in their runs, and she had some instinctive way of sensing the danger. Whatever the explanation, it was one outstanding exception to an almost general rule.

She dropped her cigar and I picked it up; there was no obvious sign of damage and it had not been dead very long. The mole is a very well sealed little package and the gases of decomposition soon inflate it to considerable pressure, into a turgid furry black zeppelin, making it even more cigar like.

Shortly after the incident with the mole, Ferdi slipped away again and we completed our walk without her. When we got back into my field, the dogs showed more than usual interest in a particular rabbit hole, close by one of the hedges. I wandered over to join them. Ferdi's presence was only betrayed to me by the shower of soil and stones that sprayed from the hole. After several minutes, she backed out, face covered in fine dry soil particles; she shook herself, turned that big open-mouthed grin on us – she had obviously been aware of our presence above ground – and proceeded with both hind and forepaws to push clear the smooth mound of debris that had built up until it was in danger of obstructing the opening. This cleared, she dived out of sight and faint scrabbling noises sounded from below but this time there was no cascade of soil. I put my ear to the ground at several positions until the noise was immediately below me. She was a long way in, about eight feet from the mouth. She seemed to clear the tunnel behind her by several stages before the spoil was finally ejected. I left her to it, and walked back to the cottage, wondering how long she had been working on that particular project.

As Christmas came along, Ferdi's preoccupation with things away from home continued; there was rarely a week in which she did not have at least one full day and night away. Once she was away for three days – this was her longest absence since way back when, a half grown cub, she'd unclipped her line and Sniff and I had searched the countryside for a week.

Even after three days I had no particular anxieties, for this was not a novice cub dragging fifteen feet of line behind her, but an unhampered, competent, experienced vixen.

During her numerous away days, without setting out specifically to search for her, I had thought it an interesting exercise to try to discover where she got to. It was conducted in a very casual manner. I directed our walks to various places in which I recalled her having shown more than a normal level of interest, called and whistled her occasionally, and left any more serious investigations to Mr B and Sniffy.

We checked out the warren in my hedgerow, obviously. She had intermittently continued her work on the one particular hole, but there was nothing in the reaction of the dogs to suggest her recent presence there. We took a look at the old railway, the gully, the field where she'd staged the rabbit hunt.

The dogs got quite excited occasionally, but there was never anything to convince me that it was Ferdi's trail they'd picked up. It was quite likely that they'd crossed the recent track of another fox. That it was a fox I'd little doubt from their behaviour, and indeed once they found some visible spore, beautifully recorded in soft brookside clay.

I'm sure that they were in no doubt as to whether or not it was Ferdi's scent, but even Sniff, Big and I did not communicate that well. Since they never persisted on the trail for more than a few yards, I strongly suspected it was not Ferdi's, remembering the miles that Sniffy had tracked her at the end of the big search.

One weekend when she was away, we had a good hike over to the old 'Pit Hole'. I had visited this fascinating place on several occasions since the time I was searching for the cub. It had not altered much since the last visit. The trees were bare of course. The steep banks that had crumbled beneath boots and paws like flakey chocolate were now slick and slimy and more slippery than ever. The gouges that scarred a portion of the bank at one end of the pool told of a farm trailer, loaded with straw bales, getting too close to the edge and tipping its cargo into the pool.

That end of the pool resembled a giant's bowl of breakfast cereal. We tobogganed down the steep face, the dogs under reasonable control on stiff forward braced legs. I for the most part on my back, colliding with trees like a ball-bearing in a pinball machine.

Once again there was plenty of evidence that the set and the earth were still used. The soft clay was patterned with prints.

The dogs very excitedly weaved in and out of the eroded caves beneath the tree roots. I do not know from where she came, but suddenly she was there. The steep sided pit confined the sound and rang to the excitement of her greeting.

I looked across the pool and there opposite me at the water's edge, in a tail-thrashing huddle, they were celebrating their re-union in the usual style. The three then came round to my side where Ferdi gave me a less raucous greeting, producing her soft throaty yuck-yucking sound. When we set course for home, she did her usual roving escort job and we all returned together.

Since it was a place where I could happily spend another half day, and Ferdi and the dogs seemed to thoroughly enjoy it, I decided to revisit the 'Pit Hole' the following day, but next morning she was busy at her excavations in my field. She interrupted her work briefly to greet us each in turn, then went back to the job as though she'd never been away.

19

The Lady Kept Her Figure

Unlike the interesting rigours of the early winter, the infant year struggled its wet shivering way through its first couple of months of life. Almost permanently wellied, I slipped and squelched my way about a soggy countryside that oozed water and was drably decorated with black rotting leaves. March roared in in traditional fashion, bowing trees, angrily blasting away clouds that had far too long sat like latter day puritans casting a gloom over the land. Its rage sucked up vast quantities of water, so that when in mid month it spent its fury, peace returned to a land that was a drier, brighter place.

One early evening while it was still quite light, we returned from a walk. The whole team had left and returned together. As we approached my field, Ferdi slipped off and busied herself with her civil engineering project, of long standing, beneath the overhang of the hedge. I wandered over and watched her for a while, not that there was much to see. She was a long way in, as well as could be judged by placing an ear to the ground she was working twelve or fifteen feet from the entrance, and from the occasional spray of finely graded soil that showered from the opening, she had evidently gone through the dark fibrous leaf mouldy layer into tawny yellow sand.

We left her to it and wandered back to the cottage.

When I fed the menagerie, Ferdi did not put in an appearance, and so later the dogs and I returned to the digging; it was now several hours after sundown and fully dark.

The patch of yellow at the entrance was considerably larger, but there was no sign or sound of Ferdi. It was Sniff who insisted that

Ferdi was at home, when I was inclined to wander once round the field and back to the cottage. Sniff was right as usual, Ferdi murmured softly from deep in the burrow, and then continued to do so when I talked to her. But she showed no sign of coming to the entrance.

It took a long time to persuade her to come out; she went through her usual greeting to each of us in turn. Even in the dark, the happy, mischievous 'aren't I a smarty?' look was very apparent. I expect that she could tell from the dogs' breath that she'd missed feeding time, so she trotted back with us. I picked up her grub and with her circling me, her head tipped back to look up at the bowl, I walked over to the compound, fed her, and shut her up for the night.

It was a cold night, with a sharpish frost, and a night in which Ferdi must have gone through the trauma of having very powerful natural instincts frustrated and, typically, eventually accepted the inevitable, compromising in the most practical way possible and making do. How hard she worked and how desperately she delayed things, before accepting what to her was an unsatisfactory compromise, I can only guess from subsequent evidence.

For me, knowing her as I did, the mental image of that beautiful anxious little vixen working in the darkness to put right what I in my ignorance had upset, is both moving and conscience-touching.

Next morning was Sunday, it was a pity that I was late getting out and about. It was probably 10 o'clock before I wandered over to Ferdi's compound. Her sleeping 'kennel' provided the only cover inside the compound at this time of year. Long grass and a bed of nettles would later on fill one end.

With a prickle of anxiety I realised that she had not popped up on top of the kennel at my approach; indeed she was not to be seen at all. By the time I was standing at the wire itself there was still no sign of her, except for a patch of very still russet fur showing through the small entrance to the kennel. I gazed at this and at an area of disturbed ground in front of the kennel – it had been scraped up in an attempt to dig, but there was wire buried an inch or so in the ground and it was merely raked up through the mesh of this re-enforcement.

With a sudden shock, something I've experienced many times

with animals, I found myself looking at two little bodies. Dark short fur, with that wrinkled, compressed look and disproportionately large head of the very young; blind and lifeless the pathetic little parcels lay. I opened the door in the wire and dived through – they were both stone cold. One had a delicate veil of membrane wrapped about its head; I peeled this away and dropped the icy little body down my shirt front while I cupped both hands into a ball around the other and panted hot breath through a gap between one finger and thumb. After several minutes of this, the forlorn little corpse moved very feebly in my hands and squeaked the faintest complaint. I quickly swapped their position, popping the squeaker down my shirt and panting over the others. I got no response from the second one, but continued the treatment all the way back to the cottage, where I placed them on the carpet, contained them in the triangular space between three cushions and focused my infra-red lamp upon them.

Big and Sniff were mightily interested in all this, but to avoid any unnecessary disturbance I shut them, to their disgust, in the kitchen.

I went back to the compound and lifted the hinged lid of the kennel. Ferdi looked up, quite unconcerned and yucked quietly at me. Contained in the warm coil of her body and suckling steadily were five more dark little parcels almost black in colour except for the tiniest smudge of reddish-brown on the tiny forward folded ears.

I stroked and congratulated her. She was completely at ease, and raised not the slightest objection when I gently touched the cubs. Everything now fell into place. 'Sorry mum,' I apologised, rubbing her head. 'I've been pretty stupid; I guess I messed up your well made plans.'

What ever the traumas of the night, she now seemed very content and prepared to accept the congratulations that she obviously considered well merited. Satisfied that all was well in the compound, I returned to the cottage.

In the nest of cushions one of the plump black sausages was moving about and squeaking quite vigorously. The other alas, although now well warmed by the lamp was dead, probably suffocated by the enveloping membrane.

I returned the survivor to the compound, showed it to Ferdi; she gently took it from me and plonked it down among its brothers and sisters. It immediately struggled to an unoccupied tap and began to suckle, joining the quiet chorus of contented murmurings. I closed the lid on the nursery and returned to free the dogs.

That afternoon, while Big and Sniff mooched along the brook, I sat with my legs dangling over the bank and thought about the latest development in the story of Ferdi, vixen extraordinaire. What a remarkable creature she was to move so freely in two worlds something most of us fail to do in one. The events of last night emphasised perhaps more than anything to date, what a completely wild creature she was. A wild creature exercising a free will, obviously accepted by wild foxes, among whom she had found a mate, yet of that free choice seeking my company and that of Big and Sniff for a considerable part of her time. I got quite a lump in my throat. I felt she had paid me an enormous compliment, that I was a most privileged person, to be on such terms with a wild creature. Oh, that all 'sportsmen' could know that feeling.

She obviously intended to continue our close association even through this new adventure, when her first instincts would be for the well being of her cubs. There was no doubt that she had intended to have them in the enlarged burrow at which she'd worked so steadily and from which she had been so loath to be persuaded last evening.

She had preferred to bring them back to us, instead of setting up home in the 'Pit Hole' which I suspect had been a focal point in her recent life. Perhaps she trusted that the degree of protection afforded by the dogs and me would extend to her cubs, perhaps she wished to continue happy bonds. She had, after all, managed two lives in perfect compatability so far. On which side of that normally impenetrable barrier, through which she could pass so lightly, she would raise the cubs, would be yet another fascinating development. As I considered the events of yesterday evening, I greatly regretted my interference. I should have known that in matters foxy, she knew better.

I decided that I would give Ferdi every opportunity to 'move house' back into the earth, but already I might have disrupted her plans too much, and she might opt to stay put.

The dog fox – what part might he take in the proceedings? Had the cubs been born in the earth under the hedge it would have almost certainly become Ferdi's permanent home for the next six months. Her mate would probably have fulfilled his normal role and the cubs would have been reared as completely wild foxes until late in the year when they would be sent off to make their way in the world, fully trained and equipped. The more I considered it, the more I could have kicked myself for my stupidity. My brief intrusion had completely disrupted a situation which the foxes had under perfect control.

If Ferdi was not prepared to transport the cubs across to the earth, it would be expecting a lot of the dog fox to constantly visit the enclosure, so artificial and reeking of man and dog, a combination he had good cause to regard as his most dangerous enemy. With the compound door permanently open the cubs would be much less safe than had they been underground. This might be a way of encouraging Ferdi to move them, but it would have to be tried in daylight when I could keep a distant watch on things. The problem here would be that in daylight she would probably be disinclined to risk the transfer of the cubs being observed. Yet at night I would not want to leave the door open after I'd turned in.

There would be times when, of necessity, Ferdi would leave them. Stuck up there above ground they would be awfully vulnerable to a stray terrier; I shuddered to think what would happen if JR reappeared and got among them. Perhaps I should have encouraged Big to bite his head off, while we had the chance.

Perhaps she'd be sharp enough to move them at dusk, while the dogs and I were there as escort. Then again if I did leave the compound open all night, perhaps the dog fox would lend a hand, standing guard over the cubs while Ferdi made the transfer one by one.

There were so many possibilities, but it was all down to what she decided was best under these imposed circumstances. This time I would not presume to interfere.

I was not prepared to make excuses, but the real deception had been in the superb way she had kept her figure. I now recalled a few weeks earlier having said to the dogs in one of my ridiculous conversations with the team, 'Do you think that slinky little sexpot is in the family way?' Neither Sniff nor Big had answered, they hardly ever did. Ferdi herself was equally unforthcoming. It had been almost imperceptible and could easily have been a recently gorged half rabbit. I never noticed it again and her agility was unimpaired.

When one reflects on the ungainly waddling condition most human mums-to-be find themselves in, it was quite remarkable that she could carry seven cubs so unobtrusively.

There had been an unfortunate coincidence the previous evening. Had I fed her as usual with the others on the cottage lawn, she would have been free to slip off, back to the earth. But because she missed feeding with them and had taken so long to be tempted back above ground, I had fed her in the compound and shut her up while she was feeding.

It was sad to interpret the likely happenings in the compound after I had left. Driven by a powerful instinct to have her family in the earth, she had painstakingly prepared and now finding herself shut in, she must have attempted to dig her way out. Frustrated in this by the wire in the floor of the compound, she must have persevered, delaying the birth as long as she could, until she actually started to drop the cubs in the open compound. There was then no alternative but to use the only shelter available.

I think she had the remaining five inside the kennel, although it is, of course, quite possible that she transferred some indoors that had been born in the open. Whether she then became too preoccupied to retrieve the two I found in the compound; whether, in nature's way, they were written off rather than hazard in the slightest degree those that were safe and sure, I will never know.

The dogs had returned to nudge me in inquiry if all was well. So, poked out of my reverie by cold noses, I got up to complete the walk. When we returned we made straight for the compound. Ferdi acknowledged our arrival without emerging from the kennel.

I opened the compound door and we all went inside, and I raised the lid. Feeding or sleeping, four lay much as I'd last seen them. The other two had come away from the 'bar' and were not rucked up under Ferdi's chin. Sniff pushed her head through the entrance; without changing position Ferdi rolled her head round for a nose touching, 'Hello, look what I've done.'

Sniff promptly began washing the two cubs that were within her restricted reach. When she was concentrating, Sniff had one particular facial expression, which on the human countenance would have been a worried frown. As she carefully licked away, her creased brown face added authenticity to the role she had adopted. She was suddenly the mother, fussing and concerned that her little girl had grown up too quickly and obviously could not have the experience to cope with a family of her own.

Sniff had no need to fear incurring Ferdi's resentment; from the very first day Ferdi with complete trust allowed Big, Sniff and me to handle, lick or sniff, depending upon our individual preference, the cubs. With a very practical attitude she accepted any assistance that was offered. This was just another manifestation of the remarkable bond that existed between four creatures of three different species and greatly differing function and experience in life.

It was an attitude which I was soon to discover, she extended to include the two cats. With one remarkable and, to me at least, quite inexplicable exception, it was Ferdi's attitude throughout the early life of the cubs.

Sniff would not vacate the entrance, and in any case Big could not get his head through the opening, so he looked over the top. Whereupon, Ferdi carefully stood up, rolling the cubs back into the straw, and poking her head out of the top of her kennel for a licking, nose-touching greeting with Mr B, who after listening to the explanations, lowered his head into the kennel and showed a very polite interest in the new arrivals.

Ferdi hopped out through the roof, yawned and stretched luxuriously, before, accompanied by Big, she took some exercise around the field, content to leave Sniff to launder the cubs, which she did most thoroughly, rolling them over despite their protests and me, no doubt in charge of security. I watched them to see if she'd visit the earth but I don't think she did. After about ten minutes she returned to take charge again, trotting into the compound and with a forepaw tapping Sniff on her backside, which protruded from the kennel opening and completely obstructed it. It took several taps before Sniff backed out, I suspect to the relief of the cleanest cubs in the world, and Ferdi resumed charge of the nursery. She arranged the cubs to her own satisfaction, picking them up and plonking them in a corner without fuss. Once she'd got herself into position they all scrambled their blind way back to the bar and the contented little chorus began again.

I closed the lid and left them to it.

In the late afternoon when light began to fail, I decided on the first experiment intended to persuade Ferdi to move the cubs into her earth. I would leave the dogs in the cottage and go alone into the field. From what had happened earlier in the day I felt it would be very easy for Ferdi to slip into a routine in which the willing Sniff would do the baby-sitting while she took her exercise or did a bit of hunting, with Biggy and I acting as additional guardians.

I did not want this arrangement to get established until I was pretty sure that she had decided not to use the earth. She was not dependent upon us and I did not want my error of the previous night to make her so, even temporarily. I slipped quietly into the field and moved slowly through the dusk towards the compound.

A large fox drifted out through the open gate in the compound's outer wire and glided down one long side of the wire netting, checking briefly to look back in my direction. In the failing light he looked much bigger than Ferdi, half way between her's and Mr Big's size, was my impression. Ferdi I could just make out on top of her kennel.

'Damn!' – I wished I'd taken the chance and left the pen door open, for that must surely have been a likely time for them to have moved the cubs. As it was, my approach would do nothing to encourage the dog fox to keep visiting the compound. He must already be thoroughly confused by the behaviour of his mate. I would open up the pen. I did not suppose he had gone far, and Ferdi would soon find him if she wanted to, then perhaps they would return together to the unguarded cubs.

Ferdi greeted my approach without looking at me. She was still on the kennel top gazing up the field in the direction the dog had taken. I was looking at her and beyond into the gloom.

'So that's the one who's had his wicked way with my daughter is it?' I asked her. My foot hit something soft and yielding, sending it rolling a few feet. It was a grey squirrel. 'He's evidently prepared to provide for his family.'

She 'yucked' at me and as I unlatched the door, jumped down, poked her head through the kennel entrance, then slipped past me, through the outer compound, along the side the dog had taken and was immediately swallowed up in the gloom. I listened carefully but heard nothing to suggest that they had come together.

Without lifting the lid and letting the warm air escape, I put my arm into the kennel. At first my gently groping hand found nothing. Then feeling my way through a thin layer of wood-wool and straw, I located a tangle of soft furry bundles that glowed like a Ready Brek advertisement. Warm and snug the mound moved beneath my hand as though it were one composite creature.

I considered the situation. Had I not been there, Ferdi would probably not have left the cubs, but if I stayed there it was highly unlikely that the dog fox would return with her. I decided to move some distance away and sit quietly for a while to see what would happen.

I was well prepared for a vigil, having pulled on a track suit over my normal clothing and an anorak over that. I left the compound, picking up one of the old cages as I did so, walked off about thirty yards, plonked down the cage in a patch of long grass and sat upon it. I was nice and warm, and quite content, for a while at least, to sit quietly in the gloom listening to the sounds of the night about me. Little owls that had been noisy among the oak trees all afternoon, continued to shout; wavering voiced tawnies called from opposite sides of my field and set some blackbirds chink-chink-chinking nervously in the high hawthorn. But I heard not a fox. Within fifteen minutes I could no longer see details of the compound. I knew from experience that in this light the foxes could pass before me unseen. I sat on, wondering how long she'd be and hoping it wouldn't be much longer, wondering where, in the darkness, she was and what she was doing, whether she was with the dog or not.

I had no doubt that she considered I had been left in charge of the cubs. For how long, I wondered. I did not expect her to be gone for more than half an hour or so. Even in that cosy huddle in the straw I wondered for how long day-old cubs would generate enough heat to keep themselves warm on a cold night. The wind chill factor would be far worse above ground than down an earth. I was quite confident that brand new to motherhood though she was, she'd still have everything under control.

My thoughts were interrupted by a distinct crunch, crunch, crunch, from the direction of the compound. Something was eating the squirrel; the thought was chased by another one – or the cubs – I shot up and ran to the compound.

There was no alarm, she knew it was I. Her tail dusted the ground at my approach while she continued to munch away.

'I didn't know you'd got back,' I told her. 'Where's the boy friend?'

She polished off the squirrel in swift order – every single bit of it.

I continued my one sided conversation. 'Would you like me to put 'em all in a box and carry 'em over to the earth for you?'

She 'yuck yucked' softly, sniffed at my hand and swished her tail over the ground again. This was a standard reaction and did not constitute any sort of reply to the question.

Ferdi poked her head into the kennel, checked things out for a few seconds before easing herself inside. I gave the matter a few minutes' thought, then decided to take the chance involved in leaving the door open. If the dog fox came back they could sort things out for themselves.

I returned to my kitchen and swiftly prepared a bowl of grub for Ferdi; the squirrel apart, I'd no idea if she'd eaten anything while she was away, but since she was now going to convert a portion of her intake into milk for six cubs, I was fairly generous and finally topped the bowlful with a raw egg and a good splash of milk.

Big, Sniff and the two cats gathered in the kitchen in anticipation of an early meal and were still milling about looking a trifle disappointed when I dived back into the darkness leaving them unsatisfied.

Ferdi had assumed a different position and was lying with her chin protruding, like a wedge of Leicestershire cheese, through the kennel entrance. She murmured softly and lapped some milk from the circular puddle that it had formed round the island of solid food.

'I wonder how many nursing vixen get served supper in bed?' I asked her. She slowly disengaged herself from the cubs and emerged to finish off the bowl of food. Squeaky protests emitted from the black interior of the kennel at this interruption to feeding time. I could almost read her thoughts – I'd had the same ones many times myself – now I'm up I might as well take a pee, before I settle again for the night.

She trotted out of the compound, relieved herself against one of the stout corner timbers (actually split railway sleepers), raising her hind leg forwards, not back and sideways like a dog, or squatting like a bitch. She immediately returned and slipped back through the kennel entrance to more squeaking from within.

I left the door open and returned to the cottage, fed the others since they'd obviously still got food on their minds, then headed off through the darkness, checking Sniff and Big as they made for my field, and deliberately moving downhill in the opposite direction. I had decided that they could have Ferdi's company during the day light, but for the time being the night would be reserved for her mate.

We wandered down to the old railway, dropped into the cutting and followed it along for a mile, then moved across to the river's confluence. It was an unusually dark night, relieved only by the city's glow on the western skyline.

Next morning, after a preliminary recce I took the dogs over to the compound. Ferdi and the cubs were still in residence and the format was much as yesterday with Sniff acting *au pair* while Ferdi and Big took a spin.

There was some fresh rabbit fur blowing about the pen, but whether this indicated that the dog had been back with fresh supplies, or merely that Ferdi had left the cubs for long enough to pick up a rabbit, I had no way of telling with certainty. But since Ferdi had devoured a squirrel, and a bowl of meat and meal, and possibly picked up a few snacks on her own account the previous evening, I doubted that she would have hunted again during the night.

20

Great Oaks from Little Acorns

As I looked at those doughy, puckered little black bundles, five inches long, blind, helpless, lost in a box, in an unkempt field, in square miles of other fields well off the beaten tracks of teeming humanity, I would probably have offered odds of millions to one against their becoming minor celebrities, being known to many more people than I ever would, and arousing far greater interests; having a thriving fan mail; and being sought after by a wildlife television personality. That they were to achieve this within a few weeks of birth was, as I say, something for me to view in retrospective wonder.

Ferdi continued to ignore the opportunities to move house and after a week or so I concluded that unless there arose some specific threat to the cubs' safety, she was now unlikely to do so. With this conclusion came the daunting prospect of trying to raise the cubs to enjoy the same freedom and special both-world skills upon which it depended, as Ferdi enjoyed.

She would presumably transmit to the cubs her own trust in me and the dogs; this and the fact that they must already know our scent and would see us regularly from the moment their eyes started to focus should make part of the job easier than it had been with the completely wild cub Ferdi, whose only previous experience of men and dogs had been a wholly terrifying one. As for the rest, it would depend largely upon what Ferdi and perhaps her mate did.

I couldn't possibly devote the same time to each individual cub that I had done to Ferdi. Alternatively the task of finding six suitable, by my definition, homes for the cubs would entail a lot of care in selection, assuming I could find that many people interested in taking charge of a cub in the first place. My ambitions for the cubs were not quite as well-defined as they had been for Ferdi, but I resolved that they should never live out their lives in a cage. They would either go wild and take their chance, become the pets of caring people who could give them the freedom of many acres, or, like Ferdi, perhaps some would learn the skills and diplomacy, the passport to both worlds.

It all came to pass in a variety of ways that I will recount later.

If things developed in such a way that homes would be needed for the cubs, then the first part of this problem began to resolve itself in a quite unforeseen way.

It was very early on; the cubs were still blind, pug-faced, plasticine objects.

I was startled one evening to receive a phone call from someone at the local commercial TV studio. They ran a nightly chat-around-the-region-style programme, half an hour of topical events. Could they send someone out to get some film of the cubs and do a short interview? There would not be a fee!

I was so surprised, that I failed to enquire if that meant they wouldn't pay me, or I didn't have to pay them. I asked how they knew about the cubs.

'Don't know,' he said, 'I've just been left a note to contact you and fix it up.'

That mystery was cleared up later the same evening when a friend phoned and asked for David Attenborough. His next door neighbour worked at the studio and that was the link. He thought it very amusing.

The actual event was disappointingly anticlimactic. There was no preliminary interview with some eminent wildlife photographer, during which I passed on the benefit of my experience, explaining where best to set up the hide in order to film Ferdi crossing the threshold between her two worlds; going out to take meat from her mate and returning with it to the compound; how I alone would have to do the filming, since any other presence in the hide would disturb Ferdi; where best to site the camouflaged outside broadcast vans; how long all this equipment would need to be left for familiarisation before we attempted the first evening's filming etc., etc.

My dreams of a whole new career opening up before me collapsed, when a couple of days later, instead of a convoy of outside broadcast vans threading their furtive way down the lane, a typical rep's Cortina roared up, sending the gravel of my drive bouncing off the hull of my sailing dingy, which sat quite inoffensively on its trailer in no one's way at all, and slewed to a wheel-locked halt.

The man who emerged to a blast of local radio, which was promptly chopped off by the crash of the closing door, was not the archetypal wildlife photographer. He would have been conspicuous had he been dropped into the middle of the Milky Way, and he contrived to make a noise to accompany every movement.

I had a wild hope that he wasn't the man from the telly, just a flamboyant traveller who'd got lost in the lanes while seeking a short cut, and had stopped to ask directions. He cruelly crushed this hope by announcing himself: 'Jim Varley, come to film your foxes.'

I'd just brewed some tea so I offered him a cup.

He explained his plan – it was very, very cunning. 'Show me where it is, I'll get some film shot, then we'll have another cuppa and you can tell me about it.' He was evidently 'our special reporter on wildlife' as well as 'our specialist wildlife photographer'. I got the impression we were talking about an ancient building or a vintage car.

The Cortina was still emitting muted noises which again exploded into a pop song as he opened the door, and fished a large leather case off the rear seat. This time he did reach over with a stiff forefinger and stab the radio into silence.

He took his ciné camera from the case, checked the footage indicator and a few other things, before raising his right arm to rest the camera on his shoulder, lense pointing at 45° to the sky, and saying, 'Let's go.'

By now I was probably looking for faults. It was probably the obvious way to carry the camera, but a snide thought slipped into my mind – this joker has been watching newsreel of war photographers going out on patrol. The camera was a Bolex, and I was sure a splendid instrument: it certainly made my twin turret Bell and Howell look like an archaeological treasure, but even this was vaguely disappointing to my now highly critical frame of mind. Where was the mighty telephoto lens that could melt the miles and bring the game into one's lap? This man had come equipped to photograph tame rabbits in a hutch.

A few yards into the field I stopped and turned to face him. I think I had given up the whole thing as pure farce.

'Look,' I said, 'if you want some film of the vixen, we will have to take things very gently indeed; we're not approaching someone's pet cat – she's a wild animal and if she detects your presence you'll be lucky to see her, much less film her.' I had that doomed to failure feeling, for the chances of us getting any worthwhile footage seemed very remote.

I had kept Big and Sniff in very close and they stayed there, just about, for they were obviously bursting to rush off to the compound. I could think of two possible ways to tackle the problem. The first would be easy enough. If I left my cameraman well out of sight and went over to the compound, I should probably have little trouble in shutting Ferdi in the pen. He could then crash-bang his way over at his leisure. I knew perfectly well what Ferdi's reaction would be, and from a personal point of view, I'd no wish to have the viewing public left with the impression that I kept a terrified vixen trapped in a cage, albeit a big cage. Not only would this appear cruel, but it would take away the very element that gave the story its interest – the free association of a wild vixen with myself and the dogs. Caged foxes are, alas, all too common, and genuinely tame foxes are not uncommon pets.

Idea number two I put to Jim. 'Can you film a fox from fifty yards away?'

'Yes, I can pull her in pretty close,' he said.

I suggested we try to get Jim set up in the nearest cover. This was a patch of tall grass, nettle and cow parsley straw so tangled that it had supported itself throughout the winter.

I would then go over to the compound, Ferdi would most likely come out, and he might be lucky to get some film of her having a chase round.

'Won't the dogs scare her off? I thought you said she was wild.'

Confirmation that the rarity, possibly the uniqueness, of the circumstances were lost on Jim and probably on whoever had sent him.

I took a deep breath: 'She is wild. The dogs will not scare her, neither will I; but you certainly will unless you're very careful and lucky. She's as sharp as a tack. You'll have to be well concealed, and set up ready to press the trigger so you don't have to move again.'

That we got to the chosen patch of cover apparently undetected could only have been due to the fact that Ferdi was inside the kennel suckling the cubs, or she had already left the compound. For Jim turned out to be one of those people who does not crouch down or move on half bent legs, so that although low in the cover, his head remains the highest point, enabling him to be aware of what's happening around him, and how well he is himself concealed.

Jim adopted the philosophy, unkindly attributed to the ostrich, that if he couldn't see Ferdi, then she couldn't see him. With sloping back and head well down, but backside at normal level, he moved through the grass like an animated anthill. It looked most uncomfortable. I hoped Biggy wasn't feeling amorous.

With Jim installed and at last getting quite interested, the dogs and I headed for the compound. Ferdi was in the kennel, and in no hurry to come out – it was evidently feeding time. It was five minutes before she and Big skipped out into the field. I watched over the side of the compound wire. It looked as though, against all odds, Jim was going to be lucky, for they did not immediately move away. I was looking back to the tall grasses when there was a noticeable disturbance.

Ferdi took off like a greyhound leaving the trap, and vanished into the long grass.

I walked back. 'What did you do?' I asked him. He shrugged and pursed his lips. 'Only moved the grass a bit.'

'I saw that, but why?'

'I wanted to get a better position.'

'Wildlife photography is not your speciality is it?'

He laughed. 'I was getting really keen, and she didn't look wild, playing with the dog, so I decided to chance it.'

'She looked pretty wild when you startled her,' I said. 'It was a pity, I thought you were going to get some reasonable stuff.'

'I did,' he replied, but I wasn't sure whether that was merely to mask his embarrassment or if he really had run some film.

However, I warmed to him a little. For the first time he seemed to have lost his crash-bang, let's-get-this-boring-job-over-with attitude. He appeared to regret having lost his subject, and now asked what she'd do and, hopefully, if there was any likelihood of getting another chance.

It was remarkable; he obviously wasn't a wildlife enthusiast and had almost certainly considered himself lumbered when he was given the job. He had been exposed to that exuberant free spirit for twenty seconds and was already regretting the brevity of the experience. Such was Ferdi's magic.

I resisted the temptation to tell him that it was entirely his own fault, that I'd briefed him, very accurately as it had turned out, as to what to expect and how to prepare for it. He obviously wasn't going to say so, but his questions and quiet bearing suggested he acknowledged those facts.

I said there was little chance of his getting another shot, without a long wait and maybe not then, since she would be doubly wary after what had happened. To keep her from the cubs would probably cause her anxiety, although I thought to myself, it might be another inducement to shift them to the earth, when she next had the chance; but to keep her away a long while might be detrimental to the cubs.

I told him the quicker we got his film of the cubs, and moved off the sooner she would return. I warned him, 'The next sequence will not be action packed, the little devils haven't opened their eyes yet.'

We had our second cup of tea and a chat. It was quite apparent that the whole point of interest was not appreciated either by Jim or the people who had sent him. Their requirements were very shallow; just a few bundles of fluff for viewers to 'Oo' and 'Ahhhh' over while they were having their tea. My feeling that the whole project was farcical made a strong recovery. They could far more easily have got what they were looking for at the children's zoo or pets' corner in any of a half dozen parks in the city. I did not extend an invitation to come back and do better next time.

When the item was screened it was even shorter than I had anticipated. But my attempts to emphasise that fox cubs born to pet foxes were common enough and that the special interest in Ferdi's case lay in the fact that she was not a tamed pet, had apparently made some impression at last. A commentator said, 'What a surprise!' while a film of the cubs ran for one minute – the cubs filmed through the open lid of the kennel, with Sniff's head poking into view through the entrance; the cubs, three on each of my hands, only my hands were shown (as some rude friends pointed out, it was early evening and children would have been watching); the cubs on some straw outside the kennel. Finally, a glimpse of Ferdi vanishing so quickly into the grass that few people could have managed to focus their eyes upon her.

While this confusing sequence ran, the voice explained that I'd had a great surprise when a wild vixen that had become friendly with my dogs, had presented me with six cubs. It was rather ambiguous and I'm sure a considerable number of viewers must have concluded that Big and Ferdi were more than just good friends. I could imagine a lot of biology masters being asked if it were genetically possible.

It had, at least, been made to sound an extraordinary event.

Apart from the inevitable leg pulling that I had to endure, the upshot of this unpromising bit of TV coverage was a surprising and most useful rash of correspondence.

It was an insight into the power of television when such a crumb, of which, I was quite convinced, most people would not be able to make head or tail could stimulate so many to write to me. I had an indication that some correspondence might be on the way when I received a phone call from the TV studio saying that several people who had been interested in the item had called them to say they wished to contact me and was it in order for them to pass on my address? I was a bit dubious, but after a quick think I decided that if I should need to find homes for the cubs, such contacts might be useful.

Quite a number of letters were from people who merely wished to learn more about Ferdi and her family, but perhaps twenty also enquired about the possibility of having one of the cubs. Most of these were pleasant letters, but one in particular aroused my suspicions – it was either a very arrogant epistle or the author lacked the vocabulary and eloquence to gentle the message. It was most abrupt and to the effect that he would do me the favour of taking all six of them off my hands, and might even pay me a few pounds. My immediate thoughts were of pet shop or fur trade.

Cyril, who has featured earlier in this tale, suggested another possible explanation. He told me that some hunts, particularly in areas where their range has been reduced by development or the fox population has dwindled, will establish artificial earths, from which on the day of a hunt, particularly a meet when they entertain distinguished guests, the foxes are flushed by putting terriers down the drainpipes from which the 'earths' are made. Cyril did not seem very sure how it was organised, but I got the impression that it was usually done by the local keepers or some such person paid a retainer by the hunt committee. In any event, Cyril reckoned there was a market in fox cubs for this purpose, and he added credence to his contention by adding that he'd had a few quid out of it in the past, although he'd come to see things differently and would never do it again. I suspect the latter was added purely for my benefit.

Whatever the motives behind that particular letter it was the only one to which I did not bother to reply.

During the few days following the television appearance, there was to be a further surprise for me and an exchange that left me most disappointed with the person concerned.

I answered the phone; my caller announced himself – not one of the better known television wildlife personalities, he had nevertheless made several TV appearances and had a couple of books to his credit. If not a household name, at least reasonably well known and, it appeared, in his own estimation an important fellow.

I was probably a trifle hesitant, while I considered the possibility of another leg pull, such was the sense of humour of several of my friends. After a couple of questions, during which he became quite irritated, I decided he was the genuine article. His assumption that his name opened all doors and that once known it guaranteed compliance with his requests, I, in turn, found irritating.

He wanted all the cubs, and he must have them before their eyes opened. He intended to conduct the most detailed observations of the foxes' lives and his plan was to be accepted so that he could observe, photograph etc., etc., quite freely and without inhibiting the foxes' behaviour in any way. To this end he wanted to be the first thing the cubs saw, he wanted to 'imprint' them upon himself so that he could assume the role of parent fox. They would live their lives in a large enclosure where they could follow a normal fox's existence, while he was free to move among them etc., etc.

I believe that I was as close to a wild fox as anyone gets to be; and from this privileged position I secretly, conceitedly, considered myself a highly experienced man on the subject of fox behaviour and specifically the sort of relationship he seemed to be talking about. An unacclaimed expert. Yet here was an acclaimed expert, talking what I was convinced was the most impracticable nonsense. Was he serious about this project, or was it just a story which he'd spun to me, the gullible layman? If it was just a story, then what was his real reason for wanting the cubs?

Ferdi had never been imprinted upon me, nor even upon Sniff in the true sense of the term. Yet I knew that she had an extra dimension to her experience, an additional way of thinking. I knew that there were circumstances in which her reactions would not be those of a completely wild fox, which lacked that extra experience. I believed that on balance it was to her advantage, and how extraordinarily lucky we had been in achieving that precise blend, when perhaps one extra degree of sophistication would have put her at an extremely dangerous disadvantage. I expressed doubts about the feasibility of his scheme. I said that even if it were possible, and I did not believe it to be, in order to play the role of parent fox without influencing the training and development of the cubs unnaturally, the enclosure would have to be the size of the countryside itself if it were not to inhibit the foxes by the limitation it imposed.

This was not well received. I was obviously a presumptious upstart.

He was evidently quite prepared to accept a high mortality rate by taking the cubs so young and unweaned; this it seemed did not matter as long as a few survived, preferably of both sexes. I told him that I was not prepared to hazard the lives of the cubs or to distress the vixen, who was obviously full of milk, by so early a separation. If, in a few months' time, when I'd had a chance to see how things developed, he was still interested, I might reconsider. I was accused of not cooperating in an important experiment, and he again insisted that he had to have the cubs before their eyes opened.

The conversation had become quite acrimonious, so I concluded by saying that I did not believe there was much that was not known about the domestic habits of the fox, but if he did have any questions he could always drop me a line. He did leave me a phone number for future reference, but I determined that his address was one that the cubs would not share.

I rather wished that his readership and television audience, who only knew him as a man oozing concern and care for wild animals, could have eavesdropped that phonecall. It's a great pity to have that sort of experience, because it leaves the sneaking thought, how many more of those passionately concerned men are really firstly concerned with what's commercially viable, and only secondly with what's good for the animals? Even the genuinely well meaning can bring about disaster. I was recently told by a fellow who organised fund-raising activities for the World Wildlife Fund, purely on a voluntary basis, that, thanks to the publicity given by a particularly famous TV programme about a troop of mountain gorillas, the entire troop was exterminated by poachers to satisfy the demand for gorilla-associated nick-nacks, souvenirs and baby animals. I certainly cannot vouch for the authenticity of this report, but it accurately illustrates a recurring paradoxical dilemma. How to stimulate public interest and support, appreciation and enjoyment of wildlife without providing the 'bad guys' with a larger market and a better chance to exploit it in all its evil forms.

I surveyed the letters with some relief. Here, if it were later needed, was an excellent start towards finding suitable homes for the cubs. I settled down to produce a circular in which I set out the pitfalls and special requirements both personal and in terms of facilities, space being the main one, for those who would raise a cub.

I stressed the time and patience demanded, and frustrations likely to be experienced. I concluded by saying that when and if the time came to dispose of the cubs, only people whose ambitions lay far beyond merely imprisoning their fox in a cage, would be considered.

I had gone into quite a lot of explanatory detail as to what could be reasonably expected, and I was fairly pleased with the final result; it was more a treatise than a letter. The very act of exchanging correspondence was a screening process, for now they knew that there would be several months before I should be looking for homes, if indeed it became necessary to look at all. Those who continued to write enquiring about Ferdi and the cubs were obviously the seriously intentioned ones, while those who had merely experienced a fleeting fascination with the idea soon lost interest.

I received one very gratifying letter from a schoolteacher clergy-man who also ran a scout troop and cub pack. He was very flattering about my 'most excellent letter'. He said that he had originally considered having a cub with a view to teaching care and respect for animals in a practical way. Thinking that if the cub became tame enough it might be adopted as mascot of the cub pack, perhaps going to parades with them.

He thanked me for pointing out the pitfalls, in particular the danger of producing an animal that was too wild to enjoy the freedom of a domestic pet, yet had been put at a disadvantage should it be turned out into the wilds. He said he had a large high walled garden on the edge of the village and if I was stuck for a home when the time came, and I'd care to go and see him, he would take one of the cubs if I approved of the place in which it would be kept. Otherwise he hoped he might continue to write to me on the subject but would no longer consider himself a candidate for custody of a cub. In the meantime, he said, he had breached the copyright laws and run off copies of my letter to use for educational purposes.

When I considered some of the comments my essays had drawn from schoolmasters in the past, I was greatly flattered.

Another correspondent, a lady, who had from the start no intention of having a cub – she lived somewhere in the city – continued to write, always eager for news of Ferdi, the cubs and the dogs.

Although the variation provided by the television episode and what had followed it had been quite amusing and educational, I was glad when the period of intense correspondence abated. It had been very time consuming, but I regarded that as a good invest-ment, for the prospect of finding suitable homes for the cubs now seemed much better.

I turned my attention back to the foxes. What potent little catalysts the cubs had turned out to be. They had not yet taken their first glimpse of the world, yet more incident and interest had revolved about their first shuttered week, than about the previous ten years of my life.

They were still in the kennel, the door had been left open but Ferdi seemed to have settled to a routine which satisfied her and it began to appear unlikely that she would move them. I saw the dog fox only once more, skipping away, as I approached through thick plates of mist that floated over the field, flat and firm looking in a very still after-dawn. Unfortunately the dogs were with me and chased after him – it was the exception to the rule, I'd been in the habit of taking a preliminary look before letting Sniff and Big go visiting.

I never again found any evidence of his having brought food to the compound. I think he gave up on his strange mate who took such outrageous liberties with a man and his dogs. It must have made him very confused and uneasy. I have never been quite sure about the dog fox's contribution to the rearing of the cubs; I suspect it varies quite a lot from individual to individual. There would appear to be an obvious survival factor in having the vixen away from the nursery earth for as short a period as possible during the very early days. In this period, at least, I believe even the least domestically inclined dog fox will bring food to her and take a turn with the cubs to allow his mate some exercise. The latter being the role that Sniff had so willingly taken on.

There was still one show of interest to be displayed by what is popularly termed the media. I imagine that the cubs' fleeting TV appearance was what prompted a large provincial newspaper to contact me. They were featuring a game fair at a local 'sporting estate', and thought it would be a good idea to run a feature on Ferdi and the cubs together with this article, to complete a full page of country matters.

It is only as I seek to jog my memory by looking out the large photograph that they eventually presented to me that I realise how early in their lives did this take place. They still have the puckered, compressed for better packaging, look about them and appear still to have their eyes closed.

It was all done in a great rush. The reporter arrived to do the photos and interview on the day that the article was to be featured. He evidently did not make his deadline since neither story nor pictures appeared in the paper.

My only souvenir of the incident is the aforementioned photograph.

A diary I kept at this time shows that I began to keep progress records from the first days. Commencing with a sketch of the sad little corpse at day one, and tracking their early progress.

Beneath the sketch I made the following notes:

Proportions better than in many young animals. Part of a litter of seven (4 dogs and 3 vixens). One of the two dropped outside the kennel, probably died of suffocation since membrane still in place over head. Both stiff and very cold but other recovered on being warmed.

5½ inches long plus 2 inches of tail.

Fur all over except ear flaps which fold forward and are flat against sides of head. Eyes closed. Muzzle carries whiskers. Mouth teethless. Pads pale pink with distinct claws – 5 per front pad, 4 per rear (no dew claw).

Colour – slate. Slightly darker back than underside; white blaze chest and tail tip, quite distinct.

Limbs remarkably sturdy and tail thick.

At one week I wrote:

Length varying 6 inches – 7 inches plus 2½ inches of tail.
Fur beginning to redden, particularly about sides of face and base of ears.
Their eyes are still closed, but they have become quite mobile and move strongly in the hand.
Ears which were almost bald at birth now have dark fur and begin to stand away instead of lying forward closely against the head.
Face and muzzle still very broad and square – showing none of the characteristic angular features.

It was on 11 April that I first noticed teeth showing through and very quickly they all had a palisade of little white needles.

During the second week they had begun to open their eyes. Their puckered faces gave them a heavy lidded look, like someone very tired and scarcely able to keep his eyes from closing. It was to be a few days yet before their muzzles began to lengthen, ironing out the wrinkles to reveal those moist sapphires in all their big blue beauty. To lift the kennel lid was like opening a jewel case.

At three weeks I have recorded:

Strong – mobile – have teeth – eyes open.
Still confined to nest – little extra evidence of colour change.
They will scrabble the straw about vigorously, will hold my finger strongly in their mouths.
Length approx. 11 inches plus 4 inches of tail.
Weight 1 lb 6 oz – 1 lb 1 oz; 2 of the dogs are top weight at 1 lb 6oz and 1 lb 5 oz.
Fur quite long and silky – 1 inch – 1½ inches.

I have also made a note at this time that the cubs show slight signs of fear, moving to the extreme corners of the kennel.

As the cubs became better able to tackle solid food I would attempt to give them individual portions. It was a completely futile exercise, since in their enthusiasm two or three cubs would demolish the morsels on one saucer then scramble for whatever the others had not already disposed of. Sometimes a furious fight would break out, which invariably scattered the contents of the untouched saucers.

At regular intervals, usually on Saturday mornings, I'd move camp into the compound. I'd take food, kitchen scales, tape measure, probably still and movie cameras, notepad and anything else that seemed appropriate at the moment. Sniff and Big never missed these parties and sometimes one or both cats would also be inside, when I closed the door behind us and settled down to an hour or two of filming, photographing, feeding, making notes, weighing, measuring, but mainly just being amused.

It was an hilarious pandemonium and a wonder that I ever recorded any data at all. The cubs would be doing their best to avoid another washing from Sniff, trying to dodge round her to get to me since I had the food. Once she'd caught one and was giving it the business, the others would take advantage of her preoccupation and scramble for the titbits. The victim would then struggle frantically to escape its ablution before its brothers and sisters scoffed all the grub.

Big was very gentle with them – moving very carefully when they were around his feet, he'd often sniff them and, in the fashion of dogs, it was usually the rear end that got the attention. Often he inadvertently lifted the little back legs off the ground. With its rear half riding on Big's black nose and its front legs stumping away, they'd move slowly along as though competing in a wheelbarrow race.

One of the cubs was particularly fascinated by the large white tag at the end of Big's tail. When he was lying or sitting with his tail along the ground the cub would struggle over the furry object, which at this time was as thick as the cub was fat. His little legs could just straddle it, and with his right legs on one side of the tail and his left legs on the other, he would work his way down to the white tip – about three inches long. Here he would sink down on to his luxurious mattress and watch the white bit. Each time it moved he would try to check it by placing his front legs on top of it. Lying like that they looked very funny, a couple of hugely ill balanced bookends. The cub, evidently very comfortable, seemed content to stay there, and usually did so until Big stood up and tipped him off.

Ferdi tolerated the riotous confusion with good humour, except for one quite inexplicable incident that was to occur a little later on.

When the cubs, still black and pudgy, first began to tumble through the kennel opening and embark on wobbly legged explorations of the compound, Ferdi seemed to limit their exposure to the great outdoors fairly strictly.

The corners of the kennel stood on four pieces of timber which raised it about two inches off the ground, to keep it dry and avoid rot in the floor boards. Even if they wanted to, the cubs couldn't get back up this step and over the baton that helped prevent straw and woodwool from spilling out of the kennel. But Ferdi would suddenly make up her mind that they should all go back indoors, and picking them up one at a time she'd carry them back to the kennel and push her head through the entrance hole and drop the cub into the straw. Often when she picked them up she would adjust their position in her mouth with a few quick grabbing movements. It seemed that the cub was released, but before it could fall it was repositioned by a quick movement of the head. It looked fearsome, not unlike the action of her jaws when she was cutting up a dead rabbit. I'm sure the pressure and control was precise, and it was done with such casual confidence, that one was left once again acknowledging the performance of an expert. It also indicated that, conditioned as we are to the frailties of the human baby, it is easy not to appreciate just how tough and hardy very young animals can be.

The dogs' reaction to the treatment meted out to the cubs was also interesting. There was absolutely no doubt that just as Ferdi was an integral member of the group, so also was the tribal circle immediately thrown around the cubs. It offered protection and concern. With me acting as Godfather to this highly unlikely but very agreeable combination of dog, bitch, vixen, cubs, tom cat and she cat. The cats, as is their nature, were only on the fringe, Elsa being more sociable than Tom, but they would both muck in with group activities occasionally.

It is fascinating to reflect on the possibilities for twelve to eighteen months from this time, had it been feasible to give the cubs the individual attention that we had been able to lavish upon their mum. Of course it was not; but might I have been roving the countryside in the company of seven foxes, two dogs and the occasional walking cat?

We could have held our own meets and chased fox hounds.

Sniff, like Ferdi, was very business-like when dealing with the cubs, her maternal instincts apparently telling her that firmness was the only way. She was quite capable of plonking her foot on a struggling cub while she gave it a wash. It looked bruising, but like Ferdi she seemed to know just how much weight to use without harming the cub. The vixen seemed to approve of the treatment for she never showed any anxiety for the cubs' safety.

By contrast, Big did occasionally display concern for the quite robust fashion in which the cubs were managed. He also, apparently, was not quite attuned to the dextrous no nonsense ways that were necessary when the welfare and protection of six cubs was being managed.

While the cubs were still at the waddling stage they discovered sanctuary from whatever particular piece of discipline they would avoid, in the narrow gap beneath the raised kennel. Once discovered, it became a regular hideaway for them.

The first time that I saw two or three of them hole up in there, Ferdi eventually decided she wanted them out where she could see them. She could not reach them with her muzzle, but lying down and looking under the kennel she made some quiet noises which were, presumably, the foxy equivalent of 'OK you sprogs, the joke's gone on long enough.' The delinquent cubs disagreed and nothing happened. The kennel was in a corner of the compound, hard against the wire on two sides. Ferdi patrolled the exposed sides of the kennel a few times while she considered this mutiny, then lying along one side of the kennel she pushed a front leg into the gap and with vigorous sweeping strokes kicked them none too gently out into the daylight. A bumping on the underside of the kennel as they were bowled out of that narrow confine, apparently counted as a spanking. From then onwards until the cubs themselves became too big to get under the kennel, it was Ferdi's normal method of dealing with would be hideaways.

Big's concern and naturally protective disposition got the better of him one day. Two cubs had already been booted out, all ways up, from beneath the kennel, and Ferdi was vigorously raking away, trying to locate the remaining one. It was all too much for Biggy's kind heart, and seemingly very embarrassed by it, but with the resolute step of one who sees his duty clear – 'A dog's got to do what a dog's got to do' – having carefully disengaged himself from a couple of other cubs who had been using him for mountaineering practice, he got up, crossed the compound and with a great horny paw gave Ferdi a gentle tap on the back. She, lying down with one leg thrust beneath the kennel, rolled her head to look up at him in some surprise. She extracted her leg and sat up lifting her head to touch his, her ears laid back, a posture of hurt indignation at this breach of etiquette. Her whole attitude held the message, 'I'm not hurting them. Don't worry, you big softy, I know what I'm doing.'

Big stood back, duty done, a bit embarrassed. Ferdi lay down and evicted the remaining cub.

Big, when he was not acting the idiot, lying on his back trying to fend off the attacks of Sniff and Ferdi with his great feet, was an immensely dignified brute.

This dignity was badly ruffled on one or two occasions by the cubs. When he lay down they were quite likely to use him as a general exercise area, which he bore with good humour. But there are certain things at which a strapping dog has to draw the line.

I saw Big flinch and heard a muttered protest. He stood up almost lifting a needle toothed cub off its feet. The optimistic youngster had attempted to take a drink and finding the bar closed had tried to open it. Big looked down at the taker of this enormous liberty with immeasurable disdain and indignation. Thereafter if he was lying down when the cubs came along, he usually got to his feet.

Sniff suffered the same treatment, less embarrassing for her but no less painful when the frustrated cub tried to uncork the bottle with his teeth.

At about three weeks the cubs had graduated from licking milk off my fingers and had started lapping from a shallow bowl. Their initial attempts were amusing; they invariably, in their enthusiasm, dipped too deeply and withdrew, spluttering with milk white whiskers and bubbles blowing from their nostrils. But they soon mastered the technique and were all lapping competently.

Within a couple of days of this milestone they started tackling solid food; initially this was taken in suitably small morsels from my fingers, biting the fingers quite painfully in the process, often drawing blood. This I'm sure was by mistake – they snatched the food, taking finger as well as meat. Ferdi had done the same when she began taking from the hand.

Their jaw power was remarkable; even at this early stage there had been a few trials of strength, two cubs locking together and shaking each other in a fury of squeaky anger.

I have picked up one of a pair of fighting cubs and the other has been still dangling in its jaws. It is surprising, in view of the punctures they made in my fingers, that no harm was done.

Already individual personalities were being displayed, and I began attempting to identify them.

One had earned a name, 'Bridget', after the famous sex kitten of yesteryear, and was just as beguiling. She was the second smallest and by far the tamest – she would play with me very much as a kitten will. Probably because of this confidence, she was first to lap and also to take meat from my fingers – definitely a trend setter.

At the other extreme, one of the dogs, the smallest, was very nervous.

The cubs were now perhaps at their most attractive, in the cuddly toy sense of the word. Still lacking the slender, angular muzzle, and lean rangy look of the adult, they were now well into their conversion to ruddy brown livery. The black fur in which they'd entered the world had gradually lightened as the guard hair of their first true coat had grown through it, until they had become an unmistakable foxy colour. Their ears were now pricked and ever moving in tune to the sounds of the world beyond their compound. Their eyes now focusing sharply were tracking every movement about them; big clear blue marbles, bright and mischievous in arresting contrast to their ruddy coats. They were a sharp little crew.

After the first week, recovering from the trauma of the birth, the dramatic change of environment, their progress had been rapid. It was a growing time of year, and the bed of nettles that colonised one end of the enclosure had thrust up its fresh growth from an underground web of roots. The fresh bright nettle patch became the cubs' personal jungle, from which they pounced upon each other in clumsy ambush, into which they vanished if startled by an unexpected noise or presence. It was then always worthwhile to sit quietly for a few minutes, while curiosity overcame fright. Little faces would poke out of the leafy screen. Bright shining blue buttons would suddenly stud the fidgeting green drift of leaves. Another pause before, slowly, very alert, one would emerge. It was invariably the precocious Bridget that led the way.

It was a source of interest and some surprise to observe the range of reaction of the cubs.

Since Ferdi in her wisdom had opted not to take the cubs into the earth, I had decided that it was unlikely that they could be raised as genuinely wild ones. It followed from this that I should probably be looking for foster homes in a few months' time, and so without planning a deliberate programme to tame the cubs, I was happy to let them get used to Sniff, Big and me. If the job were half completed by the time they went to a new owner who could give them individual attention, then it should not be too difficult to get them tame enough to be able to enjoy a lot of freedom – as ever my goal.

This, at least, was the theory.

I had expected them all to be tame; they'd known my scent and that of the dogs since their first few sniffs at the open air. We had been among the first objects they had focused upon, no doubt vague and blurred at first, becoming sharp as the faculty came to them.

I assumed that Ferdi's relaxed confidence would be communicated to them, and would be absolutely reassuring. I'm certain all these things had an enormous influence on the cubs and, of course, by comparison with a similar litter down an earth somewhere out there in the countryside, they were remarkably tame. Yet despite all these powerful influences, the instinct of suspicion and unease at the close presence of man was evidently still a potent force. This well justified and vital survival factor was more manifest in the three dogs than in the vixen, and much more so in the smallest of the dogs than in any of the others. They had by now all acquired names: the three dogs were Freeman, Hardy and Willis; the vixen Bridget, Brit and Gina.

Willis and Bridget represented the two extremes of reaction. If I was crouched in the compound, Bridget would often sit on my foot. She was quite prepared to include my fingers among her play things, to try out her teeth as readily upon me as on her brothers and sisters.

Willis was very timid and suspicious, it took vastly more patience to win him over and then the winning was an edgy sort of gamble on his part, rather than trusting confidence. He would stretch from as far away as possible to snatch a bit of meat, then immediately scuttle away with it.

The other four ranged in their confidence between these two, but were nearer to Bridget than to the wildy. He was definitely exceptional.

Referring to my notebook again, I find that at five weeks I again recorded the cubs' vital statistics and also attempted to log features by which individuals could be identified.

At 5 weeks

♂	♀
1. Largest cub – 2 lb 1 oz. Pronounced white tag. White fur on chin and blaze on chest.	1. Smallest of all at 1 lb 8½ oz. Small white tag.

172

2. Large – second largest
   at 1 lb 13 oz. Easily
   identified, the only one
   without a tag.

2. At 1 lb 10 oz with small
   white tag, difficult to
   distinguish from (1).
   Slightly darker face.
   Tamest of all. [This was
   Bridget]

3. Smallest dog at 1 lb 10
   oz. Less pronounced
   white tag. Tends to be
   wilder than the others.
   Mainly identified by
   nervous temperament.
   [This one was Willis].

3. Largest vixen, equal in
   weight to second largest
   dog at 1 lb 13 oz. Large
   white tag.

A footnote states that: Generally – fur whitening on chest and chin and eyes beginning to lose their intense blue coloration.

It is now difficult to measure them.

Indeed it was: depending on temperament they would regard the measuring process as a game and be for ever grabbing at fingers and tape measure, or as something scarey, and be trying to escape. In either case there would be a great deal of wriggling going on, which is probably why no lengths were recorded.

From the time that the cubs had first left the kennel, Ferdi had become noticeably more house-proud. As with most of what she did there was a very practical reason for her sudden concern with good house keeping. Prior to the arrival of the cubs she had spent most of her time out of the compound, and on the occasions when she was shut in for lengthy periods, the size of the enclosure was sufficient to naturally absorb her excretions so that the minimal fouling of the area that occurred went unnoticed.

Following the cubs' arrival, she spent vastly more time in the compound, and of course the 600 per cent increase in the population of the area made hygiene a problem requiring some action. Particularly in the early days of their clumsy bundling exploration of the compound, they were likely to get themselves fouled up if their droppings were littering the ground.

I discovered Ferdi's arrangement for dealing with this problem quite unexpectedly.

One day I suddenly spotted a small mound of soil and vegetation litter in one corner of the compound. It must have been growing slowly for days until it reached a size that proclaimed its presence, and left me wondering how I had failed to notice it earlier. From outside the compound I tried to reason out what it was. A molehill? It didn't look like a molehill, there was too much vegetation in it.

A rat had burrowed in? No! it would have had to burrow out to leave the spoil heap on the inside. In any case it would be a bold and short lived rat that broke into a compound full of foxes. A stupid idea anyway since a rat would merely scuttle up the first few inches of wire netting skirt, recently fixed in place to prevent the cubs crawling through the chainlink, and pop easily through the large diamond spaces in the chainlink itself.

Accepting my shortcomings as a Sherlock Holmes, I gave up the guessing game, entered the compound and with my hand wiped the top of the mysterious mound. With some surprise and no delight I discovered I'd put my fingers into a noisome treasure trove.

Ferdi did not actually laugh out loud, but she did wander across to see what on earth I was doing to her loo. Belatedly it was all too obvious. Wiping one hand on the ground I scratched her head with the other, 'Ha ha! Very clever,' I told her.

Subsequent observation revealed that not only had she appointed that corner her personal latrine, but when the cubs began to pass solid matter, she would collect these miniscule droppings and place them in the same corner, covering the mound periodically with scrapings of soil and vegetation. Once I'd learnt how the system worked, I'd shovel it out once a week; it only took a couple of minutes. A most efficient method of sanitation.

I've heard people say that foxes are dirty animals and in this respect bear unfavourable comparison with badgers. Badgers are very clean animals, judged at least by the frequency with which they change the bed linen, and their well organised latrines. I have never had any reason to consider foxes to be dirty. Ferdi kept herself in superb condition. The times I can remember Ferdi being noticeably anti-social were when she was frightened and discharged from her scent glands a pungent defensive smell, an action

characteristic of many animals in those circumstances. The only
other time she used to get a bit high was when she indulged in that
practice so beloved to dogs – rolling on dead things.

Why this is such an obviously enjoyable pastime, and what its
purpose is, I'm not sure. It seems to be a habit almost entirely
confined to predators. Is it done to overlay their own scent with
that cloying sickly stench of decomposition, intended to improve
their chances in the stalk should they get on the wrong side of the
wind? The prey would be unalarmed by the sweet stink of death,
but very alarmed by a whiff of live hunter. Whatever the reason it
must have some ancient innate origin, for domestic dogs to whom
stalking is no longer relevant, indulge in it to their joy and their
masters' chagrin.

Of the herbivores, elephants in particular have a fascination for
the dead of their own kind, to a degree where they will attempt to
raise a recent deceased back on to its feet, almost as though
believing that if they could once get it back to a standing position it
would begin to walk again. They will also show great interest and
excitement on coming across a corpse in advanced decomposition,
even a skeleton, which they seem to recognise as one of their own.
This is presumably due to very strong social bonding, and quite
different to the cavorting upon a corpse as practised by predators.

Foxes sometimes make an earth in a discarded badger set. If the
part of the set they fancy is still occupied, foxes are reputed to
deliberately foul the entrance to induce the fastidious badger
to leave home. If this does happen, and it's one of the many
classic country lore clichés that never seems to have actually
been observed, I'm sure that the practice is discontinued once
the new occupants are in residence – just a sharp trick to get
vacant possession of a desirable residence without any hard
work.

I can't think of any animals I consider dirty when in their natural
habitat. There are important advantages in not being so. The old
maxim about not fouling one's own doorstep is a very valid
philosophy. Apart from making an unwholesome place to live,
which may or may not be important to the owner, there is a much
more practical reason for cleanliness. A smelly home would
advertise its presence to passersby, far and wide, shrieking to all
with a nose to hear – excuse the mixed senses – here is an earth, set,

holt, drey or smelly semi-detached, as the case may be: highly undesirable for the owner.

So, whether for reasons of cold practicality, or delicate sensibility, or both, I don't think there are any dirty animals, save perhaps those that live in the filth that man himself creates, in sewers for example.

Harking back to my forestry days, one of the charms of one of our areas of woodland was that it contained an ancient set. Even back in those days the Forestry Commission to its credit encouraged badgers, despite the fact that fence line inspection patrols usually discovered two or three places where the badgers had left the wood by the simple expedient of lowering their heads and walking through the rabbit-proof fencing, leaving a characteristically smooth semi-circular tunnel of raised wire to show who was responsible.

The wire netting, when the fence was erected, was taken one foot deep into the ground and then two feet away on the outside – I think these were the specifications, I remember they were quite precise. Soil and turves were replaced over the layer of wire, and in due course became integral with the vegetation on the outside. The theory was that a rabbit attempting to get into the wood, came up to the fence and burrowed down only to be frustrated by the wire lying beneath the ground. Control the rabbits now wired in and most of your saplings will survive until they're large enough to be immune to bark stripping by rabbits. So ran the theory. Squirrels and deer are a different problem.

The badger is a powerful animal and if the soil over the wire was not firmly compounded and woven together with roots, he could push hard enough to raise it, forming a neat little tunnel, tightly moulded to the shape of his body and an easy way in for rabbits.

Since those days I believe badger gates have been introduced; these are basically a heavy wooden pendulum suspended to obstruct the opening to a tunnel through the wire. The more powerful badger can swing it aside, but the rabbit cannot.

Despite spending a long time close to badgers, I rarely saw one. Like the majority of people I guess, most of the badgers I have seen have lain dead at the roadside. In fact as I pen this note, one such stands on a small table at my elbow. He was a splendid old boar and has already featured in this tale during the early stages of his re-creation. Eventually, after a lot of work, he turned out to be one of my better attempts at taxidermy. I'm very fond of him, but I wish he was still trundling his nocturnal way about the countryside.

The badger is a likeable, bundling, ancient animal. Happy like most animals to be left alone, to go about his own night-shrouded business; but that alas has not been his lot. If man should be full of remorse for his treatment of wild creatures generally, he should be doing the most stringent penance for his conduct towards the badger. A creature almost wholly beneficial to man, subjected to centuries of barbarous treatment in the name of country sport. When precedent, no matter how bad, has been established for long enough it gets labelled tradition and then becomes, in the minds of those who wish to practise the tradition, inviolable. We are enjoined by the car stickers to, 'Keep your hands off traditional country sports'.

When, comparatively recently, the badger was at last given some respite, officially at least, by being afforded legal protection its troubles were far from over. Ironically, the establishment that gave it long overdue protection, almost immediately condoned its slaughter as a suspected carrier of bovine TB. Hundreds of sets have been gassed in this campaign.

Here the ultimate irony is that where TB is present, even endemic, in badger populations, it was probably originally contracted from the forebears of those cattle, which the slaughter is intended to protect. The principle being familiar and fairly typical – 'We gave it to you, and now we'll kill you to ensure you don't give it back' – a very reasonable code of conduct by any standards.

Even the name of this maligned creature has become synonymous with bullying and maltreatment. To be 'foxed' is quite amusing, it merely means having the wool pulled over one's eyes; to be 'badgered' is much less amusing.

I confess not to know the badger well. I've certainly not had the privilege of getting to know him as I have the fox. I may well be doing him an injustice, he probably has a fine IQ, but when comparing the physical performances of the badger and the fox – the one comparatively slow, steady, business-like in a methodical way, trundling and powerful, the other a superb athlete of fast movement, fine balance and hair trigger reflex – it is easy to imagine that their respective mental performances would match the physical. In which case, in a battle of wits old brock might well get 'foxed' out of his home. Neither has any natural enemy in this country, excepting, of course, the universal enemy.

I love them both. Good luck to them!

21

Progress for the Cubs

The cubs progressed, becoming very active and taking a great deal of exercise in climbing the wire sides of the enclosure. They usually climbed in one corner where a supporting timber formed a ledge three inches wide about half way up the side.

They were like a troupe of circus tumblers, forming a crude pyramid as they clung to the chainlink, each trying to get to the top. They climbed, their paws hooked through the gaps, scrambling against and over each other in an upward migration, like a fur drape hung in the corner.

When the top of this animated tapestry reached the roof wire four and a half feet above, the leader with pressure from below and nowhere to escape to avoid it, usually became dislodged; so tight was the press that he usually brought the troupe peeling off the wire with him, each knocked down by the one immediately above. For a second it would cascade plump little furry bodies, which landed on top of each other in great struggling confusion in the corner, before they extracted themselves and started the next attempt on the summit.

Another form of vigorous exercise provided by the chainlink fencing was an individual activity. When one had climbed the fence, for the moment without interference, he would grip the plastic-coated wire with his jaws, hook his front paws through the gaps and kick furiously with his hind legs, so that his rear end flew out into fresh air then thumped back against the wire to be kicked out again as he shook and bounced on the fence. They were already getting very fit and could keep this bouncing going for several minutes. There was a lot of give in the chainlink and the performance looked like a workout on a vertical trampoline.

When they'd thoroughly exhausted themselves, they'd amble as a troupe over to where Ferdi would be stretched out enjoying a siesta in a sunny corner. They'd walk all over her and flop down at random, sometimes right across her face. It must have got very warm under that lot but Ferdi was very tolerant.

Their increasing skill at climbing the wire led to a breakout. Arriving at the compound one day I found two cubs wandering about on top of the roofing's wire netting. They had happened to climb up the chain link of the side fence just below where the roofing had been a few inches short and I'd laced it to the chain link with copper wire – the gap in some of the lacing was obviously too wide. The door was open and Ferdi could easily have hopped up and brought them down had she wished, but she seemed quite happy to let them explore, idly watching them from below.

I mentioned earlier an inexplicable exception to the general rule of complete harmony and trust between the foxes and all regular visitors to the enclosure. From the start, Ferdi had trusted the dogs, cats and me with the cubs, without showing any anxiety. The cubs, with great impartiality, had climbed over any of us who were sitting or lying down. The cats were perfectly prepared to touch noses and show an interest, but drew the line at this over familiarity and merely moved out of the way. The cubs had no fear of the cats or dogs and tended to come to their visitors rather than move away – except for their attempts to escape Sniff when she was on one of her cleanliness kicks.

The incident occurred one afternoon when Big, Sniff, Big Tom and I had been in the compound for about half an hour. I think I was preoccupied with weighing or photographing; everything seemed to have been quite normal. Tom had rubbed up against Ferdi, had inspected the cubs, while avoiding their more precocious advances.

I noticed nothing to account for what followed.

Suddenly, all hell broke loose. Ferdi launched a furious attack on Big Tom. The cat seemed taken totally by surprise; so fast was her first pass that he was knocked flying before he could blink, and she was instantly upon him pinning him down with jaws and feet.

Tom managed to break free but the door had swung closed and with such a low roof there was nowhere for him to go. He leapt for the roof wire and hung from it upside down. It was only four feet six inches high and Ferdi easily jumped up and pulled him down; she didn't manage to pin him properly this time and he fled into a corner where he turned and, having recovered from the initial surprise, at last began to put up some effective resistance, creating a bit of a stand-off in the confined space tight in the corner.

The cubs had vanished like magic into the nettles. The two dogs, I think as completely taken aback as was I, now charged across to the war zone; they didn't take sides but I think their arrival distracted the combatants.

I opened the door and Tom flew out of what he obviously considered a madhouse, to the safety of the wide open spaces, with trees to climb and other desirable mod cons.

As soon as he had gone, Ferdi settled down again as if nothing had happened. Alert little faces began to appear on the fringe of the nettle patch and life in the compound returned to normal.

I gave the incident a lot of thought and I'm sure something happened that caused Ferdi to consider Big Tom to be a threat to the cubs. What Tom could have done to transmit this fear to her, I've no idea; if indeed man has the faculty to know what passed between them, then I missed it.

Ferdi, alarmed by what ever it was, had instinctively vied on the side of the cubs' safety, by launching what in international affairs would be termed a pre-emptive strike. There was little difference in their size, and a large tom cat is no mean adversary, but such was the speed and ferocity of her attack, that poor old Tom, I'm sure without a nasty thought in his head, was completely surprised and absolutely demolished.

Was it that strange law of nature operating. The one that seems to decree that the animal defending its territory will generally outface the intruder? Almost as though righteous indignation strengthens one's resolve and a guilty conscience weakens the others. Not, in this case, that I think poor old Tom had any reason to feel guilty. I once saw an incredible piece of film of an elephant apparently giving way before the territorial display of a crowned plover.

I never did arrive at an explanation that satisfied me. In fact I only ever put together one sort of theory to explain the apparently inexplicable. The next day, still wondering about the incident, I was in the compound and I noticed that one of the posts had a woolly look about it a couple of feet above the ground. A closer look revealed that the cats had used it as a sharpening post at some time.

A cat doing that great hollow-backed stretch and reaching up to rake its claws down a post is a fairly arresting sight, and I found it difficult to believe that I should not have noticed; but could it have been that Tom was doing just that, and Ferdi misinterpreted it as a display of aggression, and as the classic rugby footballing excuse goes, got her retaliation in first?

The cubs were all tackling solid food – exercising their jaws, crunching gamely away at chicken necks and tough leathery gizzards. It became obvious that they had progressed to a new phase, in which Ferdi began to introduce them to the idea that food did not merely appear every time they were hungry, but had to be worked for and searched out; that those who worked hardest and searched most diligently were the ones that ate most frequently. As soon as I appreciated this change, I altered my method of presenting food.

I was pleased that the cubs were suckling less and munching more. Well before they had arrived, I had noticed a small fatty cyst on Ferdi's stomach. It was barely detectable, and I'd only spotted it when in one of her fairly rare, most biddable moods she had been rolling on her back in the sunshine while I rubbed her chest and tum during yet another of my one-sided conversations.

Unfortunately, the cubs had mistaken this slight lump for a nipple and had mauled it about. As Big and Sniff had discovered, if the nipple was unyielding the cubs became very impatient and used their teeth in their attempts to induce it to provide a drink.

The cyst had become very angry looking and a small abscess had formed; it was taking a long while to clear up under the constant attention of the cubs, and must have been very sore.

Hitherto I had been in the habit of putting down several bowls of food and milk, so that in the free for all that followed they each got some grub. Ferdi eventually got her message across to me, after I observed her engaged in a quite hopeless task. She was quite apparently trying to prevent the cubs taking food from the plates. She would fill her own mouth until she couldn't flick up another piece from the plates without dropping a piece already in her mouth, but even at full gape, with a red and pink frill hanging out all round, like a puffin with a beak full of sand eels, there was always too much left over. The cubs, naturally, instead of chasing their food around the compound took the easy option and went for what was left upon the plates. This did give Ferdi a chance to hide bits in the nettle patch, and to make a shallow scrape and drop in a titbit before nosing it over.

It was obvious that I was providing too much and too many sources for her to get this game of hunt for your supper going properly. I started using just one bowl and feeding a bit at a time, or giving it out of my hands directly to Ferdi. Now the cubs really began to work for their supper.

She'd walk around the compound with her head held high, and the cubs bundling about her, clumsily leaping for the food that hung out of her mouth. When she let them get hold of it, she'd then make them jerk and wrench at it in a bouncing tug-o-war, before she let it go; very much the exercise they'd been practising upon the wire.

When they'd all got a piece, she'd take advantage of their preoccupation to hide more bits. Soon they knew this game well and would sniff around, scrabbling here to uncover a morsel or searching the nettle patch. Not only did they have to pit their strength against Ferdi in order to obtain food, but now that there was no longer more than enough for everybody at any one time, when two or more cubs managed to wrench the same pieces from Ferdi, they had then to pull it to pieces or one had to dispossess the others.

It was all vigorous exercise, quickening and strengthening, establishing a solid foundation of physical fitness, greatly to the benefit of the cubs, whatever their future held, whether wild skills or domestic habits were eventually to be built upon this foundation.

Ferdi seemed to regulate things very well; despite the obvious element of competition there was no serious dominance by one or two of the larger cubs to the detriment of the others.

That great killer of wildlife, the motor car, has always provided me and my animals with a steady supply of rabbits, pigeons, pheasants, hare, squirrels and, from time to time, quite a variety of other things. The most spectacular to date was when quite recently, an unfortunate red deer hind has a fatal altercation with a lorry immediately in front of my car, providing me and friends with a supply of venison that lasted for months. For although I absolutely deplore this slaughter with its supporting cast of a million hedgehogs, I see nothing wrong in taking advantage once it has happened.

It was about this time that I started presenting such things to Ferdi as nature intended, or perhaps modified to a greater or lesser degree by the passage of a motor vehicle, but at least recognisable for what they were. Ferdi, who had spent very little time away from the compound in recent weeks, had returned from one of these rare trips with a half grown rabbit. Presumably to avoid raising a family with a supermarket mentality – milk comes from a cardboard carton and meat is always covered in clingfoil – without any guidance she presented the rabbit to the cubs and seemingly left them to do some exploring and come to a few conclusions. They seemed to have some ideas about it, but whether they recognised it as meat or merely as a new plaything, was not immediately obvious.

A rabbit has so many extremities that each cub could obtain a firm tooth hold. Then to the accompaniment of throaty little growls, they proceeded to drag the rabbit and each other all over the compound in erratic wanderings, depending upon which direction the resultant force of that moment took them. It was like a seance gone out of control, where instead of the glass moving around the table, the whole circle rushed about the room.

Apart from pulling out large tufts of fur which stuck all over their faces and set them sneezing and coughing when they inhaled it, and had them rubbing away with forepaws in a comical fashion when it irritated eyes or nose, they seemed to achieve very little but exercise.

She let them persevere for a long time, but the nearest they got to obtaining a meal was to give the ears a good chewing. She then took it off them and dismembered it, leaving each cub to drag away a more manageable portion which had, in at least one place, the flesh well exposed.

Ah! so meat isn't always bald. Sometimes it comes in a furry wrapper and a funny shape. Quiet growlings were coming from all parts of the compound as each struggled with his prize.

A couple of days later I picked up a pigeon from the roadside. That evening I gave it to Ferdi, who again left the cubs to their own devices. The basic principle, that underneath the fluffy wrapper it was good to eat, had been well learnt. Within a few minutes feathers were everywhere, drifting in the air, rolling over the ground, rumbling cubs struggled in a haze, they coughed and spluttered, some had so many feathers sticking to them that they appeared to have grown their own.

I had seen flying foxes, but never before feathered ones.

The cubs were by their sixth or seventh week probably as tame as they were to become. When I approached the compound the three vixen would often come out to meet me, wagging tails much in the manner of their mother. The three dogs were rather less overtly welcoming, but would turn their attention upon me from a position farther back in the compound. Even though the door was regularly open to the field outside, I think these short excursions to meet my approach were the only times that Ferdi allowed them out unaccompanied.

Whether I was bearing gifts or not, my arrival and that of Sniff and Big were enough to bring the vixen playing around, worrying at fingers while I rolled them over, when they'd kick themselves free and bounce back for more. The dogs, and particularly the extra shy one, needed the lure of a few snacks to bolster their courage and bring them scrambling around my feet. They would rarely play with me merely for the fun of it. Daily they became stronger, more agile and very difficult to weigh.

I found on the compound floor what appeared to be round-worms, and decided on a general dosing of the entire menagerie.

The dosage is by body weight and each patient required a different technique, the two extremes being the cats, particularly Big Tom, and Mr Big. Biggy was as ever the perfect patient. I got out the bathroom scales, weighed myself, scooped a surprised Mr B up in my arms and stepped back on to the scales, to discover Biggy was about half my own weight. I counted out the appropriate number of tablets – about eight if I remember correctly – spoke to Big to attract his attention and proceeded to throw the tablets to him one at a time. He caught and swallowed them, caught a couple of biscuits that were his bonus, and that was that.

The cats and Sniff knew the routine well enough and had I not shut them all in the kitchen before revealing my intentions, they would have been long gone. No amount of subtlety would prevail when dosing the cats. There must have been a telltale scent to the tablets. I knew from past experience that to crush up the tablets and mix them with food or milk did not deceive them. They had to be subdued in hand to hand combat.

First prepare, so that everything is quickly to hand when the moment is ripe. Liberally grease the tablets with butter or margarine so that they will stick to the end of your finger, but will slide easily, and their chalky absorbent texture will not cause them to adhere to the cat's throat. Next, with large towel, car rug or other 'swaddling clothes' endeavour to mummify your cat so that only its head protrudes and hopefully its feet are securely contained beneath. Sit on the floor, on your heels, knees apart. Jam your towel-bundled cat between your thighs so he can move neither backwards or sideways. With the fingers and thumb of the left hand take the cat's chin and pull the lower jaw down, hook fingers over lower jaw and push thumb up firmly against the palate to hold mouth open.

At this stage one may feel one is sitting on a bucking bronco, for the bundle will be performing all sorts of gyrations. There is, however, a very good incentive for holding tight and ensuring that the patient does not get its feet free. Pick up the tablet on a finger tip of the right hand and push it as far back down the cat's throat as one can reach, past the point of no return. Remove the finger and release the dosed cat.

It merely requires a bit of confidence and practice. The quicker it's executed the better. The power/weight ratio of an alarmed cat is quite remarkable, and can serve to remind one that over confidence is a dangerous thing.

Talking animals, one evening in a pub, one of the circle told me that their cat had worms and had defied even the attempts of the professionals to dose him. The vet had eventually suggested that they take him to the surgery, tranquillise or anaesthetise him, and then administer the dose.

I should have known better – nobody doses an animal more

competently than the vet. 'I don't normally have much trouble, I'll have a go for you, if you like,' I said airily.

The cat's owner was a rugby playing friend I'd known a long time. He maliciously accepted my kind offer, in terms that made it quite apparent that he regarded it as a challenge and that his money was firmly upon his champion. It was during the long light evenings. The idea was taken up enthusiastically by all present – it seemed to assume the role of some gladiatorial contest; I don't think side bets were placed, but it almost came to that. With the promise of a bit of a party back at Clive's place, we all left the pub while there was still plenty of daylight.

'Tinker' was sitting at the edge of the fish pond casually watching fat orange fish drift around just out of striking range. He was BIG. He was friendly enough, unsuspecting of the treachery I planned. He was hard; he felt hard to the touch; he pushed hard, with his head, shoulders and arching back, against your hand. He was heavy and moved easily even in quite a firm experimental grip. My confidence was ebbing.

Clive was encouraging: 'Want a stiff drink before you start?' he said.

'What's your blood group?' someone else joined in.

'I'll just polish off this little job,' I said, 'have that drink, then if there's anything difficult you'd like doing, perhaps we can get it over before the party starts.'

The barrage of comment made it clear that as far as they were concerned the party had already started.

In fairness to myself I don't think Tinker was a cat, I believe they'd found him at the Safari Park and dyed out the spots. It took several attempts to get the blanket around him; in the process he had twice got a front leg free. I had refused the offer of leather gardening gloves, since they would be too clumsy for holding his jaws apart and picking up the pills.

By now the backs of my hands were seeping fine evenly spaced lines of blood in columns of four, and had that raw sting to them that you get from cats' claws or blackberry brambles, and the battle had not started yet.

I realised that I'd got this thoroughly aroused, pulsing, writhing, wild thing as well wrapped as I was ever likely to. Yet the blanket was far too slack and he moved far too freely inside its folds. There was a lot of laughter, cheers and counter cheers. I knew the portents were bad, it was really time to give up; but I'd already been wounded, and Tinker was way ahead on points.

I subsided virtually on top of him, my thighs crushing hard in on him from both sides. Keen to get it over as quickly as possible, I grabbed at his jaw; after a lot of head bobbing like a boxer evading a succession of punches, I managed to get his mouth open, to a cheer from those crowding around, at a safe distance.

This was the limit of my success.

I thought Tinker was already going flat out, but on receiving this treatment he changed up a gear.

'Ouch!' I yelled. There was a simultaneous burning in both my thighs; in his frantic scrabbling to get a firm purchase, an anchorage from which he might force himself out of the enveloping blanket, his claws had passed through the blanket and he had found his purchase, deep in my thighs, and was now shoving against it with all his might. I tried to ease the pain by moving my legs apart in an attempt to disengage his steely hooks. Feeling the side pressure slacken, he merely thrust himself backward until I was almost sitting on top of him. Now fearful of what he might next sink his claws into, I gritted my teeth and sprang up, tearing my legs free. Resisting the temptation to boot the whole thrashing bundle into the fish pond, I stepped back. The blanket gyrated wildly for a couple of seconds, then Tinker exploded from within its folds and hurtled down the garden and up a willow tree.

All around me was hysteria; my trousers were torn and red. I'm slightly allergic to cats' scratches and already, apart from being sore, the insides of my thighs and backs of my hands were itching like mad.

Someone, laughing so much that he was slopping beer all over the place, pushed a glass into my hand.

I said, 'When they're trying to treat one of those, they shoot them first with a tranquillising dart, from a safe distance. I've watched it on TV.'

'At least you got his mouth open, which is all the vet managed,' Clive consoled.

I looked at the baleful Tinker staring at us from his high perch, as one of the girls presented me with a bottle of TCP and led me off to the bathroom.

Thank God Tom and Elsa were not like Tinker!

Dosing two cats in the presence of each other is tactically unsound; the most difficult part of the operation is catching the second cat that has just witnessed what happened to the first. Sniff, also, is very familiar with the process and by now will be forewarned and alarmed by the treatment so far. Big's excellent example of how to deal with such things without trauma is completely lost on the others.

Sniff usually contrives to make a small profit out of the business. By moulding a good layer of one of the pastier dog foods around the tablet, rather like a scotch egg, and suddenly throwing it to Sniff so that she tended to make a sudden unconsidered snap at it, I could sometimes get her to swallow the lot with no more trouble than that.

If she had seen the preparation, it never worked, but otherwise, if the Trojan horse was disguised among several other titbits, it would give a fifty per cent success rate. But once it failed it would go on failing all night. Sniff was quite happy to swallow the meat, but just as I'd think I'd succeeded, there would be the tablet, slimy with saliva on the kitchen floor. It was then a matter of opening her mouth and shoving my hand so far down her throat that the pill was beyond recall. It was amazing from how far down she could retrieve it. She did not like this treatment and was not at all cooperative.

I did not want to scare the cubs by such man-handling, and so I was relieved when they proved highly cooperative. All that was necessary was to take a piece of meat of a size they could bolt down, stick a sharp knife into it to form a slot, push a crushed tablet into it like money into a purse, and present it to the cubs rather like a carpet bag steak. They were so ready to take it, that the only problem was to ensure one did not end up with three times the dose while two others got no dose at all. Ferdi was as easy to treat in exactly the same way.

While establishing the dosage for the cubs, I weighed them for the last time. These data recording sessions had always been amusingly chaotic and by now they were no less hilarious, but as an exercise to record accurate data had become nigh on impossible. With their narrow base and large pan, my kitchen scales were a most unstable instrument, just about adequate for coping with inert heaps of flour and currants. When a young fox, determined it seemed to prove some law of physics concerning perpetual motion, was dumped on the pan, he invariably leapt off in one direction while the pan and scales leapt with a great clatter in the other direction, affording me about a tenth of a second to decide on the mean position of the wildly swinging pointer. For the purposes of the worming dosage I have noted that their weights varied between three and a quarter pounds and three and a half pounds – very approximately! – on 16 May. That would make them just over seven weeks old.

The cubs were now very foxy in appearance: their muzzles had sharpened, their colour change was complete except for a few persistent dark patches about their faces. Their eyes had almost lost their startlingly beautiful bright baby blue colour, now becoming a golden green, flecked, on close inspection, with very fine dark radiating lines, squeezing the pupil into a black sliver in the bright midday sunshine. Foxes have 'cats' eyes', the pupils contract not by diminishing circles, but from huge round pools in the dusk to vertical slits in bright light.

They could occasionally show very aggressive tendencies, usually towards each other in some dispute over possession of a choice bit of meat, but also increasingly towards Sniff. This latter development surprised me since she had played baby-sitter to them from the earliest days. Whether she had been a bit too rough with them and now they could resist, they were doing so; whether it was the result of a confusion of mind on the cubs' part, between instinct and experience; or merely that she had tried to baby them for too long, I do not know. When they turned on her, not in robust play, but in obvious anger, she looked quite hurt and bewildered for a few moments. A situation with many a parallel in human parent/off-spring relationships, particularly when the latter explanation is correct. There had never been a similar phase at the same stage in Ferdi's development. She had accepted Sniff as a substitute mother/big sister from the start, and I could not recall a blow struck in anger.

All that now remained to change these cubs into foxes, physically at least, began to happen very rapidly. It was a drawing out and stretching process. They became very sinuous, stretched and lean, long and supple in the spine, tall and rangy in the leg, with that definitive ID of the fox – the tail was unmistakably becoming a brush.

Their thin summer coats lent them no bulk, and at one stage they became quite gaunt by comparison with Ferdi, who still retained her dense winter coat of rich red/brown, to the cubs' paler yellow/brown. Had I not seen wild juveniles with the same stretched appearance, I should have been concerned about their diet, but they all seemed very fit and healthy, and when their permanent teeth arrived, they were pefect. Very soon they could all produce the archetypal toothpaste advertisement smile. Without having any pretentions to being an authority on diet and nutrition, I did know that diet is particularly important during periods of rapid growth in young animals. Deficiencies at this stage may inhibit development in ways that can never be made up later; also that trace elements in quantities so small that they may seem insignificant, can in fact be very important.

There was one slight hiccup in their otherwise healthy development, that may well have been due to such an apparently trivial deficiency. One day I noticed that two or three of the cubs were lame; it was nothing dramatic, but just enough to spoil their usual fluid movement, and the contrast was very marked. They were, in their weight distribution, favouring one or more of their legs. When the condition had persisted for a couple of days, I asked the vet to take a look at them.

As the stranger approached, Ferdi, as usual, reacted like a wild creature trapped in a cage. She became nervous, anxiously prowling the distant end of the enclosure, then lying down, never taking her eyes off him. I wished I'd had the forethought to let her out into the field before he arrived, but I'd forgotten and the door was shut until we approached. The vet I knew well, he was Mr Harrison who had already made Ferdi's acquaintance, and who had that totally unconvincing theory about horses on three legs.

He knew Ferdi's story, and so I felt none of the embarrassment I usually experienced when a stranger came to look at her, when her behaviour must make it appear that for my own amusement I'd deprived a wild creature of her freedom, to keep her, terrified, in a cage. This is a major crime in my personal code of required standards, and acceptable only under very special circumstances where the actual survival of the animal is at stake. On these occasions I would be copious in my explanation of the true circumstances, and end up with the uncomfortable feeling that he would probably think that I did indeed 'protest too much' and that his suspicions were confirmed. To convince my visitor finally that things were as I described, to his surprise I usually finished by releasing Ferdi, who vanished at high speed into the great beyond, while I casually informed the visitor that she'd come back of her own volition once he'd gone.

The irony was that what a stranger thought about my relationship with Ferdi was, because of my principles, probably infinitely more important to me than to him. Perhaps when you have few principles, you become keen that those you do possess are not misunderstood.

At this particular time there was a more practical reason for wishing Ferdi was not behaving so nervously. Either her unease had transmitted itself to the cubs or she had sent them into hiding. In any event they had dived into the nettle patch and were doing their best to become invisible. With their increasing size and the wear and tear on the nettles, this was becoming more difficult, but by flattening themselves and remaining absolutely motionless they managed a reasonable job of concealment.

I eventually got them to parade in the open spaces sufficiently for the vet to get a good look at them. He thought it might be due to dietary deficiency, I can't remember exactly what sort, and provided a blanket-style additive which would cover several alternative possibilities.

The diagnosis was evidently spot on, and by the following weekend all was once more balletic. As a safety precaution I continued to add the magic mixture to one or two meals each week and there were never any further problems.

The cubs continued their rapid development. The last vestiges of their hilariously heavy foot bundling about the enclosure had been replaced by the agile grace of adult foxes.

I now began to notice a change in the mood of the cubs; at my approach they would move to the far end of the compound. A frieze of silent lean shapes, heads lowered, watching me with a fixed stare from beneath their brows. Statuesque, suspicious – no panic – but an instinct to distance themselves from me, and to shy away from the old intimate contact with the dogs. Nor were these changing moods reserved for my presence. Sometimes they would range themselves about Ferdi in this silent tableau. There was something timeless about these lean angular shapes, so still, yet epitomising the latent energy of the wilderness. For me a Kiplingesque quality drifted about the group, stilled as if by a camera. I have a copy of *Jungle Book* in which each chapter starts with a stylised pen drawing. The silent group around Ferdi was so like the gaunt lean wolves about the council rock. I could return their silent stares, quite fascinated, for minutes on end.

In a group, Ferdi was no longer immediately distinguishable from the cubs. They were still very slightly lighter of coat both in colour and density, and had a leaner look. In size, several were as big as she, and no doubt the dogs would soon be bigger.

The original kennel had filled up weeks before. Initially Ferdi had taken to sleeping outside to give the cubs more room. It was one of those situations that had crept up on me. Ferdi drew my attention to the chronic housing problem one morning after a night of rain, by the simple but effective expedient of shaking herself while I was having a chat to her, and showering me with spots. I quickly installed a larger second kennel. Very soon the cubs had been able to leap on top of both kennels, a feat which Sniff, heavier and shorter legged could not emulate.

With their growing aloofness it was difficult to decide whether their games with Sniff and Big were still for fun or whether they were genuinely trying to escape. In any event, they gave Sniff a great run around. While she scampered excitedly below, they leapt from kennel top to kennel top, a distance, I suppose, of six or seven feet.

They flowed across this gap like a group of crag-hopping chamois, often passing in mid air in opposite directions, while a frustrated Sniff shuttled excitedly below, head up-turned, barking. If Big joined in, standing on hind legs and effectively occupying one landing area, sometimes all six cubs would be left struggling to stay on the roof of the remaining kennel.

My belief that the cubs were now slipping back as far as their tameness was concerned, advanced by a few weeks a decision that would have to be made. It now seemed highly unlikely that they could be given the full range of experiences that thousands of wild cubs would be receiving at this time. Too many influences had intruded upon a normal pattern of development. They were well exercised and undoubtedly very fit and fast; Ferdi had made them search for hidden food and work to take food from her. They had been introduced to a variety of prey species, both furred and feathered, and could easily dismember a large rabbit, but they lacked field practice. Ferdi had had few chances to put a fine edge on their natural instinct to hunt, to coach them, to teach by example.

She had introduced them to the larder in the basement of the grass meadows, where she had made her own first moves towards self-sufficiency. Some weeks ago, before their sudden change of mood, she had taken them all to the wildest part of my field, up near the far hedge, where coarse grasses and thistles discouraged the grazing horses. Here they had spent most of one afternoon trying to catch the scuttling furries in the galleries below. They had lost their fumble-footed cubbiness, but were now a bit gangling and under-powered. I recalled how instinct alone had drawn Ferdi to the same practice.

It was incredible to think that she had once been as inept as they were now. Even so, before the afternoon was out several of them had managed to trap a probably equally inexperienced young mouse. Whether all the cubs were successful, I could not be sure. I saw most of them eating at one time or another, but Ferdi, when demonstrating the art, invariably allowed one of the cubs to take the morsel from her.

The tuition took the form of an interesting progression. Initially the cubs had merely been enjoying a romp, chasing each other and treating the outing in a completely frivolous fashion. Then, either by command or by the change in her manner, Ferdi's intense concentration as she located hidden snacks beneath the grass stilled their wild tumbling and held their interest. After she had performed the trick a few times, their attention was undivided. They followed her in close formation, and each time she pounced there would be a wild scramble for the titbit. This was little more than showing the kids where the sweet shop was to be located and popping a sweet into each mouth. Now they were to be encouraged to try shopping for themselves.

Ferdi now altered the routine: she'd snap a victim but leave it deep in the grass. On seeing her pounce; the cubs again rushed in for a free hand out, sniffing and worrying about her mouth; when this proved unrewarding, they began nosing excitedly about in the grass. They knew they were close and became very busy indeed until one located the snack; there was a great scrabbling with paws and thrusting with noses, two of them extracted the little morsel and shared it by pulling it in two.

Later in the afternoon I realised she'd again changed the programme. I returned to the field and eventually spotted them when Ferdi arched into view above the long grasses and vanished again in a typical mouse hunting pounce. Ferdi, having trapped the victim by collapsing the gallery about him, did no more. The cubs tumbled over each other to dig him out and despatch him.

As I watched, I realised that some were already showing a degree of independence. The ever sharp Bridget was one who continued to show a lot of interest in the exposed gallery after Ferdi had moved on, exposing more by bulldozing along it with her nose, undoubtedly learning about the smell imparted by those who used it, so that from above she might detect the lie of these interesting tunnels beneath the grass.

Later, Ferdi lay down and left them to practise and work things out for themselves. Now, like Bridget before them, they spent a lot of time going over already disturbed ground as if expecting to find another meal in the same place, but no doubt learning even from this abortive exercise.

Eventually, one of them quite obviously located a furry troglodyte. Just like Ferdi's earliest attempts, the cub merely flopped down extending his forelegs on to the grass, covering a considerable area but without the impact to collapse the tunnel and trap his supper. In great excitement he thrust his nose into the fibrous tangle, which, as when Ferdi behaved similarly, brought the others bustling around. The mousey creature, whatever it was, had of course scuttled away long before the gallery was opened.

Nevertheless, a major milestone had been reached; it now remained for them to learn to locate more accurately, get up high and thump their weight down on the right spot; and they need never starve when there was a good grass meadow with its metro system and soft fibrous bundles of dormitory and nursery just below the surface.

There was no individual coaching. It was squad training, but seemed to have the advantage that she was teaching the brightest member, and this was not always the same individual. Whichever one seemed to make most progress in a particular respect, was quickly copied by the others. Big and Sniff were banned on such occasions, since they created too great a distraction. I also stayed as distant as possible, doing most of my observing through binoculars, while I perched on the stable roof. During the next week or two I'd wander into the field and eventually spot them when one rose above the grasses. They were invariably working in the rough near the top hedge, sometimes with Ferdi, sometimes alone, although she was never far away. They all seemed to have adopted the correct technique and I was confident that they could all catch mice.

I think that this was all the hunting experience the cubs had received. They became so jumpy, so quickly, that I was convinced they would scatter far and wide if they were completely free again, and had for several weeks now confined them to the enclosure. I wondered, if they went free, could Ferdi reassemble them as a family unit, or would she even try? For a while she had been far less tolerant towards them, occasionally turning on a particular offender quite savagely. By the calender of the wild fox it was early in the year for cubs to be packed off to seek their fortunes, but I suspected that the confines of the compound and other artificial influences had probably imposed strain and confusion that had perhaps accelerated matters.

The enclosed area was no longer big enough, the nettle patch had worn away to a few sad stalks, as had the grass. The threadbare grass tended to be puddled into mud during a wet spell. To alleviate this, I practically returfed it with sods cut out of the field. Keeping the enclosure reasonably wholesome was now a daily chore.

What are the factors that determine when the wild fox family fragments to go separate ways? I am unsure!

Does the parent fox assess the cub's competence, his fittedness to survive, before turning him out? I think this most unlikely. It is probably the result of a time and tolerance balance. The wearing and wearying effect on the adult fox of a long hard spring, summer and autumn, of feeding, schooling and generally promoting the

8a No nonsense . . . 'Ferdi would suddenly make up her mind that they should all go back indoors, and picking them up one at a time, she'd carry them back to the kennel . . .'

8b No peace . . . 'It must have got very warm under that lot, but Ferdi was very tolerant . . .'

9a The great outdoors. An early excursion beyond the compound

9b Posing for the camera

9c 'There was a lot of give in the chainlink and the performance looked like a workout on a vertical trampoline . . .'

10a 'Any more cheek from you and . . .'

10b Photocall. 'I would probably have offered odds of millions to one
against their becoming minor celebrities . . .'

11 'She checked and turned to look towards us . . .'

welfare of six or seven cubs undoubtedly leaves a rather jaded animal as winter approaches.

I have seen wild cubs in early summer, no older than Ferdi's and apparently unaccompanied, but whether the vixen was there, unobserved, or had perhaps been killed, I do not know. On one occasion two young cubs behaved in a very naïve fashion, casually trotting along a rusty railway line, pausing to look back at me until I was no more than twenty-five yards away, then, without urgency, moving into the tangle of cover on the embankment.

This sort of blasé behaviour is increasingly observed among the city foxes, for whom familiarity seems to have led to a feeling that man is a fairly harmless neighbour, and a bit of quiet human watching holds no real dangers, but not among their sorely persecuted country cousins.

The family is subjected to similar pressures to those now evident inside the enclosure – too many large animals living too close together – tempers get frayed. Perhaps the cubs themselves decide when it is time to move away.

It is probably a combination of various influences, but like most things in the natural order it is beautifully synchronised and evolution's slow ruthless elimination of errors guarantees that it has a beneficial effect.

The period of tolerance is long enough for the cub to be self-sufficient by the time he departs. The pressures that split the family group do so just as the tougher times begin leading up to the belt-tightening and hanging on of winter in the wilds.

When the cubs are born in early spring, the fox population in the immediate locality is suddenly increased by 350 per cent if, as in Ferdi's case, there are seven cubs. As the growing cubs demand more food, so more food is easily available as the easy time keeps strict step with the demands. The hedgerows are hopping with young rabbits; the nests of rats and mice are full; young of ground nesting birds get trapped by the wet grass; insects teem in the fields.

As the year winds down, all the easy pickings upon which the cubs could practise have been picked, so by now they must be efficient. Now the area that supported nine foxes in the easy days can no longer do so without serious risk of them going short of food, with consequently reduced chances of surviving the rigours of a hard winter. So, for the cubs to disperse to new territories in which they will subsequently breed is a major survival factor to the benefit of the individuals and the species at large.

The precise length of fuse on the vixen's temper is not then the casual, insignificant piece of personal temperament it might at first appear. If it burned too quickly, the cubs might be driven out before being fully equipped for survival, if too slowly, it would put the entire family at a disadvantage.

Contrary to what many countrymen would have us believe, it is not only the irresponsible, unknowledgeable towny that lets his dog make mayhem in the countryside. There had been several unfortunate incidents fairly locally which had prompted my concern for the safety of the cubs exposed in their above-ground accommodation. This had meant that I'd tended to shut them up at night and so restricted the opportunity for Ferdi to take them on those nocturnal rovings, when the wild fox plys his trade; certainly, not since they had been big active animals, had she had much chance to do so. Whether or not she'd trotted them out in the moonlight to meet their dad during the first few weeks, when I was giving her every opportunity to move into the earth, I had no idea.

I should think that a great deal of what a young cub is taught, as opposed to its instinctive knowledge, is learnt at night: where to go and what to avoid; is the farm dog chained or free? Perhaps something about traps and poisons, although I think when such nasty devices are avoided, it is not out of knowledge but out of instinctive suspicion of something strange, particularly something strange associated with the smell of man.

Although deficient in this and much other experience, there were growing signs that the cubs wanted to go, and that Ferdi's fuse had nearly burned down. I have a great respect for the fox's ability to adapt and learn; I'm sure they arrive with a very useful set of basic instincts, and I had the superb Ferdi before me as an example of what a self-taught fox could achieve. If they did go it alone at this stage in their young lives, I felt that they could probably sustain themselves initially on insects and mice, while they perfected other skills. There would be plenty of food about for some time yet. But they would not be exposed gradually to the big world, as had Ferdi. They would be into it once and for all, quite on their own unless she went with them.

I could not quite bring myself to open the doors and leave them to sort it out for themselves. I had the uneasy feeling that this would be a washing of hands, the easy way out of a situation for which I was responsible. So, the alternative was to find suitable homes where the cubs could get the individual attention that was obviously necessary if they were to become tame enough to enjoy another sort of freedom. If this was to be done, then it needed to be done as soon as possible, before they became quite unmanageable.

I contacted some of the more promising names and addresses that I had on my list. They were all still keen and I was asked to go and visit some of their homes to see what they proposed for the cubs.

Within another week, thanks to a couple of visits and several lengthy telephone conversations, I was reasonably happy with the homes available for three of the cubs. Their owners elect seemed to have the right attitude and their homes were suitably situated.

One lady, I believe she had been the first to write to me, from near Penkridge in Staffordshire, lived in an old farmhouse and owned a few acres, including a splendid old high-walled paddock. The mellow, well weathered wall enclosed about half an acre and contained some fruit trees, with a few clumps of bramble and other rough cover. Her husband used to shoot a few pigeons and rabbits, so diet was no problem. Her plans were to tame the cub so that it could accompany them on walks and so enjoy a wider freedom, while its 'at home' accommodation would be the paddock, in which it would either dig its own shelter or use one she would provide. Access to the paddock was through a heavy, well fitting oak door, set in an arch in the wall. I considered this to be the best accommodation so far on offer to any of the cubs.

Another was at a large house, on the fringe of a highly desirable residential development of about a dozen dwellings, that had been built into the margin of a tract of woodland, so that the very large gardens all enjoyed a woodland glade appearance. The wood itself was the edge of the open country. I dreaded to think what it would cost to park one's car on the drive for an evening; but they were very nice people, attentive and keen for advice, with a son who had a passion for wildlife.

The third foster parent had already had some experience with a pet fox. He was a zookeeper from, by coincidence, the zoo where that sad brown bear had shuffled across his concrete cell, when I had gone to practise skiing years ago. Perhaps he still did, by now surely no more than an animated vegetable. The keeper did not want the cub for the zoo, but for himself – he had tamed an orphan cub some years before; it had died the previous year and he was keen to have another one.

All these homes were in or on the edge of open countryside, so in the event of an escape before the cub had become properly tamed, it would find suitable cover and have a reasonable chance of survival and conversion to a truly wild condition.

I was asked how much I wanted for the cubs by each of the potential new owners. I did not quite know how to handle this matter. I did not want to appear to be making a profit out of trading in fox cubs, yet to ask for a fairly stiff sum of money would be a way of further testing the interest and enthusiasm of the new owner. I decided to rely on my impressions, and gut reactions of those concerned, and merely said all I wanted was to be assured that the cubs would be treated kindly and that the objective of the exercise, to give the cub maximum freedom, should always be uppermost.

I had not given it prior consideration, but said it on an impulse, first time, and thereafter repeated it to each one. It was to the effect that if, after a few weeks, they were not making reasonable progress in taming the cub, they would let me take him back. I decided that I'd then turn him loose at home, where he might still get assistance from Ferdi and where I could leave food out and so perhaps take some of the pressure off while he struggled to adapt.

I thought back a few months, to Bridget in particular, but also several others, gambolling over my feet and playing with my fingers. Given individual attention at that stage, without any particular effort on my part, they certainly could have been as tame as, and lived the life of, a domestic pup. But I'd not wanted to do anything that might close the door on their ultimately living the lives of wild, free foxes, and it now looked as though I'd fallen between two stools, something I'd so dreaded when considering the cub Ferdi's future.

Three homes had been found, three owners had not been discouraged by my warnings. I had selected several of the sounder cages and taken them down to the cottage for overhaul; they would become travelling cages for the cubs. Predictably, the first to phone to make final arrangements to collect their cub were the lady from Penkridge and her husband. They arrived the following day complete with brand new collar; we 'worked' this until it was very supple and then went out to the compound. Anticipating their arrival, I had let Ferdi out half an hour before; as we entered the field she, Sniff and Big were busy along one of the hedges. My visitors were intrigued, but Ferdi denied them a closer look. As the dogs spotted our approach and galloped over to join us, she slipped into the hedge and vanished.

The lady from Penkridge was clasping her hands together with excitement. 'I do hope ours will get on as happily with our old dog. They would get lots of exercise if they could be left together in the paddock.'

I asked them their preference – dog or vixen – they said vixen. I told them all about Bridget; I guess she had been my favourite from the early days, even now she was probably a little less skittish than her brothers and sisters. I had been tempted to keep her, and several times later was to regret not having done so. Because I could not imagine ever finding a more suitable home than the old farm, I thought I'd like her to go there.

I slipped into the compound, closed the door and, after a lot of coaxing, managed to pick Bridget up. She was not at ease, but while I talked quiet nonsense to her and she was preoccupied with the two strangers outside the enclosure, she let me put on her collar. She had no bad reaction to this strange thing about her neck, merely having an almost absentminded scrape at it with one front paw, while her unwavering gaze fixed the two strangers. I ran a couple of fingers inside the collar to check its tightness, then eased it firmly forward to ensure that it would not ride over her ears and off. Fortunately, the fox's broad triangular head makes it possible for a collar to be fairly slack, and yet secure.

I delivered my lecture on the dangers of fitting collars to young animals that still have a lot of growing to do, citing once again, for impact, the horrific story I had heard from Mr Maylor, the keeper, during the big search for Ferdi. Ferdi's cubs were now of a size where this danger had virtually passed, unless the collar were fitted ridiculously tightly in the first place.

It had not occurred to me before, but that at least was a plus mark for having delayed their departure so long. As a tail piece to my discourse on collars, I suggested if they wished to label the collar – Ferdi carried her name, my address and telephone number – that it should be engraved on the brass strip and not dangled from the collar as a separate disc. If the animal did find itself in the wilds, such a disc, jangling against its collar, would be a considerable handicap, rather like the practice of 'belling the cat' to stop it catching birds.

I carried Bridget over to the cottage, holding her with fingers through the collar, and enfolding her against my body with enough pressure to cramp her limb movements but without crushing her so uncomfortably that she'd start a frantic struggle to get free. Even so, by the time I put her well into the cage and rapidly shut down the end flap, she was giving off the pungent defensive smell of the frightened fox.

The estate car was going to be pretty high by the time Bridget reached her new home. Not that my lady friend seemed to care or even notice – she scarcely took admiring eyes off the little vixen while repeatedly telling me what I already knew. 'She is beautiful!' She was still turned in her seat to watch Bridget in the back of the estate, when the car slipped round the corner and Bridget, the sex kitten, the sharpest of them all, was gone from my life forever.

I hate endings, but I pushed a feeling of sadness out of my mind and prepared for the people from the expensive pad among the trees, who were also due to collect their cub that afternoon.

Little did I realise that by evening, the future of three of Ferdi's cubs would have been decided.

22

The Cubs Make Their Choice

It had evidently taken the foster parents about a week to make their final arrangements for the cubs. Since it was then Friday, Bridget had already been collected; one more to go that day, and the zoo man to come over during the weekend.

Sniff, Biggy and I wandered back into the field. Up at the far end we were joined by Ferdi. As so often before, she suddenly material-ised, one moment I looked round at the dogs in the hedge bottom a few yards behind me, a moment later I glanced back and there were three. 'One of your kids has left home,' I told her. She looked up briefly at the sound of my voice.

I was so reminded of the way she used to come and go, drifting into and out of my company during our walks. I reflected that the four of us had not had a good long walk together for months – not since the arrival of the cubs – in fact I could not remember being in her company, outside my own field, in all that time. Perhaps this indicated just what a preoccupation the cubs had been. I wondered if there'd been any permanent change, or if things would slip back to normal when the cubs had gone.

My reflections were interrupted by the sound of a car slowing to make the hairpin turn into my short drive.

Except for their choice – they decided they'd like one of the dogs – the procedure and various pearls of advice were as before. He took a while longer to coax than Bridget had. Then we discovered that, as I had requested, they'd brought a strong, light collar, but had left it back in the car.

'Never mind,' I said, full of confidence, 'it's always a good idea to slip your fingers round the collar when you need to carry the little brute; but you can manage quite well without. I'll show you how best to hold him.'

I enfolded him with a good steady pressure, tucking his legs in and restricting their movement with hands and arms, and in lieu of a collar, taking a good grip on the loose skin of his neck. They were duly impressed by the amazing display of bush craft, and we set off across the field.

The cages were about three feet, six inches long, the whole of one end hinged up from the top to expose the full two by two foot section. They were constructed of one inch square wire mesh on a skeletal timber frame. The particular cage lay on my lawn, end already raised to receive its charge. I put the cub into the cage as far as I could reach, so that his head was virtually touching the wire at the far end.

I would not have believed that any animal in such confined circumstances could move so quickly. He had first to turn round in a space two feet wide. It was as though the steady pressure I'd been applying had compressed a spring, which on being released displayed a startlingly fast recoil. Being in a full crouch, I was slightly handicapped. Nevertheless, he passed over my withdrawing arms before they had cleared the cage. Before I could lurch forward to block the opening with my body, he was through the gap, he ran up my chest and over my left shoulder. Getting a good thrust off the platform of my shoulder, he landed two and a half yards away in the middle of the lawn, before streaking across the garden, threading through the hedge like a high speed bobbin and disappearing up the field with the dogs in joyous pursuit. The cub apart, the dogs were the only ones that had reacted at all – the rest of us stood in numbed surprise.

The aura of the infallible 'animal man' collapsed about me, rather like a supermarket display when someone pulls out a can from the bottom row. Recovering, I whistled back Big and Sniff, I didn't want the cub chased any further than he might decide to go. I grinned rather sheepishly, 'And that's not the best way to handle your fox cub.'

Later, after they'd driven away with another cub safely caged in the back of their car, I turned my attention to the escapee, and what to do about him. With a wry smile I realised that it was Freeman – it seemed appropriate. I wondered if Ferdi had been close enough to be aware that he was now free. It had happened at a bad moment – when he was thoroughly scared – he might have run a long way.

There seemed to be only two possibilities to getting the cub back. Depending on how well he made out, it was conceivable that finding himself alone in a very large world for the first time, he might drift nervously back to what was familiar and the lure of easy food. If, however, he had some quick success in his hunting forays, or if he'd run so far in such a confused state of mind that he couldn't easily find his way back, then it would be entirely up to Ferdi.

I considered this further – a frightened fox leaves a strong scent, strong enough to be detected by that comparatively insensitive organ, the human proboscis. For this reason I was certain that Ferdi could find him if she chose to, also reasonably certain that however far he ran, once his panic was over he'd be capable of back-tracking his own scent if he wanted to return.

The dogs, also, certainly Sniff, could track him, but the chances were that when we got close we would drive him farther away.

The only out-going expedition that might bring him back would be Ferdi alone; whether she could, or would try to bring him back, I thought doubtful. Unless he came close, I could not take any part in it. The most compelling reason for his return would be the lure of food, so I'd set up a few traps about my field and let fate take its course. There were still several cages on the lawn and they could be the basis of cage traps.

I made and fitted simple 'ride over' catches to the bottom rail at the hatch end of the cages. The falling flap passed over the top of a leaf-spring and into the cage shut position, the spring then flipped up again to lock the cage.

The tripping mechanism was even simpler: I tied a piece of cotton to the wire floor of the cage, well to the back, ran it vertically up through the mesh in the top of the cage and forward to the raised flap, where I tied it to the free edge, with a cotton length that set the flap at about 45 degrees above the cage top. To prevent any pull on the cotton raising the flap up through the vertical and merely letting it flop over backwards on to the top of the cage, I fixed a couple of bits of wood to provide a stop and prevent the flap exceeding 45 degrees above the horizontal. Now any pull would break the cotton and release the flap. A few experiments showed that it worked, and once closed, the trap was quite secure.

So, when setting the trap with serious intent, tie a sliding loop in the cotton inside the cage, pull it firmly up, on to a good lump of meat, fix to the flap as before, and presto! I had an infallible trap?

By the time I'd converted three cages, it was late afternoon. I had interrupted proceedings at one stage when Ferdi joined us in the garden. I shut the dogs in the cottage and went back into the field with her to see if she had brought Freeman back home. We walked around the field but I could see no sign of him, nor did her behaviour suggest that he might be about. As we came back to the enclosure the cubs were all up on the kennel tops swishing their tails at her approach. She decided to join them and I let her in. They gathered about her as usual, sniffing excitedly at her muzzle and shoulders, they were usually keen to explore what new scents she'd brought back from her trip.

Brit and Hardy were particularly persistent. It was like watching people exchange information in a language that I was not privileged to understand. I wondered what they were learning; was the smell of their brother fresh upon her? Were they missing the extrovert Bridget?

I watched with interest for any sign that she was aware that three were missing. She responded to each as it fussed about her in what I thought to be the closest domestic scene I'd witnessed in the compound for some time; this may have been coincidence or merely that I was looking for it. It was easy to imagine that she was counting them. With such a sudden depletion in their ranks from six to three, I'm sure she realised that some were missing. Indeed, the compound appeared almost empty. I was relieved that she showed no sign of distress.

That evening, while there was still light enough to see what I was doing, I set two traps in positions along the hedgerows and one close to the compound. Next morning I did a dawn patrol but none of the traps had been tripped.

The early part of Saturday morning was busy. My parents arrived for the weekend and the zoo man arrived to collect his cub; fortunately, he brought a travelling cage with him, since mine had been converted to traps.

This time there were no mishaps. As one would hope, he was

much more relaxed and at ease with the cub than had been either of the other two, never moving suddenly and talking almost continually to the cub in a lulling quiet voice. I was not this time instructing, but swapping opinions and experiences with a knowledgeable man. We chatted for a long time before he departed with Brit. A conversation of little sentiment, but much practical, caring, good sense.

It rained during the latter half of the morning and activities were restricted to indoors and in shed. Early afternoon Dad had wandered off on his own. He came back into the garden twenty minutes later and called that all the traps had been sprung and to go and see what I'd caught.

The furthest trap was tucked in close to the base of the hedge and partially hidden by a fringe of tall grass, even through this I could see at some distance that there was a movement inside the trap. I ran up to where Dad was standing grinning at me.

Sniff was a most expressive little dog, and now she did a passable impression of the little boy caught in the pantry with jam all over his face. With ears drooping and head bowed, she turned those melting brown eyes up to me from beneath brows creased with worry, while her tail, held low, tapped rather uncertainly on both sides of the cage. She was an emotional cocktail – guilt, apology, shame, embarrassment.

Laughing, we let her out. Pleased to be free, and from our laughter, judging her crime not to be as serious as she had first imagined, she frisked about, standing up against our legs to have her head scratched, mightily relieved to find the incident acceptable and, in marked contrast with a few seconds before, seemingly quite pleased with herself.

All the traps had been emptied. Mr B was quite prepared to bluff it out; he'd even had the cheek to bark at Sniff while she was in the cage, evidently finding her discomforture a great joke. But circumstantial evidence was strongly against him. Biggy would, in order to get into the cage, have practically to lie down and wriggle; there would still be a lot of Mr B on the outside when he broke the cotton. The flap would merely give him a tap on the backside. He would reverse out with his snack, the flap would eventually slip off the back of his head and swing down to be locked shut. The trap sprung and locked but the bait missing and nothing caught – what a mystery! Big kept his bluff going until I stood him beside a trap and without making a sound I pointed to it and kept my arm extended; slowly his tail stopped wagging and his head drooped just a little, while he also turned a big pair of brown eyes upon me.

'You crafty old rogue,' I said, gently cuffing his head. His tail swished wildly and he planted front paws in the middle of my chest, while catching me under the chin with a flick of his nose. I could readily picture one of my mates giving me a hefty thump on the back and saying, 'What's the matter, can't you take a joke?'

We were intending to go for a walk, so I reset the traps, and kept the dogs out of the field until we were ready to depart.

It was an interesting comment on fox behaviour and instinct; without giving much thought to the traps I had, before taking the zoo man over to the enclosure, let Ferdi go. She'd been free for a couple of hours before appearing in the cottage garden, yet unlike the dogs she'd not been lured into the traps. Set in such safe and familiar surroundings and permeated by my friendly scent, these cages, that had so suddenly appeared intruded in such stark angular contrast that they prompted caution even in a fox familiarised by daily sight of and contact with rows of the strange see-through objects. These same objects, set about the field with their yawning mouths and inviting titbits, were apparently sufficient to trigger some deep preserving instinct, which in turn generated unease in her mind and out-weighed the temptation of easy pickings.

If the inexperienced young Freeman had inherited equally compelling instincts of self-preservation, I was probably wasting my time. Then, perhaps hunger would eventually out-weigh caution.

An early Sunday morning round revealed two traps still set. Big and Sniff were showing great enthusiasm about the third, which was not visible, but I knew it had been tripped, since the flap no longer angled up above the grasses. I trotted up to find we'd caught a cat. It had apparently had such a fright when the trap sprung that it had not even eaten the meat. Now with the dogs galloping round the cage like redskins around a covered wagon, the poor old cat was fluffed up like a huge ball of wool.

Big and Sniff were keenly anticipating the release; no doubt to put the wind up a cat was a perfect start to a day. I decided it better be a handicap event and managed to give the cat a good start. It reached the sanctuary of an oak tree without much difficulty.

The dogs came back, muttering together – something about 'a . . . spoil sport'. I was a bit surprised that neither Big Tom nor Little Elsa had got caught.

The traps took nothing more during the weekend.

Freeman's last known meal had been taken on Thursday, so assuming that he'd come to no harm, he was either a very hungry cub or was managing to turn his instincts and brief tuition into a food supply.

Of those that had recently departed for new homes, the first news I received came on Monday evening. It was from Hardy's new owner, to tell me he was no longer Hardy's new owner.

Hardy had also opted for freedom when the opportunity had arisen, escaping from his pen in the garden when being fed during Sunday evening, and vanishing into the adjacent woodland.

They asked for advice on his recapture. They were obviously worried about him and feeling very guilty. I could well imagine that there had been considerable soul searching as to whether or not they dare report the escape to me.

I indulged in a characteristic piece of human double standard-manship, with a flare of annoyance that I'd entrusted the cub's welfare to them and they had failed me. I cooled off when I reflected that with far more knowledge and experience I had still allowed Freeman to escape under their very noses. That they were prepared to endure the embarrassment of telling me, in the hope that I might be able to improve their chances of getting him back, indicated that their hearts were in the right place, and their prime concern was for the good of the cub.

I could give them little encouragement, explaining that with all the advantages I had in my home situation, I had failed to recapture Freeman. I related what I had done, said that I thought the chances of getting him back were remote, but that I would, one evening during the week, endeavour to get over to take a look. They wanted reassurance, and I found I could honestly say I had increasing confidence in the cub's ability to survive, as long as he avoided any major misfortune like bumping into some gun-toting nasty, before he got to know his new environment. They then asked, rather nervously, if Hardy had gone forever, would I let them try again with one of the remaining cubs. My first thoughts were that I would not let them have another, taking the rather harsh line that I might just as well turn them loose in my field as hand them to people who turned them loose fifteen miles away. These thoughts remained skull bound, for I realised that my annoyance was out of my own concern for the cubs and the still strong doubt that I had done the right thing: perhaps I should have done precisely that and turned them loose in my field. I was taking my concern out on these kindly, well intentioned people, and there was no reason why they should not have another one – suitable homes were not that easy to find. I compromised, saying that I thought I'd got homes for the two remaining, but I would keep them in mind. They promised to phone immediately if they had the good fortune to get him back.

That week my own traps took quite an impressive haul. I inadvertently captured a large brown rat, two hedgehogs together in one trap, a crow and Little Elsa. These were all duly liberated. Of Freeman there was no sign. Whether or not Ferdi met him on her nocturnal wonderings and, if so, whether he benefited from continued association with the vixen, was entirely a matter for conjecture.

On Thursday evening I drove over to see if I could assist in the hunt for Hardy. We toured the adjacent woodland, inspected three traps – they had acquired two more. I did not like these, brand new and brilliant in their galvanised weather proofing, they sat among the blends of greens and browns as conspicuous as the proverbial brass button up that most private part of the sweep's anatomy. The cub had certainly got himself an attractive new home. I think I was a major disappointment, but at least I came away fairly happy for Hardy. From the start of my house hunting I had, while taking a look at potential foster homes, been casting a sideways glance to assess the surrounding area for what it would offer an escaped cub, while he was adapting to a new lifestyle. Cover and not too much human activity were the main criteria.

One place that provided these requirements was at Sutton Coldfield. A royal borough that has for administrative purposes at least, and almost as a physical fact, been engulfed by that great urban amoeba, the City of Birmingham. It is nothing to do with my tale and I have not researched these facts, but I believe that the monarch who bestowed the royal charter did so to mark his pleasure in hunting over adjacent lands, part of which now forms a large natural park, to which the town gives its name.

Sutton Park is a large tract that contains woodlands, heath, bog and several lakes; it supports a good variety of wildlife, including a considerable fox population. The house in question stood in a large garden on the park boundary.

They had been to see the cubs in the early days; he had seemed all right but she had gushed Oo's and Ah's, leaving me with the impression that the cub might be treated like a cuddly toy, with an irate vet being called in every time he sneezed.

I had two cubs to place. There was the reluctant clergyman (in an emergency); the folk from Sutton Park; and the, briefly, erstwhile owners of Hardy.

I thought that with patience any of them might do well with Gina, but I did not fancy any of their chances with Willis, who seemed to be more skittish than ever since the disappearance of so many of his brothers and sisters. Willis the wild one! He was my main concern, and as I considered the situation, I realised that the man best equipped with the patience and understanding to have won the confidence of Willis was the zoo man – I should have asked him to take Ferdi's least tractable child.

The idea, when it came, was so contrary to all the basic principals and goals that I always pursued and considered sacrosanct in organising the future lifestyle of the cubs, that even to find myself giving it any thought was quite a surprise. Of all things, I was thinking of a zoo! Not any zoo, but a specific zoo and, more precisely, a specific enclosure in that zoo.

23

The Snakeman

It was a small zoo in the Staffordshire countryside. Several years before, I had become acquainted with the keeper of reptiles.

On the couple of occasions that I visited the snakeman, I was given a conducted tour, while the grounds were closed to the public.

I was, as usual, disappointed by the space allocated to the big cats and I was glad that there were no tigers, perhaps my favourite of all animals, but I thought that lions, pumas and lynx were badly off, although the pumas had just produced three beautiful kittens (I had not realised until then that puma cubs are called kittens). As with most zoos, certainly small zoos, there seems to be a law of inverse ratio between the animal's degree of spectacle and potential danger, and the adequacy of its housing.

The zoo was in the grounds of an old manor house. The grazing animals did quite well, with large paddocks in the parkland. The smaller predators also had quite generous enclosures. The snake pit, as is usual in this cold country, was utterly unspectacular, the overhanging concrete wall containing a large rockery that appeared to be littered with dead sticks. So torpid were the serpents, that despite the list of deadly names on the glass-fronted information board, I'm sure one could have walked bare foot through their midst without the slightest danger – they appeared in a state of permanent hibernation.

But the keeper of the reptiles was quite young, a bit of an extrovert, and a touch inclined to show off. His quarters were a large caravan, and as one entered it was a bit like walking into a bakery. All that excess heat was not because he suffered from the cold. It was for the benefit of the snakes and his sense of showmanship. He'd no intention of having a guest leave with the impression that he was a zoo man in charge of dead sticks. There was a fluid pouring movement about the caravan. On a stand immediately above the headboard of his bed was a large aquarium, inside which a cobra tied knots and slid out of them, like a flowing stream. A soft dry rustling, restless fluency, that checked briefly now and then as the nose and small beads of its eyes came level with the top and its tongue appeared, flicking inquisitively in the one inch gap formed by the wooden corner blocks that supported the glass cover. The cobra appeared to extend a couple of times around its tank – apparently it was almost seven feet in length and was fully equipped with fangs and venom glands. The tank was wider than the single bed; the top appeared to be only normal window weight glass, not the hefty slab of plate I would have expected. There was no additional weight on top of it and that muscular animated bowline inside looked well capable of pushing it off.

There were two more tanks, but they contained far less sinister tenants – a boa and a python, both beautifully marked and very friendly. Soon I was festooned in boa constrictor, probably a very disappointed boa constrictor – he was used to better things. Around the walls of the van was a very racy exhibition of photos – a stunning collection of girls, some well known actresses, clad in very little but boa (not the feathered variety) or python. In fact a couple of very well known ladies wore snakeskin alone, the coils more or less strategically placed.

Here, obviously, was a very admirable bloke, with an eye for the main chance. An interesting chap! He had offered a service to various publicity agencies and was now often called upon to take his snakes to work. He got the plum job of draping the snakes about the ladies, coming over very macho and protective and apparently getting one or two unhoped for bonuses. He got to be quite well known and invited to some rather splendid parties and, as he said, 'Amazingly enough the silly buggers pay me quite handsomely. I'd do it for nothing!'

Another extracurricular project was much less frivolous but no less fascinating, something that conjures up images of hot climates – Africa, India, Australia. This was the collection and marketing of snake venom. Snake venom was apparently a valuable commodity, used for producing serums, but more recently increasingly interesting to medical research units where its properties and ingredients were being used in developing treatment for all sorts of conditions. He planned to indulge profitably his passion for snakes by getting into that business. He had already experimentally milked snakes and was absolutely confident about it. As we chatted and drank beer from the can, I reflected, not for the first time, that you never know what's going on behind the most unlikely looking wall.

My boa had disengaged himself, having presumably decided that I was not of the shape or softness he preferred, and together with the python was moving about the van. They were of similar size, about nine feet. The snakeman explained that these three, plus several more in the pit, belonged to him personally as opposed to the zoo.

There was not anywhere for the two constrictors to go and inevitably the python got on to the bed and right up to the cobra's tank. The cobra showed no reaction, but I watched rather keenly, for it seemed very likely that the big fellow would knock the glass cover off the cobra. I mentioned this as casually as I could manage, playing it very cool, as the saying goes, but secretly not at all relishing the prospect of having the cobra use me as a climbing frame as had the boa. I added that the cobra looked plenty strong enough to push the cover off for himself, without any help from the python.

'Yes,' he agreed, 'but she never does. Not that it would be any sort of disaster. I don't normally have her out while the other two are loose, just in case she does bite one of them, but they have been altogether without any problems. I let her out every night for a bit of extra exercise.'

Apparently, he occasionally let her loose outside, but had to be very careful. There was a place where one of the paths ran between walls; he used to block off one end with a large timber panel, let her go and stand guard at the other end. 'If ever she escaped they'd feed me to the lion,' he said. 'There'd be such a panic and the place would have to be closed to the public until she was found – think of the money they'd lose.'

'Do you feed her in there?' I asked.

He said he usually fed her outside in a large concrete sewer pipe;

he'd blocked one end and had a large piece of perspex with which to seal the other, after the cobra and the unfortunate food had been put inside.

I felt sorry for any plump rats or chicks shut in a drain pipe with that lady, still flowing about her tank as we talked. She was not due to be fed again for several days. There was something very compelling about her, and I wasn't sure whether I was disappointed or relieved that I was not to see her kill. She was obviously his favourite and by far the most valuable of the three.

The second time I saw him was a few weeks later, and he was a mess. I'm still not certain if the spitting cobra is a specific cobra variant, or if all cobras can spit venom, but he had had venom sprayed into his face. Fortunately, he wore spectacles which gave his eyes some protection; it must be pretty caustic stuff, for even then, over a week later, he had great red blotches about his cheeks and forehead and was wearing dark glasses. Loyal to his big sinister pet he said it had been his fault, but did not enlarge upon that.

This then was how I came to know of one particular enclosure in one particular zoo, which might possibly be an acceptable home for Willis.

I went back to the zoo. As I have remarked, some of the small predators were quite well provided for. The enclosure I was interested in was next to a similar one, the home of a dingo. The enclosures in this section ran between one of the paths and an old high wall which had once enclosed the very extensive gardens, and now did the same for a considerable part of the zoo. Trees and shrubs still grow along the base of the wall, providing some cover for the animals. The distance between the wall and the path was around forty to fifty yards; the enclosures in this section were about twenty-five yards wide and, except for the wall at the rear, were contained by a heavy chain link fence with an inward sloping barrier on the top; the boundary margins were slabbed, presumably to discourage digging.

The enclosure next to the dingo had been empty last time I'd been there; if it was still empty, I wanted to take a look at it. The dingo was still there and seemed quite composed, having a good scratch close to the path end of the enclosure. The next enclosure was still empty, or was it? There was nothing to be seen, but the plaque said *Vulpes vulpes crucigera*, the European fox – range, diet, etc., etc.

Had they left the plaque since the last occupant departed, or was *Vulpes vulpes crucigera*, at home? The public could only approach one end of the enclosure, and if he decided he wanted privacy, there was some cover and a small shelter at the far end near the wall.

I'd just decided to go and look for the keeper of reptiles, when *Vulpes vulpes* trotted out from behind some low shrubs and stood in the middle of the enclosure to do a bit of human watching. He was a young one, although a bit bigger than Willis. He seemed very calm and reasonably content with his lot; I wondered if he was the sole occupant.

I found the snakeman. We had a chat about the venom marketing scheme which was apparently functioning in a small way, while he tested the water and built up the number of his snakes.

I asked if he'd been doing any publicity work lately. He led me round to the caravan of rustling snakes and with a tight-lipped grin and rude gesture, pointed to a large photo of him in Tarzan loin cloth; in his arms was an amazingly proportioned Jane who had lost one half of her leopard skin bra, while the python and boa coiled around them. He made a most unlikely Tarzan, not being the brawniest individual I have ever seen. It was all clowned up for comic effect, but there was nothing skinny about Jane.

I said, 'And they're still paying you?' and shook my head in mock disbelief.

He said, 'You'll never guess what we were advertising – insurance! "Don't get caught in the investment jungle". They never used it after all – not that it makes any difference to my cut.'

He introduced me to the keeper who was responsible for the section in which I was interested, who just happened to be the keeper of reptiles! (There were only four keepers all told.)

They'd only the one fox and he was sure they'd take another to keep it company, although he'd have to clear it with his gaffer. So, if I decided to let him go, Willis had a new home and some company.

By the next weekend Freeman was still a free man, and I'd not seen a whisker of his brush since it had disappeared through the garden hedge the previous Friday.

The traps were still out, but I'd not bothered to set them the last couple of evenings; instead I put out a few titbits at one or two places around the field; each time these vanished, but there was no reason to believe Freeman had been visiting. There must have been dozens of mouths about, only too willing to accept a free meal, including a flamboyant group of four jays who seemed to have taken temporary residence about my field and garden. I'm fond of these little crows, with rough-cast voice and brilliant plumage. They're not nearly so severe on the smaller birds during nesting time as are their cousins the magpies.

I had reached a stage when I felt it was going to be a pleasant relief to have a respite from thinking about the cubs' future and how best to discharge my duty to them. I was looking forward to it.

During the weekend I contacted the Sutton Park people; there seemed to be nothing to choose between them and Hardy's recent owners as potentially successful fox trainers. In fairness I had little choice; although, had I considered the other home obviously better for the cub, I would have not hesitated to use it. Before I'd known of Hardy's escape I'd told the Sutton Park people they could have Gina, and they'd spent a week building an enclosure in their garden. So by Sunday evening the compound in my field, burgeoning for so long, a bustle of mischievious activity, was strangely, sadly, still.

Ferdi and the dogs were off along the hedge, and I stood alone staring at the threadbare grass and the devastated nettle patch – it had been time for them to go, but as I've said before, I hate endings. There was a hollow, sad anticlimax about the deserted compound. The sort of feeling that weighs heavily at the end of a big adventure, when you head for the departure gate to fly off to the other side of the world knowing that you'll probably never experience those wonderful times again – never see the friends who gather to see you off, now as quietly lost in their thoughts as are you.

I'm not a particularly religious person, and I don't know to whom I addressed the request, but I looked up at a towering *cumulo nimbus*, a great thunder cloud, tiers of belly rolls like a Michelin advertisement, with a flat head that the declining sun still touched, so that it bled a rosy patch to stain its white turban. It was beginning to collapse in the cooling air. I said, 'Please keep the little buggers safe and happy.'

Gina had departed for Sutton Park during the morning.

I had taken Willis to the zoo, arriving at lunchtime when most visitors were out in the park eating their picnics. I was allowed to drive right up to the enclosure. We took the cage inside before releasing him. He was well scared and immediately shot off at high speed towards the wall and cover.

I reparked the car and returned to watch for a while. Eventually the other fox came into view and after several more minutes a cautious Willis joined him in the open. He never came more than half way down the compound while I was watching, but he had lost that panic stricken appearance. The enclosure was large enough for him to distance himself from passers by, or come as close as he chose, and as gradually as he chose. As I looked at the two of them, I was as happy with this compromise as I could expect to be.

Ironically, for the first time, to my knowledge, since that fateful night back in March, Ferdi explored the earth in the brambles under the holly tree. It was a salutary lesson in just how little interference, even well intentioned, it takes to completely upset such things. Had I, that night, deprived myself of an absolutely unique opportunity to have moved freely among a litter of wild fox cubs, with the opportunities for study that that would bring, watching them develop and learn their trade? I had been treated to some small insight into these things, but when I considered the opportunities I may have blown that night, I felt quite overwhelmed by the lost chances.

That television naturalist man was desperately – hopelessly in my opinion – trying to set up such a situation artificially, and his act could not include the parent foxes.

I may have had the perfect natural circumstances presented to me, by that most remarkable lady, young Ferdi. Like so many other things – I shall never know now.

It was as though Ferdi took a few deep breaths and stretched in languid luxury in the mellow autumn sunshine – like a business-man after a hard year's trading, recharging the batteries on a quiet, sun drenched beach. I suppose the experience of motherhood is quite a sobering one. There are a few bright young things that don't slow down a bit and display a more wistful, serious side to their character after it. Ferdi's greetings to me and the dogs were no longer the boisterous, noisy, excited boilings over that they used to be. All the welcome and goodwill was still there, but now they were the solid, more dignified, strong handshakes of old tried and trusted comrades, with a shared experience, a common history, instead of the soaring excitement of playmates just freed from the burden of homework.

It seemed that those wildly extravagant burnings-off of vast energies, for the sheer exuberance of taking themselves to the limit of performance, the unbounded enthusiasms for the fun of each others' company, had gone forever. They were less than one year older, the old energies were still there, but it was almost as though there was a quiet preoccupation about Ferdi that had not been there before the cubs arrived. Quite intangible, but to one who knew her as well as I, quite certain.

At an unhurried pace, the routines returned.

The frequency of Ferdi's 'stays away' got to be about the same as before, as did her participation in our walks.

They chased rabbits, squirrels, rats and mice, and occasionally caught one. As before, most of this was not serious hunting, but just for fun. Once they did seriously hunt rabbits, in the same field that had been theatre for that remarkable performance of many months earlier. The stage direction was almost identical, but this play, for the rabbits, ended happily.

Briefly, the old youthful zest for play returned. That great stimulator of frivolous activities, the snow, arrived. Men slide down mountains with planks clipped to their feet; otters toboggan down river banks; birds beat their wings and shower it about like a summertime dust bath. It is thrown, slid upon, rolled in, built with, sculptured and burrowed into. As long as its stay is brief, it seems a plaything welcomed almost universally for the change it brings.

The winter was not hard, the snow fleeting, but for a few days the trio welcomed it with their old enthusiasm. Madcapping in the drifts. Rolling each other beneath. Sniff's caterpillar progress, to her plimsoll line in snow, legs stretching below for terra-firma; while the other two happily pushed her deeper. A game in which Big was certain to win, but allowed himself to be dumped, to the great delight of the other two who rushed to take revenge. A game Sniff was bound to loose. A game in which Ferdi broke even, nimble feet hampered by the yielding snow, but not heavy enough to bog down, like the stocky Miss Sniff. A game played in a Corinthian spirit – every player had an occasional turn on top – no one cared whether on top or below. The fun was in the playing.

In the valley, ice follies were being performed on the frozen lakes, water birds, particularly the heavier ones, were performing a drunken ballet as they 'landed on'.

In the clear extended twilight of a sharp evening, a magnificent flock of over one hundred Canada geese touched down. For the next ten seconds they nose dived and ground looped; triple axels and double salchows were common place. Like tumbleweed in a western ghost town, they rolled and skidded to ignominious rest. Surely not the same graceful creatures of the skies, that seconds earlier had made their lordly approach, epitomising the majesty of flight, now reduced to an hilarious clod-hopping shambles. How had the mighty fallen indeed!

After their final departure from Ferdi's enclosure way back in early autumn, I was to see only one of the cubs again. It's possible that one of the wild foxes I saw from time to time was young Freeman, if so he was by then a truly wild fox, and I never got close enough to have any chance of identifying him. To my certain knowledge there was only Willis. I'd made several social visits on the snakeman, partly because he was an interesting guy whose company was always good value, mainly as an excuse to take a quiet look at Willis, when the zoo was closed and there were no people about. Had he shown any major signs of stress, I would have taken him back and released him to take his chance about Ferdi's domain.

I watched the two play together in mock fights, they seemed reasonably contented. They were both dogs and both that year's cubs. I wondered if with sexual maturity their confinement would cause stress. I was pleased that they were still no more than half tame. They certainly would not come to the wire while I was there.

Hardy was never recaptured. His short-time owners popped over to bring back my cage. After a couple of weeks they had ceased to set the traps, believing that by then he would be well on the way to being a truly wild fox. They had made commendable efforts to gain him a stay of execution should he meet a local farmer, by touring the locality explaining what had happened.

I thought back to my own endeavours to improve Ferdi's chances during the time she'd been trailing her tow rope about the countryside. She would have been about the same age as the young Hardy, and she had survived. I told the story, thinking it might reassure them of a young cub's adaptability. It was a pity, for they were so keenly interested. If I found myself in the same situation next year would I contact them? I said I would, but secretly determined that if Ferdi performed this splendid trick again, next time I would better read the signs and she should have her nursery where she chose.

Every week to ten days I would receive a progress report from the lady from near Penkridge. Bridget it seemed had settled into her new home quite well, predictably becoming firm friends with their labrador. The lady confided that it was her ambition to be able to take Bridget for a walk off the lead into the local village when she went to visit the vicar.

An ambitious goal. Bridget was developing Ferdi's very selective trust of people. From early times I had thought that she probably reflected Ferdi's temperament more closely than the others. If the trait continued she would never make that walk, unless it was at night – alone. She was quite friendly towards the lady and her husband, keenly welcoming their arrival at feeding time. She played for ages with the labrador, who spent a lot of his time inside the paddock. If visitors came to see her she merely sheered off to the furthest cover.

Generally they felt that they were making nice gentle progress with her. It was progress that Bridget dictated. The size of the paddock made it quite impossible to catch her if she opted not to be caught, so the degree of close contact which she made was of her own controlling. I was pleased that they had no intention of trying to trap her in a smaller enclosure to deprive her of these options.

They began taking her for walks on a line; she did not adapt well to this, and although they never neared the village and rarely met anyone, she was usually in a state of rebellion at the check imposed by the line. This exercise was counter productive. Being the sharp little lady that she was, she immediately changed her tactics and became much less willing to be handled, knowing that she might again be attached to the hated line.

A few weeks after her departure, I was passing close to Gina's new address and popped in to see how she was getting on. Gina had another new address – c/o Sutton Park. She had slipped out of her enclosure when someone had apparently failed to fix the door correctly. Without any panic she had wandered about the extensive garden for some time, ignoring attempts to coax her to hand, and had eventually run up some timbers on to the roof of a lean-to garden shed, from that on to the top of a high old wall, on the other side of which are the wooded acres of the park. For tormenting minutes she'd sat on top of the wall as though debating upon which side she would prefer to live, refusing to allow her judgement to be blurred by all sorts of succulent luxuries being proffered from below. She had walked a few yards along the wall and dropped out of sight. By the time a gate in the wall had been unlocked, there was no sign of her. By that time half of Ferdi's family were, one hopes, wild and free. Well before Christmas, Bridget had joined that independent band. The flow of letters from the village near Penkridge had dried up. I'd not had a report on young Bridget for several weeks.

So regular had been the reports, that I contacted Bridget's folk to see if they were all right. There were mixed emotions in the old farmhouse – concern for the cub, but excitement that on two occasions she had met them while they were walking in a nearby wood. To their amazement they had suddenly realised that Bridget had joined the labrador in a tail-swishing but silent greeting. I could easily imagine her materialising, like her mum, almost magically. On both occasions she had come within a few yards of them, but had not let them actually touch her. For me there was something very poignant about that. I had considered Bridget temperamentally best equipped to achieve a lifestyle similar to

Ferdi's own. My friends from the old farmhouse were not going to enjoy the privileges that Ferdi allowed me, but they might yet be two of a very small number who enjoyed the trust of a wild fox.

Like Hardy's owners and I had done before them, they had visited the local community with the story and a plea for leniency for the cub, should anyone meet her when he was out shooting. I must admit that although those whose pleasure it is to destroy wildlife, will, to indulge a massive understatement, never be my favourite people, outwardly at least, those I have approached have apparently been willing to cooperate. What happens in the unobserved solitudes may well be quite different, but considering that the fox is the traditional rogue about the countryside, a gross slander but one which is cherished by all who enjoy maltreating him, a tradition which sadly dies hard, I've usually found an agreeable amount of sympathy and interest in my stories.

24

Bats, Rats and Much Besides

As the new year gathered momentum, I watched Ferdi for any signs that she might have mated.

Looking at my few jotted notes of the time, I find that the longest period she stayed away around the change of the year was three days, including the day she went and the day she returned. For a while I thought that an accurate replay was probable, when on two occasions I saw her leave whatever business she and the dogs had along the hedge, and slip down her old earth. She did no further digging, there was never any fresh sand at the entrance. This demonstrated to me an advantage of an established earth. For last year the well concealed entrance might have been revealed to anyone whose curiosity prompted him to investigate the source of a scatter of bright yellow sand in the hedge bottom.

As we got into mid March, last year she'd given birth on the 23rd, I watched her figure very carefully and when she condescended to be fussed, I felt her abdomen. Again I could detect no sign, but this time for the very good reason that she was not pregnant.

Life with Messrs Ferdi, Sniff and Big and supporting cast of Little Elsa and Big Tom went on quite happily. For the most part we were sharing experiences that we had shared a dozen times before – they were always fresh and interesting, but a touch repetitious to set down in writing.

Ferdi showed me a blackbird's nest built in a scrape in the ground, actually inside the enclosure. I could not remember ever seeing one on a ground level site before. Naturally there were no eggs in it, whether this was because Ferdi had decided upon eggs for breakfast, or the incredibly optimistic bird had decided that discretion was the better part, before laying, I do not know.

The enclosure was once again verdant, with the nettles providing her ladyship with a shady lie in hot weather.

In early summer rats and bats were prevalent about my place. The bats' story was an unfortunate one. I was well aware that there were plenty of bats about, without knowing where they lived. In the light evenings the day-fighter squadrons of swallows, swifts and martins were still on patrol, when the night-fighters became operational – pipistrelle, horseshoe and long eared – and for the hour or so that their operating times overlapped they must have given the flying insects a hard time.

For no apparent reason, a bough fell off a large ash tree. The heavy timber narrowly missed the stable, the smaller end branches landing on its nearby flat roof. When I found what had happened I climbed on to the roof with a bow-saw to clear the wreckage, amongst which I found a dead pipistrelle bat. When I'd cut up and thrown down all the debris, I climbed down and took a look at the main timbers. A large cavity contained several more corpses. The hollow branch had obviously been a bat roost, it had fallen during the day when the colony was probably asleep; some had evidently still been inside when the bough landed and some of these had been killed by the impact and recoil.

Ferdi had been shut in the compound and when I let her out she explored this new feature and quickly located the dead bats. It was good fresh protein and grist to the mill as far as Ferdi was concerned; she ate the two I extracted, pushed her paw in and scraped out another one. She seemed to regard these rather crunchy novelty snacks as a nice change, so I climbed back on to the roof and tossed down the other one.

It was several days after this bat disaster that I found both cats and Ferdi in the stable, which seemed a bit unusual, so I also went in to see what was so interesting. Apart from where shrinking planks allowed thin laths of sunlight to angle through, the only opening was the door. My swift transition from bright sunshine to gloom left me almost blind, while my eyes sorted themselves out. Even after a couple of minutes I could still not see what made this hot place that smelled of ammonia and seemed to have cornered the market in flies, so fascinating to Ferdi, Elsa and Big Tom.

After breaking off whatever business they were about to come over and say hello, they all went back to one of the rear stalls into which the stable was divided, and sat, heads tilted back, looking and sniffing at the ceiling. It seemed to be some sort of secret society initiation ceremony, so I thought I'd better join. I looked up and suddenly realised that there were dozens of dark little packages hung up on the ceiling. The bats had moved to the more modern residence next door. They continued to roost in the stable for most of the autumn, before finding somewhere smaller and cosier for their winter hibernation.

I never discovered where the rats came from, but I seemed to be the only one of the tribe who did not. They all got into the act; Ferdi and Sniff weighed in with a great toll, both cats seemed to be averaging one a day. Mr Big, who I don't think was particularly interested in rats, also chopped a few.

They were brown rats and most of the victims seemed about half grown, but several large adults were also killed. It went on for several days before it abruptly stopped; whether by then the rats had been exterminated or whether a population had moved through and were then clear of the area, I do not know. I like sleeping with all my windows open and I was glad when they'd gone.

For a week, almost every time I went into the field Ferdi would have a rat, she and the dogs, particularly Sniff, killed them very quickly. To Ferdi they were a natural part of the diet and she carried them off or buried them. The dogs left them lying around. The cats brought them home.

The cats also ate them but rarely managed a whole one, so the bits of rat that littered the lawn were cat kills. Fortunately Sniff and Big would usually scoff these leftovers, so keeping the place reasonably tidy. This was a bit surprising since it was rare for either of them to eat a rat they had just killed.

I have already dwelt upon my attitude towards rats. I'd always discouraged them from house or garden – like mice they can be a damn nuisance in shed or garage, gnawing away at all sorts of things. Farther away from home I find them not repulsive animals. If one could put aside one's prejudices, except for their mangy looking tail, they are not unattractive. But after that display of tolerance and fairmindedness I must confess if there is one place I can manage without a large rat it's my bedroom.

Since the days, years earlier, when Big Tom and Elsa used to deliver live rabbits in the middle of the night, I had received no such visitations. What prompted the cats to revert to their juvenile generosity I cannot imagine, but one of the sweet little souls caught such a magnificent specimen of *rattus norvegicus*, the brown rat, that he just had to present it to me as a sign of his esteem and affection.

So the brainless bugger dropped it, very much alive and vigorously kicking, through the bedroom window. Normally all the interior doors were left open, giving the animals full range, with the cats free to come and go through my bedroom window. The dogs never slept on the furniture but otherwise were free to pick their spot. Favourite positions were the angle of the stairs, the landing, or the mat beside my bed, usually the latter. I surfaced from sleep with heart thumping and adrenalin flowing by the gallon. What manner of thing was attacking me?

There was a snarling and scuffing, my bed was being buffeted, a thunderous growl sounded almost in my ears, that had been from Biggy. I got the light on, blinking like an owl in sudden sunlight. Sniff was on the window side of the bed, lying almost on her side, in her attempt to force herself into the three-inch gap beneath. Big on the otherside, with front legs flat along the floor, and head down, barked a couple of times deafeningly in the confined space.

I yelled at them to stop the noise and for Sniff to cease her attempts to destroy my bed. With her still muttering to herself in sheer frustration, I took a look underneath, bringing my reading lamp down to floor level and laying myself down beside Big. There, pressed against the wall at the headboard end, was the plump and furry answer to the mystery.

Sniff, sudden death to rats even out in the fields, had apparently been outraged when one landed in my bedroom. In her furious attempts to get at it she had actually moved the divan on its casters, even with my weight on it. I decided to maintain the status quo while I considered the matter. My bedroom is never the tidiest, but if that rat were forced to make a run for his life, I could see them turning it into a shambles.

Now a rabbit is a friendly pacifist, even when scared and cornered. Although he possesses a similar set of chisels to those of the rat, he never thinks of being sufficiently disagreeable as to sink them into your hand – he is a nice guy – in fact the only rabbits that have ever bitten me have been tame ones. But you get a squirrel or rat in the same situation and it's a virtual guarantee that you're going to have two pairs of opposing incisors meet in the middle of your thumb. It follows from this, that extracting a large rat from the small space under one's divan or wardrobe poses a few extra problems. On top of which the midnight rabbit hunts were in the days before my wife decided to do her midnight hunting with someone else. Two of us had a chance of using pincer tactics upon the rabbit. I still possessed two pairs of heavy leather gauntlets but they, of course, were in the shed at the top of my garden. Cursing, I took a final sighting of the rat, still motionless beneath the bed, not that he was likely to bolt with a well stirred up dog on either side, but if he did have the luck to get past Big and dive downstairs, they might have wrecked the entire cottage by the time I returned.

I went down into the kitchen, stepped into a pair of wellies, picked up a torch and headed up the garden. As I went I addressed the cats, no doubt somewhere, invisible in the darkness, with the message that if I got my hands on them I'd turn them into carpet slippers.

I flashed my torch around the shed and eventually found two of the gloves; naturally they were both for the left hand – in any case, from long neglect the leather had become so hard and insensitive that they were about useless. I spotted a length of plastic down pipe for roof guttering. If I blocked one end and offered ratty the other as a nice dark bolt hole, would he oblige by diving into it? I returned to the bedroom with this ingenious invention, plus a long stick for goading purposes. I left the kitchen door open, just in case ratty got downstairs.

Back in the combat area the troops, to my relief, still held their positions in a deadly concentration of silence. I lay my plastic pipe on the floor, but it was too large a diameter to slip under the bed. I should have to ease the bed away from the wall at my side, while keeping it firmly in contact at Sniff's side, so that she wouldn't try to force herself into the gap and panic ratty into a desperate run for his life.

Very slowly I angled the bed to leave a wedge shaped gap between the wall and the headboard, half way along which crouched the luckless rat. He had now another option, he could go upwards between wall and bed – I hoped he would not. With the end of the pipe slipped slowly to within six inches of him, he began to twitch and fidget and back off towards Sniff. Like a good collie with a rebellious sheep, she grumbled a warning and checked him.

He was obviously driven by panic to the verge of some desperate action, so I left the pipe where it was and brought the stick in a slow sweep from the foot of the bed. Threatened on three sides by vastly superior forces he found the enfolding blackness of the pipe more comforting than the bright splash of electric light up above him. So having made his decision, with a sudden movement, emulating his proverbial counter part, he shot up the drainpipe and vanished into the sheltering darkness. I eased the pipe out, held a piece of cardboard over the open end and the capture was complete. I'm not sure that Big or Sniff knew where he'd gone, for they remained in the bedroom as I carried him away.

On this night when everything was happening I was greeted in the kitchen by Ferdi. She had failed to return with us after a walk and had still been away at feeding time. She had probably provided for herself and in any case at 3.00 am I could not face the prospect of feeding her and shutting her up in the compound.

I dropped the pipe on the edge of the lawn. I told Ferdi, 'If you're hungry, your supper is in there and if you don't fancy supper out of a drainpipe – eat the bloody cats!' I closed the kitchen door.

The rat had been terrified; there might be some disinfecting required beneath my bed – that could wait until morning. I shut the window down to the first notch and got into bed, as I switched off the light Sniff was still peering beneath, not yet satisfied.

Next morning the plastic pipe was empty, but whether the rat had provided supper for Ferdi or whether she'd not been hungry enough to outwait him, I've no idea. After all that had befallen him last night I could almost find myself wishing him good luck and hoping he'd got away.

It was high summer when I next got news of Ferdi's brood.

Some friends from New Zealand had arrived on a two-year working holiday, married, both teachers, she a Kiwi on her first trip to the UK, and keen to see and do everything. He a Brit, had seen it all before and during the long summer holidays had got himself a job delivering ice cream in bulk to various outlets.

The wife, Jan, and I had decided to take a canoe trip. Nothing very ambitious, twelve to fifteen miles as the river winds, downstream to a small town with conveniently placed roads and car park. As usual with such a trip the only real problem is organising off water transport. Take two cars to the destination, drive one back, canoe down to the other car, plonk canoe on top and drive home.

The real bind comes if you happen to break your boat at the mid point. Not much danger of that on our quite large, but placid river. We arranged that we might meet Arthur, Jan's husband, in the car park at our journey's end. This had to be a very loose arrangement since we did not know what lay between and how long it would take us to negotiate. He was making a delivery at our destination, but obviously couldn't hang about all day.

It was a bikini and swim shorts day and, taking in the sun, we floated pleasantly down and rather to everyone's surprise, met him in the car park in mid afternoon. He had a splendid tale to tell.

One of the deliveries that morning had been to the zoo and park where Willis had found his home. Arthur had remembered my saying that one of the cubs had gone there. Regarding it as one of the perks of a most undemanding job, he had taken an hour's break and wandered round the zoo, but had found no foxes. He had eventually unwittingly approached one of the proprietors and by way of introduction said that a friend of his had donated a fox cub to the collection and he wondered what had happened to it.

The gentleman's reply had begun something like this: 'Foxes! I'll never keep foxes in here again. They'd get out of a bloody safe. We did not mind them escaping so much, but they hung around the grounds for two months living off the wild fowl enclosure – they took several exotic geese, ducks and a peahen. We were damn glad when they moved off.'

That is not a verbatim quote but contains the gentleman's sentiments, expressed in similar style. Apparently the two cubs had been quite an attraction, not deigning to have close association with their public, but becoming a popular twosome by their habit of putting on a wild tail chase around the enclosure. I thought back to Ferdi's spectaculars in the days of old Blackie and his gang.

The escape had been a great mystery. One morning everything in the enclosure had been normal except that the foxes were not there. This had been so puzzling that they began to suspect that someone had deliberately released them and relocked the door. I would have liked to take a good look at the trees and back wall. Ferdi could easily gain my roof by running up the plum tree. I had only seen the trees in the enclosure from forty yards away, but if they offered a fairly rough claw hold, and if any branches extended close to the top of the old wall, that might just have been the way out.

The wall was about twelve feet high, but even if they did not fancy a straight drop, it was a very long wall and by running along it they would almost certainly find a shed or cage on to which they could drop.

The accounts of their antics suggested that they'd trained themselves to high fitness, and I conjectured that depending upon the degree of difficulty imposed by the tree, they would be quite capable of performing this feat. Lacking the personalised climbing irons of a cat, they could not merely drive in those ever sharp retractile hooks and drag themselves up the steepest trunk, but if the bowl was not too steep for too far before branches angled away to provide sure traction for rough pads and blunt claws, by emulating Ferdi's plum tree technique they might well get close enough to jump on to the top of the wall.

An unashamed postulation – it can be nothing more – my commentary on the escape as witnessed from a secret and invisible hide inside the enclosure.

The foxes' instinct for play had been turning to progressively more vigorous exercise, as inadvertently they built speed, stamina and strength. When they staged these wild racing 'workout routines', the public's gaze was diverted from the sedentary, dusty lion, yawning cavernously in his cage, overwhelmed by the utter pointlessness of life.

They turned away from the metronome predictability of the puma's swaying patrol, back and forth endlessly across the narrow frontage of her pen. A more active expression of the futility epitomised by the lion. By contrast with their sad gloom, the explosive agile enthusiasm of the two humble foxes was a cheering hymn to the joy of being alive and healthy.

A few days before I had observed for the first time an additional element introduced to the racing rough and tumble of their play – a new plaything discovered.

Willis, hotly pursued by his slightly larger buddy, had suddenly leapt sideways, hit the largest of the trees some three or four feet up its trunk, like a fairground 'wall of death' rider and bounced off again in an unslackening helter-skelter. Next time the chase took them past the tree, he did it again, evidently the new trick was fun. Soon they were both doing it and it became a regular part of the course, they bounced against the tree more often than they passed it by.

The milestones of the day had all passed – the excitement of feeding time had brought all the cages and enclosures to life, in anticipation of the approach of the tractor and trailer, piled high with a variety of diets, which threaded its tortuous progress along the network of paths.

In this small zoo the main feed is done after the public has departed and the narrow access roads are clear for the trailer. The final 'keeper patrol' has wandered the grounds; the great ancient wrought iron gate now obstructs the arch of the mellow brick work in the old garden wall; its huge bolts have been thrust into the arch above and the road below; heavy chain has been wrapped around and sags like a giant necklace under the weight of a huge padlock. All is secure. An incongruous chorus of voices from around the world float upon or rend the still, warm air of this summer evening.

After eating, the foxes had sprawled out for some time, but they are now trotting about the compound in businesslike fashion, checking, exploring the front wire and gazing beyond, now that there is no press of people behind it. The tree has become a focal point and is urinated upon and around.

Willis, on hind legs, his forepaws reaching high above his head, stands against the trunk. He arches his back in a reverse curve, pressing his chest towards the tree, and rolls his head right back until his muzzle passes the vertical position and his nose is inclined backwards over his own shoulders. A great gaping yawn completes this comprehensive stretch.

He backs away, dragging his front paws down the trunk in a

continuing stretch posture. He sits briefly at the foot of the ancient pear tree, with its dark scabs of bark that appear to have been stuck on individually. He looks up at the tree, head and shoulders moving back and forth in short jerky oscillations.

A cat about to charge, winds up with its hind quarters as the excitement of anticipation becomes unbearable; so Willis wound up with his shoulders. An explosive thrust from hind legs, a great extension of back and forepaws. He found the trunk perhaps five feet above the ground, but he had leapt too high and too steeply – his energy spent he hit the tree very lightly and was instantly falling back, despite scrabbling at the bark with his hind claws. He slid backwards down the tree, with barely sufficient time to detach himself and turn for a rather heavy landing.

I had watched Ferdi run up my plum tree many times and understood her method. Her angles of approach, timing and synchronisation had to be precise to allow her that second upward kick off the vertical trunk. The cub would need this second stage boost if he was to reach the first resting station with his forepaws. He needed to reach seven or eight feet before he could perch. At that level the old tree appeared to have been stopped at some stage in its youth, by having its top cut out. A lateral shoot had thrown a short horizontal limb, before bending back to the vertical in its quest for more light.

Apart from its hockey stick appearance, it was now indistinguishable from the main trunk, and had been for fifty years past. Above this there was a short steep run, but this supported several stout side branches and the usual fuzz of brush so typical of an untended fruit tree – easy footing for the nimble cubs. Above this there was a tangled crown of branches, several of which crushed their unruly twigs against the wall, well below the top. Far more significantly, a gnarled old limb of five or six inches diameter poked its storm-shattered end, like a dirty broken finger, a couple of feet above the wall's top and not two fox lengths from it.

Willis persisted, each time skidding earthwards down the crazed bark. He began to take off from farther away, jumping from a trot, jumping from quite a pacy approach. He was improving; his more distant takeoff and faster approach meant a slight sacrifice of height, but a flatter angle and much heavier contact with the trunk. The flywheel that was his body, now still stored some of that energy when he struck the tree. Instead of touching lightly and falling away as previously, there was now a brief moment when that stored energy pressed him firmly against the bark. Momentum was the secret.

If, during the fraction of a second that the compression lasted, when his feet were glued by pressure to the tree, he could kick again, the friction of rough pads on rough bark would provide sufficient foundation to drive him upwards.

He would have found that vital traction. Not that Willis had time for such pedantic dross; but now when he hit the tree, for a fleeting moment he felt stable and secure. His attempts to get in that second kick were too slow and the magical moments when gravity is held at bay were wasted.

Once, he almost succeeded, lifting himself up but away from the trunk, to tumble even farther than usual. He gave it up, projecting an attitude so typically human and characteristic of his mum – that of not being particularly interested – he'd not wanted to get up the damned tree at all.

Willis also displayed some of the characteristics of his little sister Bridget; although the smaller of the two, he seemed to lead by example, as she had done when the family had practised hunting the ubiquitous field vole. Soon Buddy Boy was trying his hand (or paw) at this pointless exercise invented by his pal. During the mad-capping of the day time the tree was used merely as a bouncing pole. In the more restrained time of the evening, they practised the new game.

Foxes possess the necessary athletic capabilities for the perfection of the trick that now fascinated the cubs, so it could only be a matter of time. Two evenings later I watched Willis get it all right – he rose so easily to find the horizontal limb with his forepaws, that he must have wondered why it had seemed so difficult before.

The technique was mastered and there the adventure ended. He perched, apparently well pleased and enjoying a different perspective on the zoo; there were strange shapes and movements not visible from the ground. He half slid, half ran down the trunk before detaching himself for a light touch down.

He returned to the perch on the hockey stick several times that evening, with equal ease.

There is an inexact natural law, proposed by some and ridiculed by others, which, according to its proponents, rules that once something has been achieved, the very act of achieving creates an atmosphere in which the likelihood of its being repeated by another agency is greatly increased even, they say, if that other agent is not aware of the original act.

All a bit too heavy for me!

So whether Willis succeeded because Ferdi and thousands before her had performed similar feats, I'll leave to you, my reader.

However, Buddy Boy had known it was possible from numerous, by now perfect, demonstrations, and an evening later he also could take a loftier view of his surroundings. So by an extension of their new game, the cubs one evening found themselves looking down not only on the neighbouring enclosures, but also on the top of the wall. From my imaginary hide I gazed up at the foxes, in sharp relief against the soft evening sky. I watched Willis compose himself – settling his feet in a tight bunch, with little paddling movements. I saw him lower into a slight crouch, pause for a final calculation and, with a gentle thrust, arch easily down on to the wall, with a sure balance. He stood gazing about him and for a moment it looked as though Buddy Boy would land on top of him, as back on the bough he also prepared with little dipping, reaching movements of his head.

Willis trotted along the wall and Buddy, with a lazy spring, made it look ridiculously easy. They trotted confidently, unhurriedly along the wall over the dingo looking up at them, attracted by the movement across his skyline. The wolves also showed a neighbourly interest; the wallabies did not notice.

I saw them stand together looking down on the far side of the wall. Already it was possible to look around the empty enclosure and believe it to be fox proof. I certainly would have thought it so had I not known about Ferdi and the plum tree.

I now leave my hide in the empty enclosure, inside which I have indulged my conjectures, to consider the next two months in the lives of those lively adventurers.

There is a certain poetry about the fact that the very establishment that had sought to keep them captive should now provide the easy pickings to sustain them while they honed their hunting instincts, to better equip themselves for freedom. Had they initially returned to the zoo because they had learnt to associate the quiet evenings with a food supply and, finding that supper was no longer served, helped themselves and so commenced a transition that was completed when they drifted away from the parklands to meet their fates and fortunes – two wild young foxes?

Like all Ferdi's brood, I wished them good luck.

Five out of six had won their freedom in circumstances that gave them a sporting chance. Had fate remedied my blunder of nearly eighteen months ago? Had my agonising over their futures been a complete waste of time, a penance I richly deserved to serve? Might I just as well have opened the compound and left Ferdi, fate, and the cubs to sort it out?

Of the remaining cub, young Brit, I have no knowledge. I completely lost contact. In the unlikely event of these jottings finding favour, perhaps the zoo keeper will read them, recognise himself and update me on the fate of the last of the only youngsters I am ever likely to call my kids, if Ferdi will excuse the gross presumption.

If I were placing bets, I'd reason that with 83.333 per cent known to have gone free, the remaining 16.666 per cent would also make it. I'd bet they managed six out of six – perhaps Ferdi's kids would settle for nothing less.

God bless 'em all!

25

The End

By the time the first scatter of leaves was beginning to collect in the ditches and along the lane's edge, Ferdi was spending more time away from home than she had during the summer. On several occasions she spent two or three days away, before suddenly, when one's thoughts were elsewhere, slipping back into our company in midwalk, as easily as if she had set out with us one hour before. Despite the dozens of times she had done this, there was always the little prickle of pleasant surprise and slight relief to find her among us, grinning her open-mouthed grin that I knew so well. The welcome she received from Sniff and Biggy was never flagging.

As the year wound down towards winter, Ferdi had been away four consecutive days – the longest absence I could remember since that hectic week four years before when she had taken her tow line with her. We visited the Pit Hole, but despite spending several hours on its steep slopes and down by the pool, Ferdi did not appear.

On the evening of her fifth day away, a farmer acquaintance stopped at the end of my drive and shouted above the grumbling tractor, 'Have you still got your fox?' I said she had been away five days.

'Ah, I thought so,' he said. 'I saw her last night; I was doin' some ploughin' late on by the lights o' me tractor. Saw 'er twice, just on the fringe of the spotlights' beam. 'thought it must be 'er – seemed t'know a thing or two – yer know – weren't the rush you'd see from a normal wild un, if it got that close.'

At the risk of repeating myself ad-nauseam – I hate endings. Even

237

in this, that wonderful little creature let me down gently, let me absorb the fact over a couple of weeks, and even then with Ferdi there were no definitive arrangements – she was ever the free spirit; that was what made her company so interesting and enjoyable. The feeling that this time was different grew steadily, until a fortnight later I recognised that she had decided to stay on the other side of that fence, the fence through which she had passed to and fro with such ease for four years, but which was insurmountable to Big, Sniff and me. She had gone where we could not follow.

During that first fortnight I believe I saw her once, and the two dogs met her on at least one other occasion. Walking in the dark one evening near my field, I judged from the dogs' reaction that she was close – they vanished into the darkness. My thoughts were confirmed when I heard Ferdi's voice in greeting, from the next field. The dogs eventually returned alone, nor did she respond to my call.

On the other occasion, I was, I believe, to see her for the last time, the lithe, red figure that for so long had been part of my life. Appropriately, she seemed to epitomise all that was wild and free, drifting through white scarves of mist that lay like solid plates in the breathless air, above the frost-stiffened grasses. It was at a considerable distance, in failing light, as we climbed the gently sloping flank of the valley, up from the river. I saw the fox before Big or Sniff. She was trotting along the side of a derelict barn. She was about the right size to have been Ferdi. I whistled and called her name. She checked and turned to look towards us. The dogs, alerted by my call, ranged uncertainly ahead, then they spotted her and set off at a steady lope.

For a moment she held her position, watching the approach of the distant dogs, as though a finely balanced decision was being reconsidered. Then, like a man telling himself that the choice had been made, there was no going back, she abruptly turned and slipped round the corner of the old barn, to be quickly swallowed by the veils of mist. Big and Sniff were soon past the barn and also lost, but ten minutes later, as I dropped into the lane, they returned alone. Now I knew with sad certainty that she would not come back – that the wild had reclaimed its own.

I hoped she might intercept our walks from time to time, but she never did.

The End

For a while there was a loss of direction to life around the cottage. The dogs, at first expecting to find she had returned, would still streak off to the compound as a first priority on being released. Slowly, successive disappointments dampened their enthusiasm, until they moped listlessly about the enclosure on increasingly infrequent visits.

The gap she left took a long time to close.

Epilogue

My personal feelings were that I had been very lucky to have shared Ferdi's company for so long – she taught me much, directly or indirectly. She retaught the lesson that he who looks down the sights and squeezes the trigger, whether he be pointing at elephant or quail, whale or warthog, fox or pheasant, has no conception of the miraculous thing he maims or destroys – its personality, its idiosyncrasies. If he does know, then he should be executed for the ultimate act of vandalism.

He who poisons or traps, or fells the forests or pollutes the waters is perhaps even worse in his indiscrimination. As are those of such warped values who demand coats of exotic furs, the illicit acquisition of which adds to the excitement of possession and to their value, and those idiot-orientated minds that finance the cutting down of the rhino in a pathetic hope that its horn will boost their inadequate manhood. Those who parade their fur coats; those who swagger with their rhino-horn dagger handles, in their vanity they put a terrible price on the head of the innocent and condemn magnificent creatures to maiming and death, as do those, bewitched by exquisite carvings, who provide the market for ivory – toothpick or chess-man, temple or, with vicious irony, that amazing line of marching elephants, linked trunk and tail. No matter how beautiful and tempting the object, a far more beautiful creature died, more often than not in appalling circumstances, to provide it. As with many animal products, the purchaser encourages and condones the suffering. There are always two price tags, the high price the purchaser pays to line the pockets of evil men, and the astronomically high price paid by the original owner, who

240

wanted no part of the transaction. Those who provide the market are as guilty as the mercenaries who take their money.

That which I was privileged to share with Ferdi, I hope I have, in some small part, shared with those kind enough to read her story.